GOD SAVE

SeX PiSTOLs

GOD SAVE

SeX PisTOLS

EDITED BY **JOHAN KUGELBERG**
WITH **JON SAVAGE & GLENN TERRY**

RIZZOLI
NEW YORK

New York · Paris · London · Milan

First published in the United States of America in 2016 by
RIZZOLI INTERNATIONAL PUBLICATIONS, INC.
300 PARK AVENUE SOUTH
NEW YORK, NY 10010
WWW.RIZZOLIUSA.COM

2016 2017 2018 2019 / 10 9 8 7 6 5 4 3 2 1

Printed in China
ISBN-13: 978-0-8478-4626-9
Library of Congress Catalog Control Number: 2016940678

Edited by JOHAN KUGELBERG
Co-Editors JON SAVAGE / GLENN TERRY
Associate Editors JEFF GOLD / RYAN RICHARDSON
Design by BRYAN CIPOLLA
Captions annotated by JEFF GOLD / JOHAN KUGELBERG / RYAN RICHARDSON / JON SAVAGE / GLENN TERRY
Digital image preparation by BRYAN CIPOLLA / MARK IOSIFESCU / CHRIS MCDONNELL

Cover art JAMIE REID
Front endpapers JOE STEVENS, WOLFGANG 'BUBI' HEILEMANN
Back endpapers ADRIAN BOOT, ROBERTA BAYLEY

Sex Pistols materials and identity courtesy of LIVENATION

Objects from CHRIS STEIN COLLECTION / CORNELL UNIVERSITY PUNK ARCHIVE / CORNELL UNIVERSITY
SITUATIONIST ARCHIVE / ENGLAND'S DREAMING ARCHIVE AT LIVERPOOL JOHN MOORES UNIVERSITY / GLENN TERRY-
VICIOUS SLOTH COLLECTION / JAMIE REID COLLECTION / JEFF GOLD-RECORD MECCA / JOHN TIBERI COLLECTION /
JULIO SANTO DOMINGO ARCHIVE AT HARVARD UNIVERSITY / MARC ZERMATI COLLECTION / MARY HARRON ARCHIVE /
PAUL DRUMMOND COLLECTION / PETER CHRISTOPHERSON ESTATE / PETER HOOK COLLECTION / PUNK MAGAZINE
ARCHIVE AT YALE UNIVERSITY / ROBERTA BAYLEY COLLECTION / UNIVERSITY OF MIAMI / YALE UNIVERSITY

Photography courtesy of and copyright by ROBERTA BAYLEY, 244–248, 265–279 / LEEE BLACK CHILDERS, 108 /
PETER CHRISTOPHERSON, 23, 24, 41 / IAN DICKSON, 96–97 / BOB GRUEN, 123 (*above*) / HANS HATWIG, 184–185,
186 / WOLFGANG 'BUBI' HEILEMANN, 74–75 / DENNIS MORRIS, 164, 165, 228–229 / CAROL MOSS, 156–157, 162 /
BARRY PLUMMER, 85, 171, 179 (*above*) / MICK ROCK, 57 / KATE SIMON, 84 / RAY STEVENSON, 43, 45 (*below*), 47
(*below*), 51, 52, 68, 86 (*below left*), 102 (*top*), 287 / JOHN TIBERI, 183 / PETER VERNON, 78, 79 / RICHARD YOUNG,
292–293.

Special thanks to BILL ALLERTON / JACK BATES / ROBERTA BAYLEY / OSSIAN BROWN / AMY BUCKLEY /
DARREN CAMERON / WILL CAMERON / SONG CHONG / ELLIOTT COLE / MICHAEL DALEY / EARL DELANEY /
JESPER EKLOW / ALYN EVANS / COLIN FALLOWS / BILL FORSYTH / MARY HARRON / MARK HAYWARD /
JOHN HÖLMSTROM / PETER HOOK / JONH INGHAM / MARK IOSIFESCU / KAYLEIGH JANKOWSKI / GARY JOHNSON /
ANNE KENNEY / JACOB LEHMAN / EDDIE LOCK / JOHN MARCHANT / CHARLES MIERS / LESLIE MORRIS /
KATIE MURPHY / RICHARD OVENDEN / KATHERINE REAGAN / JAMIE REID / KEVIN REPP / ANDRES SANTO DOMINGO /
JULIO SANTO DOMINGO JR / AGUIRRE SCHWARZ / ANGELOS STATHOPOULOS / PETER STATHOPOULOS /
VALERIE STEVENSON / CHRIS THOMAS / SARAH THOMAS / HELEN TZAS / GAVIN WALSH / GEOFFREY WEISS /
DR LILA WOLFE / TIMOTHY YOUNG

PAUL COOK / STEVE JONES / JOHN LYDON / GLEN MATLOCK — THE SEX PISTOLS

— FOR LILA

DRIFTING THROUGH THE WORLD'S GREATEST ROCK AND ROLL SITUATION:
A SEX PISTOLS PSYCHO-GEOGRAPHY

Johan Kugelberg

A cloud of critics, of compilers, of commentators, darkened the face of learning, and the decline of genius was soon followed by the corruption of taste.

— EDWARD GIBBON,
THE DECLINE AND FALL OF THE ROMAN EMPIRE

Our goal is to overwhelm the reader with the realization of just how radical the visual language of the Sex Pistols was (still is); and of how these visuals reflect the extreme potency of John Lydon as an activist/lyricist/artist; and of the musical quantum leap of Matlock, Jones, and Cook; and of Vicious as the ultimate icon of romantic idealism; and finally, of the profound environmental artistry of Helen Wellington-Lloyd, Malcolm McLaren, Jamie Reid, and Vivienne Westwood. Every component contributed to a sum much greater than its parts.

This book needed to be a drift, a gambol, through the myriad of Sex Pistols visuals that have assaulted our eyeballs since their creation. The curatorial vision for the project was to be no more than admiration: admiration tempered by the archaeology of uncovering twin visual trajectories, the accidental alongside the intentional, as created by the band, the management, the designers, the record companies, the fans. The legacy of this majestic group is not merely music, nor attitude, nor politics, nor a rebellious stance of glowering brilliance—but a seismic cultural shift from whose impact some of us only now can get a sense of how the Sex Pistols will be considered three hundred years from now.

Frustration is one of the great things in art; satisfaction is nothing.

— MALCOLM MCLAREN,
COLLEGE NOTES, WINTER 1967/1968

My co-editors, Jon Savage and Glenn Terry, and I began this book around five years ago, deciding almost immediately that it should act as a visual companion for Jon's 1992 masterwork *England's Dreaming*. We perused thousands of objects, documents, images, and pieces of ephemera in dozens of private and public collections, and then started the delightful and odious task of distilling the materials down to a cohesive visual narrative that we hoped would come in handy for the neophyte as well as the grizzled punk-rock veteran.

All editors lie, as all of us take away even when we add. But once immersed in the editorial work that we completed on this book, we felt the task of immersion in time and place worthwhile. Drifting through this visual landscape brings about private truths and insights from the observer, which take away some of the extraordinary shock and vibrancy of stark day-glo color, simultaneously exploding and imploding at a point in time when the western world was mostly gray and beige.

In our 2013 book and exhibition, *Punk: An Aesthetic* (the opposite of an aesthetic is an anaesthetic—the punk pun truly the last refuge of the last scoundrel), we attempted to answer the question of

An authentic illustration sheds light
on true discourse, like a subordinate
clause which is neither incompatible
nor pleonastic.

— GUY DEBORD, PANEGYRIC

Is your cucumber bitter? Throw it
away. Are there briars in your path?
Turn aside. That is enough. Do not go
on to say, "Why were things of this
sort ever brought into the world?"
The student of nature will only laugh
at you; just as the carpenter or shoe-
maker would laugh, if you found fault
with the shavings and scraps from
their work which you saw in the shop.

— MARCUS AURELIUS, *MEDITATIONS*

whether punk was, is, or will become an aesthetic. As our answer was a resounding "maybe," what we are doing here with this visual journey through the original lifespan of the Sex Pistols is as close to documentary as we could muster. We are certainly standing on the shoulders of giants—those collectors both private and institutional that realized very early on that the subject of the Sex Pistols deserves passion, scrutiny, and study for decades, even centuries.

My endless fascination for studies of radical thought during the English Civil War has enabled me to find some parallels in the context within which punk materials are now held at university libraries—Cornell, Yale, Liverpool John Moores University (home of the *England's Dreaming* archive), Oxford, and the University of Miami, to name but a few—since each is indicative of the way a free society documents the most abrasive confrontations to its status quo. What we know now about the diggers, the ranters, the levelers, Ebenezer Coppe, or Roger Crab (who described Oxford and Cambridge as "the whore's great eyes"), is to a large extent due to the contemporary collection of materials by the very institutions that were attacked in their tracts and broadsides—and I don't have to reach far to compare this with museums and university libraries documenting punk.

To take this slice of pretense a bit further than that: If John Lydon had written nothing but the lyrics of 'Holidays in the Sun,' he would still remain a major British man of letters. And considering his continuing brilliant work, it is almost baffling to realize what a mind of such potency had already produced in his early twenties—a performer/agitator in the vein of Max Wall, Ian Dury, Daniel Cohn-Bendit or, hey, Byron for that matter. This is important work for the ages. And the situation that is the Sex Pistols brought into focus people and events that will take us well past the point when we finally depart the twentieth century (nope, we haven't yet) to fully understand.

Malcolm McLaren as a cultural catalyst—well-versed in the art of agitprop as well as keeping shop, in tandem with the profound deconstruction of public image exemplified in Vivienne Westwood's designs—is consistently scrutinized these days, as he well and truly deserves to be. It is almost impossible in 2016 to understand just how radical the Sex Pistols *looked.* Jamie Reid's artistic sensibility, with one foot in pop-culture detournement and one foot in anarchist community activism (and a third foot planted in hippiedom), brought about a visual language that hurled its precedents against a collective visage, the continuing trickle-down reverberation from which functions simultaneously as mass-market swill and grassroots DIY culture. And the band themselves—Steve Jones, Glen Matlock, and Paul Cook—were arguably the greatest instinctive British rock and roll stalwarts of their generation, bridging mod, glam, and the proto-punk "themness" code to the masses. The music, the stance, the glower... And finally Sid Vicious, a cultural icon stolen away by death, and preserved evermore like Shelley or James Dean as an icon for consecutive generations to discover as a romantic archetype; his name not writ in water but carved into school desks, graffiti'd on walls, emblematic as outsider code both generic and secret.

In this monograph, we wanted to subject our readers to an immersion as pure as we could in book form. The appeal of nostalgic memoirs of legendary days of yore, when people who were there will with great relish tell those who weren't there that they should have been there, was pretty limited to begin with, and at this point doesn't seem to be of much use at all. (And on that note, it is funny how social media has brought about a post-cool era in which everyone can be cool [on Instagram] and therefore no one feels cool, and how the yearning for coolness for the hyper-fragmented Millennials is often filtered through the signifiers of coolness of their parents' or grandparents' generations.)

Since the bankruptcy of ideas has stripped the image of man right down to its deepest layers, the instinctual background manifests itself in a pathological manner. As no form of art, politics, or religion seems adequate to deal with this breach in the dam, the only possibilities are bluster and total artificiality.

— HUGO BALL

The discussion of what to include and what to remove was endless. Ultimately, we hope to provide a visual companion to the music, to the films, and to Fred and Judy Vermorel's *The Sex Pistols Inside Story*, Ray Stevenson's *Sex Pistols File*, and Jon's *England's Dreaming*. We chose not to conduct any new interviews with the people involved; as luck had it, we had access to vast amounts of interview transcripts conducted in the late 1980s, in which the events of flesh had not yet been retold so many times that they read as simplistic myth even when the speaker is authentic. The quotes from insiders, key players, and scenesters on the margin reflect our attempt to provide a human voice alongside the graphics, photographs, and realia.

Sometimes I think the Sex Pistols were the greatest rock and roll situation that the twentieth century brought about; and that the events that unfolded over the absurdly brief scope of two-and-a-half years came to encompass all futurity as it was directly lived by the players, with its representation continuing to create situations all around us every day.

ROBERTA c/o Newman
163 Ocean Ave
#2G BROOKLYN
NEW YORK
U.S.A.

BY AIR MAIL
AIR LETTER
PAR AVION AEROGRAMME

CHELSEA 4.30PM 2 MAR 1974 S.W.3

6p

SECOND FOLD HERE

AN AIR LETTER SHOULD
NOT CONTAIN ANY ENCLOSURE:
IF IT DOES IT MAY BE SURCHARGED
OR SENT BY ORDINARY MAIL

SENDER'S NAME AND ADDRESS (PLEASE SHOW YOUR POSTCODE)

Katharine McQueen
c/o Ker it Roek
430 King's Rd
Chelsea S.W.10
LONDON

Send confusion to
Nympolis Fett. Johnny Kal —
Amos Y/o: Maamagerey does suppose
to schedule lighten and have
them to N.Y.C. last Feb. Anyway
if there not been packed they'll
money I will get them to them

"the dirty stripper who... on
the railings to go hitch-hiking said you
don't think I stripped off all these years
just for the money do you? THAT'S
THE NAME. sprayed onto a latex
sponge sheet and strapped over
the front of the shop. Our window
display includes one long
thigh stiletto boot, 2 real
white mice and the caption
MODERNITY KILLED EVERY NIGHT.
I've written lyrics for a couple
of songs one called Too Fast to live
do you to die (have the idea of
the singer looking like Hitler arm shaking
those gestures etc. and talking about his mum etc.
in German phrases which seen!

joy to hear Albert
[Portugal] a
breath of fresh air

FROM MALCOLM LET IT ROCK

Dear Roberta,   Thursday 21st

Received a card from you this morning which made me feel happy. Didn't even know you were in New York. Closed my shop 6 weeks ago and still fuckin trying to sell it. No luck so far. Hopefully soon I will. Because I will be heading for New York when I do.

Good to hear you like the Dolls. I haven't had a chance to hear their new album yet. Although it's been released ~~gave me~~ ~~your now~~ here a week now. I know they are ~~ever~~ ever so popular in New York from reports I get from friends there and much as writers here. Thought you might still be with Kilburn? Ever such a surprise to know that you were in New York. Are you staying there to long Because I couldn't get there for a month yet. Maybe 2 more like it. I want to come this time for a long time. At the moment I am working with friends on the shop transposing it into a RUBBER GYM. and calling it P.T.O.

clothes by
LET IT ROCK
430 kings road london
01 351 0764 & 673 0855
National Boutique Show
room 760. McAlpin Hotel
Broadway 34 St. N.Y.C.

"MALCOLM McLAREN

THE MOST AMAZING PERSON I'D EVER SEEN IN MY LIFE

VIVIENNE WESTWOOD TELLS TACKY

HER THRILLING STORY

LITTLE DID VIVIENNE WESTWOOD AND MALCOLM McLAREN KNOW WHEN THEY OPENED A LITTLE CLOTHES SHOP IN THE KING'S ROAD, CHELSEA, THAT WITHIN A FEW SHORT YEARS IT WOULD BECOME THE NOTORIOUS HANG OUT OF SEX FIENDS AND JUVENILE DELINQUENTS.

MALCOLM, SEEKING TO GIVE SOME OF THESE POOR LOST SOULS A PURPOSE IN LIFE AGAIN ENCOURAGED THEM TO START A POP GROUP, NAMED AFTER THE SHOP, THE SEX PISTOLS.

UNWITTINGLY HE HAD UNLEASHED THE HORROR OF PUNK ROCK ON A TERRIFIED WORLD...

VIVIENNE WESTWOOD, IN AN EXCLUSIVE INTERVIEW WITH TACKY, TELLS THE WORLD FOR THE FIRST TIME OF THE YEARS OF TRIAL AND TEARS, AND THE MOMENTS OF FLEETING JOY:

Teddy Boys

Q: HOW DID YOU GET THE FIRST SHOP TOGETHER?

V: Oh my god! That takes ages to explain. Well, when we started LET IT ROCK in 1971 we didn't have any money but we had this collection of '50's records and twelve pairs of lurex drainpipe trousers I'd made. We were really looking for a market stall but we were invited to take over the back of this shop called PARADISE GARAGE and we just came to take over the rest of it.

LET IT ROCK catered for Teddy Boys. We were trying to create clothing but we weren't actually designing anything yet. Just making very good facsimilies. We were making exactly what they wanted, the best drape suits tracing back to authentic materials to get that real '50's look, that sort of thing. We were attracted to Teddy Boys

because we saw them as an expression of revolt against a boring way of life.

I was a Sex fiend

Q: HOW DID THE BONDAGE CLOTHING IN "SEX" DEVELOP?

V: We just came up with more and more sexual imagery on our T-shirts and began to see the pertinence of it.

The fact is that if you really do want to find out how much freedom you have in this British society at the moment the best way is just to make an overt sexual statement and you'll have all the hounds of hell on your back. Certainly in this country its the thing that brings out everyone's emotional prejudices so much so that by the time they've finished they're really quite lunatic.

So, we began to think about sexual clothing and materials like rubber to make people much more aware of their bodies and to flaunt themselves in order to confront people. A young girl wearing a rubber skirt to the office is going to produce a reaction. That's what clothes are all about and that's why people wear them. You can't walk down the street in anything I ever made and not have people stare.

Q: THE SHOP CHANGED ITS NAME TO "TOO FAST TO LIVE, TOO YOUNG TO DIE" NEXT, DIDN'T IT?

V: Yes. What happened is that we became very disillusioned with Teddy Boys because they never changed. They are very static, reactionary people and not at all what we thought they were. Apart from which listening to the music they like you begin to realise the inherent racism of that white rock 'n' roll. When you trace it back to its black roots you begin to like that a lot more.

So we developed a feeling for the black thing behind the Teddy Boys and started to get interested in the Rockers who went to Teddy Boy dance halls. They were much more spontaneous and had more human ways of behavious and clothing themselves and anyway we'd always been into having names on the back of jackets and bits of chain and studs. So in TOO FAST we sold two things, the black rock 'n' roll look, drape jackets with peg trousers called zoot suits, and the rocker things, tiny skirts with chains, bike T-shirts and fringes.

TURN OVER FOR MORE THRILLS

VIVIENNE WESTWOOD CONT'D

The truth about Bernard

Q: WHAT WAS BERNARD RHODES (MANAGER OF THE CLASH) INVOLVEMENT IN YOUR SHOP?

V: Let's get this straight once and for all. Bernard Rhodes goes around telling everyone he designed my clothes. He told a girl from a music paper that, then when they printed it he said to me that he didn't know where the rumour started from.

He was my printer and never designed any of my clothes except one T-shirt he had the idea for. The "You're Going To Wake Up One Morning And Discover Which Side Of The Bed You're On" one. It was a good idea and he was a good printer but apart from that one thing he never designed anything.

I seduce children

Q: WHY IS THE SHOP CALLED "SEDITIONARIES" NOW?

V: Because we've always tried to confront people to find out and been concerned with changing things, giving people the confidence to assert themselves as they really are. Its just polarised into a more definite political concept now. Sedition to us means to seduce people into revolt and that's what we're trying to do.

Q: TO WHAT ENDS?

V: To grab their birthright. I bel-

ieve that people are born with un-limited potential and if they can latch on to whatever is wild in themselves that's the best place to start.

People say you can't have anarchy because you can't impose it from above. They can only think of it in those kinds of terms. But you can't say they'll never be anarchy because I am an anarchist. If everyone was you'd have anarchy in this country. People only have to take it and its within their means to so it. Its the only logical way of living.

TOO YOUNG TO DIE

Q: WHY DO YOU THINK THAT KIDS KEEP SMASHING THE WINDOWS OF YOUR SHOP?

V: I understand why its happened to me and not other shops. If you rationalise it they should go and kick in someone like Kickers because that stuff's establishment and mine is anti-establishment. But they don't because they feel emotional about my shop and they don't about Kickers.

Its strange, I call it the Time Out mentality. They think that I must be anti-revolutionary because I'm a materialist, capitalist shopkeeper. I will admit that really is a problem and you do have to walk a tightrope there, but all I can say is that if I do earn a profit then I'm going to use that money to put a few more spokes in a few more wheels.

I don't at all mind the fact that they broke my windows, it was really nice to have that boarding up and see all the graffiti that got written on it. The windows are pretty though. I can't decide which I prefer. Its up to the kids to decide, I'm giving them an open invitation to come and smash them again and drive me to penury.

GOD CAN'T SAVE HER

V: Little boys come running into my shop and say, "Do you really think the Queen is a moron?"

Of course she is. If someone came to you with a piece of paper and if you signed it another person got executed and you did, wouldn't you have to be some sort of zombie. Its not the act of a human being. Lady Macbeth could never wash the blood off her hands but the Queen wears white gloves. A callous little woman who takes off her glove to sign away a life.

You can talk about her having killed many people too by smiling on hypocrisy. Like en tertaining the Brazilian ambassador on a business level, while his country is daily torturing people to death.

If you took away the Queen the army and all those people wouldn't have this figurehead to look up to that smiles at them and pretends everything's all right.

Maybe though, she doesn't know whats going on, the old burke. In that case, let's be very kind for a minute, I feel sorry for her. I'd compare her to those people in the Polynesian Islands who are taken away at a very early age, kept in a dark room and stuffed with food. Then they bring them out once a year so everyone can revel and marvel at these very pale, fat people who can't walk but have to be helped along a sort of catwalk.

I'd compare her to them because she is a symbol of the total wastage of potential. She's prevented from being some kind of wild, crazy, intelligent, creative human being and has to be some kind of a zombie instead. She's an A-1 example of what this country is all about.

Distorted Fragments Of An Interview With

VIVIENNE WESTWOOD

Q: WHAT DO YOU THINK ABOUT THE WAY PUNK HAS GROWN?

V: I think that most of the groups and fanzines are useless. They're just old news. I hate the way people are academic and sociological about it all the time. That's why I don't like the clash. What they say is just not truthful. For example, that thing about the Rastafarians being alright, and they want a white riot of their own. Well, the Rastas aren't alright, maybe they look good which is cool, but they'd be a lot better off without their stupid religion. Without it they'd be a force to be reckoned with, not to be contained and put down as a set of nutcases. Its the same with the Clash, they've contained themselves before they've even started. All that stuff about sten guns in Knightsbridge. I don't see them taking up sten guns. They're lying. Why sing about it if its just academic?

I hate that term "new wave", it sounds like an old hair style. It just means old wave in new trousers. The music papers tried to contain punk by calling it that, new wave, something they can relate to. Punk is not a wave that will come and go, there's something happening here that's quite definite and not about to be swapped for something else pretty soon. Anyway new wave sounds poxy and punk sounds great.

DEBBIE: Punk is just another word for what kids are really. Where I come from everyone's like punks.

Nobody responds to them, they think they're just riff-raff on the street corners who are going to start a fight so they'll have to call the cops in.

V: All the football fans ran down the street outside the shop the other day after the match singing "I'd rather be a punk than a ted". DEBBIE: And Manchester United fans go into fights singing "Anarchy". All the trouble with the Teds is just because they're so jealous of this whole thing. All those Teds are just like their mothers and fathers. They're Teds because their mums and dads were, and uncle Charlie around the corner. They never change

Punks are all out for things that are new and different. In the papers they say punk is going to die out. The only reason it might is because punks have changed into something else.

Q: BUT HASN'T IT STARTED TO STABILISE AND BUILD UP ALL THESE RULES. THE RIGHT THINGS TO SAY IF YOU WANT CREDIBILITY?

V: People have had so many rules already that its difficult for them to break away. So, if they find a new rule that's more exciting than an old one they'll adopt it. But the whole thing inherent in punk is that finaly you don't need any rules, its a Catch-22 situation really. Young kids might be attracted to it thinking that you have to do things in a certain way, Honey magazine wanted me to write a thing telling people how to do your hair and eyes and things to be a punk, but the point is these superficial-

ities aren't important. Its all about attitude. Trust yourself, don't let people tell you what to do and take one little step so you're living instead of following.

Those Auntie Margaret advice columns in girls magazines stink, they're disgusting. They're trying to rationalise things for the kids so that they can live in a repressive enviroment. All those letters about "I'm worried that I'm going to make myself cheap". Fucking go and make yourself cheap. Forget the people that tell you you are and you're no longer cheap.

I think that these kids having trouble from their parents should just leave home. There's no excuse for those advice columns all they should say is my advice to everyone is leave home, the column is ended. DEBBIE: I always used to think when I was a little girl what would it be like if all the adults got blown up and the kids had to start things all over again. Would they do things exactly the same way as their parents did?

What would they do when there was no-one you had to fight against anymore. No coppers. I probably wouldn't have been half as bad as I have been if there wasn't. Because I only did things to revolt against the press and police like a football hooligan. I wouldn't have bothered setting fire to the Metropolitan Police College at Hendon...

WHAT ARE THE POLITICS OF BOREDOM?   BETTER RED THAN DEAD.

Contrary to the vicious lies from the offices of Leber, Krebs and Thau, our former "paper tiger" management, the New York Dolls have not disbanded, and after having completed the first Red, 3-D Rock N' Roll movie entitled "Trash" have, in fact, assumed the role of the "Peoples' Information Collective" in direct association with the Red Guard.

This incarnation entitled "Red Patent Leather" will commence on Friday, February 28th at 10 P.M. continuing on Saturday at 9 and 11 P.M. followed by a Sunday matinee at 5 P.M. for our high school friends at The Little Hippodrome--227 E. 56th St. between 2nd and 3rd.

This show is in coordination with The Dolls' very special "entente cordiale" with the Peoples Republic of China.

                    NEW YORK DOLLS
        produced by Sex originals of London
                c/o Malcolm McLaren
                    New York--212-675-0855
                all rights reserved

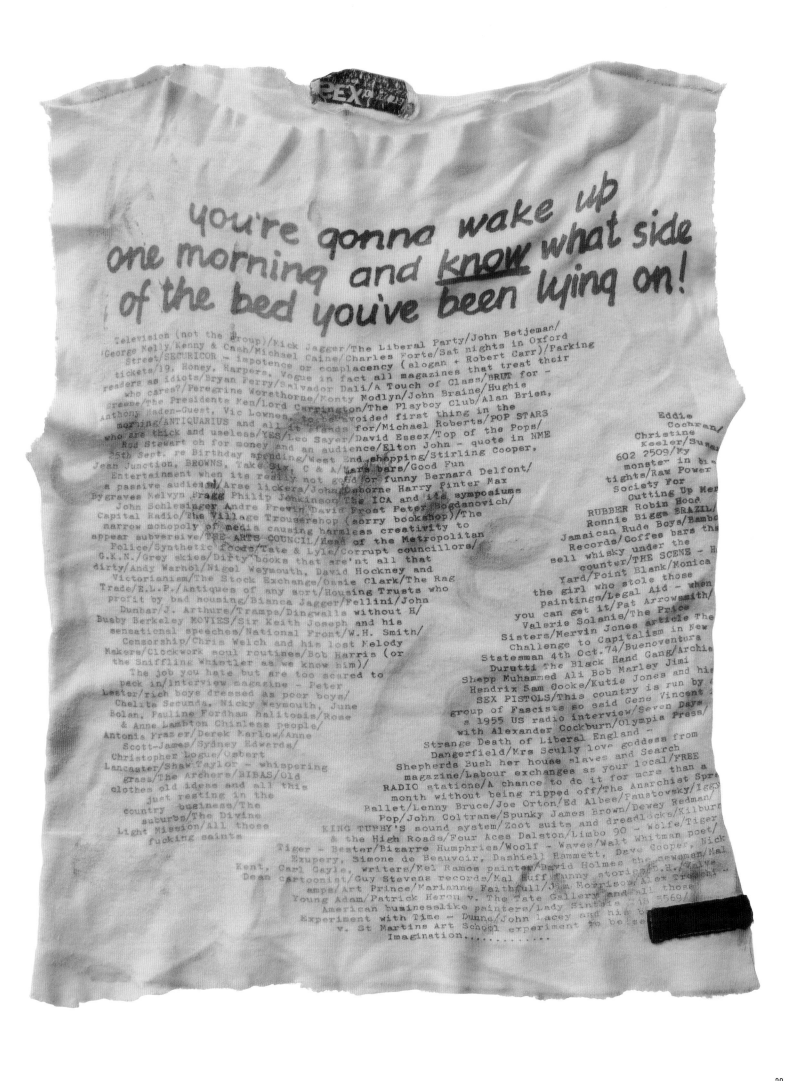

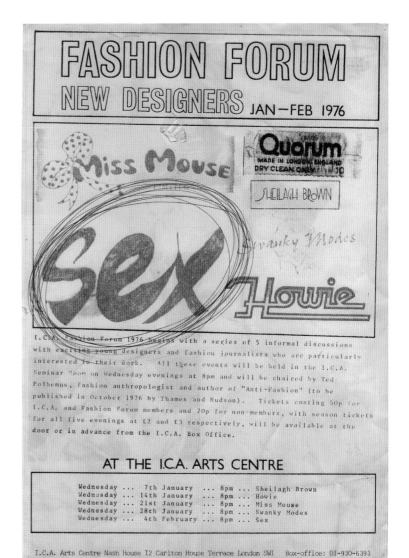

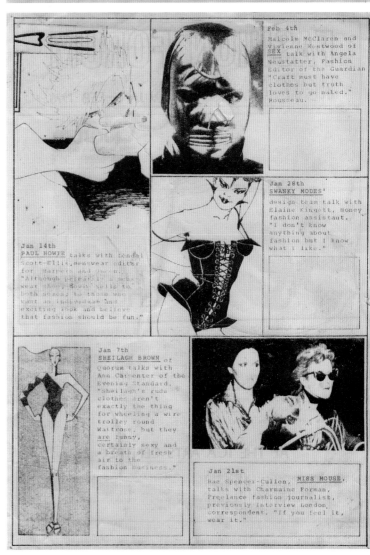

REF
SEX PISTOLS.
c/o SEX
430 KINGS RD.
CHELSEA
LONDON. S.W.10.

01-673-0855
01-351-0764.

MALCOLM

TRACY COOKLIN
Ravensbourne
College of Art.
Walden Road.
Chislehurst.
Nr. Bromley.
Kent.

Dear Tracy
          This is a short note
to confirm that the SEX PISTOLS
will appear at your college
on the 9th December and play
at 9 p.m. for 1 hour maximum.
They will arrive at 4 p.m.
and endeavour to sort out
any problems about playing
. time and equipment with
the other band FOGG. We do
have our own P.A. etc. And
everything should run ~~perfect~~
smoothly. Free beer for
the band would be welcome
          Look forward to seeing you.
then . remaining yours faithfully.
          Malcolm Maclaren.

22   9 December, 1975. Malcolm McLaren note confirming a Sex Pistols performance at Ravensbourne
        College of Art, Chislehurst, Kent.

23   Late 1975. Portraits of Glen Matlock (ABOVE) and Steve Jones (BELOW) by Peter Christopherson.

24   Late 1975. Portrait of Johnny Rotten by Peter Christopherson.

1972   **First formation**

Steve Jones   When I started going down there it was Let It Rock. I used to like it. There were the other shops, Granny and Alkasuras, there were a couple of them where all the rock 'n' rollers used to go, and Malcolm's was cool because you could hang out in there, with the jukebox and the sofa and stuff. We just used to sit in there and watch people come in. After a while I used to hang out with Malcolm, he used to go down to the Speakeasy. I used to go down there on a Friday night and wait for him to go down there, because I couldn't get in, I was only seventeen or eighteen or so. I started driving him around to all these little tailors down the East End, because he couldn't drive. I'd drive Viv's Mini, getting all the materials...

Paul Cook   Steve was always hanging around the Kings Road, and we just felt drawn towards the shop, it was different to all the others down there. It was Let It Rock at the time. Those were the clothes we were into at the time. Ted-ish, flash. John used to go in there as well, I think, with his mates, and eventually as you know we met up. We got involved with Malcolm, though he didn't want to know at first. We told him we were in a band. He was involved with the Dolls at the time. We kept pestering him. Steve wouldn't be working, you see, so he'd go in there quite a lot. I was working in a brewery in Mortlake, Watney's. Electrician apprenticeship. That was a drag, but I had to work I suppose, to get some money. I stopped just before we signed with EMI.

Steve Jones   Wally [Warwick] I knew from school and he could play guitar a bit, and we'd go round his house, and we had the idea of the band. There was Wally on guitar, Paul playing drums, I was singing, and Matlock was playing bass. I met him through the shop really, he used to work there Saturdays. I never really got on with Glen that much. I found him a bit poncified, he wasn't one of the lads. He'd have liked to have been, because I was a total fucking hooligan... but he could play, he liked the Faces, we all liked the Faces at the time. Wally's dad was under contract to do this Riverside place up, and it used to be the BBC, and there was a studio in there, and we used that room to rehearse in. All the equipment was stolen, of course, by me.

Warwick Nightingale   I suggested a group, I had a guitar and an amplifier, a Les Paul copy. I was into music, and after I left school I started to hang around with them, because I liked Steve. He was funny and he could do things. He would nick cars. Things happened around him, he would make them happen. He liked being the center of attention. I thought Steve would be a good front man. Then Paul wanted to be the drummer. He was a sensible sort of fellow. But he's always been a good friend to Steve.

3 JULY 1973   **David Bowie's "last show" at the Hammersmith Odeon**

Warwick Nightingale   Because Steve was there we could always find a way to get in for nothing. It didn't matter if we had to tear a door down. We went to Wembley, the Faces and the New York Dolls—to get in there, we had to virtually rip this door down, tore a panel out of it. We got in, got right down to the front, then went backstage, drinking all their drink in the dressing room—Rod Stewart just standing there—doing all their champagne and everything, having a great time. They didn't know who the fuck we were. They just let us get on with it.

We took the whole PA, every single one of their microphones. RCA were recording it, too, so they were Neumann microphones, about £500 apiece. There was a security guard up in the sixth row, asleep, and we walked on the stage with a pair of pliers, snipping the wires. We nicked all Mick Ronson's gear. Prior to that, Steve had gone out and nicked a minivan to cart the stuff away in. Paul didn't want to go, so me and Steve did it.

1973–1974   **Swankers early rehearsals**

Warwick Nightingale	It was beneath the Furniture Cave, King's Road. Right down the very end. "It's All Over Now," "Twisting the Night Away." Small Faces stuff, "All Or Nothing." "Sha-La-La-La-Lee." I remember Steve bringing round the first Queen album, and the Thin Lizzy song, "The Rocker." Instead of pointing the monitors in, we pointed them out, for effect, as though we were doing a gig. We were pumping out as though we were doing a gig. We could hear the music okay, but we couldn't hear Steve enough to know that he wasn't a good enough singer. He really wanted to be like Rod Stewart, but there was something holding him back. He could play drums better than Paul at that time. He's naturally talented, he had a lovely touch on the drums.
	Glen started working at Malcolm's shop, and Malcolm put him onto us. He came up and auditioned here. He could play this riff from the Faces and we thought it was amazing, and that was it, he was in the group. Just because he could play this riff. He was grammar school–educated. He came from Greenford. He was art school. He wasn't posh, but he hadn't been around too much. He was the first one to get a car, pass his test and everything, his dad's Morris Oxford. He was different, he got his gear together: he wanted a Fender Bassman, and we nicked a Fender bass, a Precision, and we rubbed it down to the wood, and he got that. He bought the cab, and he eventually bought the Bassman top. Then we got down to rehearsals. That went on for a couple of years, the rehearsals.
Glen Matlock	I met Steve and Paul because they used to come in the shop and try to nick stuff, and I had to stop them, didn't I? They came in quite a lot, and we got talking, and they had this band. Steve was a right tea-leaf, and I think the story was, they'd nicked all this equipment and didn't know what to do with it, because it was too hot to sell. One of their mates had the bright idea: "Why don't you learn to play it?" And they were like, "Oh, yeah. Hadn't thought of that." They had a band already with Paul's brother, called Strand, or the Swankers... the bass player wasn't taking it that seriously, and they found out that I was playing bass.
	I'd been playing at school, just playing in my bedroom, trying to copy Ronnie Lane. In fact, that was how I got the gig. There was this quite intricate bass part in a Faces song called "Three Button Hand-Me-Down." I know now that it had been overdubbed twice and all that, but I'd actually learned it as it was. I could play it then better than I could play it now. My first audition with them, I went round to Wally's house, and he said, "What can you play then?" Well, I like the Faces, I know this one, "Three Button Hand-Me-Down." Played it... "You'll do!"
Paul Cook	Malcolm was sort of half interested, because he was getting into the music side of things as well as the fashion. By this time we had a rehearsal place down the Kings Road somewhere, round the back there near Lots Road. Malcolm gradually got more involved. It was me, Wally, Steve, and Glen by that stage, because Glen was working at the shop.
Warwick Nightingale	The first name was the Strand, then the Swankers, which was a joke. Q.T. and the Sex Pistols was the original name that Malcolm came up with, and they didn't like it.
Glen Matlock	Malcolm came up with a few ideas. There was a few names floating around. The Damned was one of them. Kid Gladlove was another one. You got to remember the Biba thing was still going on, it was all Cockney Rebel—it was the tail end of that. Obviously that would color your judgment a little bit. Then the band was called the Pistols, and the shop was called SEX by that time. Malcolm came up with that. I think the QT was from the postcode where we were rehearsing was 4QT. He must have seen that.

EARLY 1975   **Gig at Tom Salter's Cafe, Kings Road**

Warwick Nightingale	I've been told it was in a café, but all I remember is there were these kids we knew who were into taking cocaine, who had some nice little birds with them. They lived in Chelsea and their parents had a lot of money and were very hip, didn't mind them smoking dope and things like that. [We played] probably three numbers: "Scarface," "Twisting," and something else... "Can't Get Enough of Your Love."
Steve Jones	We played in this flat in Kings Road once. These kids we knew, Chelsea kids, had a party one night and all the instruments were up there so we got up there. Did a couple of numbers. It was quite funny. We got rid of Wally, he wasn't right. It was hard to explain his attitude really. We were all having fun, and he was one of these "Don't touch my guitar" merchants, you know?

Paul Cook	I went to rehearse as normal. Me and Steve used to fall out by that time, he was playing guitar behind my back. He'd moved back home and nicked another Les Paul, a black one, and a Fender amplifier. I wasn't keen on the idea because I wanted him to be the star, the front man. I was too naive to think that he wanted to take my position in the group, so I wasn't thinking along those lines at all. I don't know what period of time it took them to decide that I was leaving and Steve was taking over on guitar. Malcolm realized he wasn't right as a singer.
Warwick Nightingale	Why it happened I don't know. It must have been something that turned them against me, because I wasn't aware of it, and neither was Glen. Glen stuck up for me. I don't think even he knew about it. It was a normal rehearsal at Riverside and Malcolm was there, and they just said, "You're not in the group anymore." That was Steve and Malcolm backing him up. It was very hard. I didn't say anything, I was virtually in tears. Didn't cry, but I was so gutted that I didn't say anything. I even went for a drink with them that evening. As far as they were concerned, it was no reaction.

AUGUST 1975   Audition

Steve Jones	Malcolm started to come down. He wasn't managing us or anything, he just wanted to get involved. He said, "You've got to get rid of Wally. You should play guitar." Then we started auditioning singers at the same time, from the shop. We had a few idiots come in, and then Rotten came in, who I didn't really like at all because of his attitude, he seemed like a real prick. He looked really interesting, there was something about him that magnetized you to him. He had all the punk stuff on, that was nothing to do with McLaren. He had all the safety pins and everything, he had the "I Hate Pink Floyd" T-shirt and his hair was orange or green. He was wild looking. His brothers were boot boys. So he came down and we tried him out. We did a couple of cover songs, "Eighteen." He wouldn't do it, he just fucked about in front of it. I started playing guitar and three months later we did our first gig at St Martin's College.
Glen Matlock	He started coming into the shop, and Malcolm suggested him. We set up a meeting and all that, and we all had a few drinks in the Roebuck. He was being particularly obnoxious, and we got him to come back [to the shop] and sing in front of the jukebox, which he felt embarrassed about so he turned it into a charade more than anything, but he was quite engaging. "School's Out," I think. We played a couple of things.
	I always thought he was a bit of a twit. Actually I still think he's a bit of a twit. There was a sort of rivalry between us and a shop called Acme Attractions. It wasn't heavy but they were, like, second division, and John was wearing a lot of things from there. Also he used to wear those horrible plastic sandals. I always thought that was the height of naff, anybody who could wear shoes like that must be a twerp. He used to come in with Wobble and a bloke called John Gray, who was around quite a lot. I think Sid was around, but I wasn't that aware of him. I think they'd all met up at this college in Kingsway, an A-Level college, and they were all called John, so they invented nicknames for themselves.
Paul Cook	It just all fell into place. It was just one of those things. Was it fate? John walked into the shop and he was perfect, you know... Glen was working in the shop and he was looking out for people. John came down one night and met us in the Roebuck, which is now the Dome... The Roebuck then was like a throwback to the 1960s, all those long-haired types. He was all right, he obviously wanted to get involved in doing something. I think he was quite thrilled that people were getting something together and he wanted to be involved in it. I remember saying to him at the time how nothing was happening in music and how the whole youth movement needed something to get them going again. That was my view, because after the skinheads, teds and mods, everything had been in a lull since about 1970, and this was 1975. Five years had passed.
John Lydon	It was Bernie Rhodes that spotted me, because he thought I looked bloody peculiar, with the spiky hair and the safety pins, and everything torn, and an "I Hate Pink Floyd" T-shirt. They thought that was stunning. All of that so-called image was out of poverty. I am a bit of a style pig, too. There was no great master plan on my part or theirs that we got together. I was asked to mime to a jukebox, to an Alice Cooper record, "Eighteen" and "School's Out," which I did very well thank you. [I was] terrified. It never occurred to me that the music business could be a place for me to vent whatever talent I had.

SEPTEMBER, 1975	**Rehearsals**

John Lydon It might have been August 1975. It was summer. They never turned up to the first rehearsal. Never bothered to ring me and let me know. I felt like a fool walking around Bermondsey Wharf, and it's dangerous down there, particularly the way I was looking at that particular time. Bright green crop, I looked like a cabbage.

Glen Matlock So we had this rehearsal down in Rotherhithe, a place called Crunchy Frog. Like a warehouse, a bit hippy dippy. We arranged to meet him down there but nobody turned up. John wasn't too happy about that. I called up the next day to say sorry, but something turned up, and he was, "I'll kill you. I will, I'll come round there with a hammer!" There we go. He's a fucked-up Roman Catholic. Lots of the lyrics he was coming out with, waiting for the Archangel Gabriel, you know, and Anarchy—I am an Antichrist. That's all part of the Catholicism in a way.

Note: during this period, the embryonic Sex Pistols were filmed by Julien Temple and were photographed by John Gray.

SEPTEMBER/OCTOBER 1975	**Rehearsals for second guitarist**

Paul Cook We used to rehearse a lot though, every night straight from work to the West End, once we got the studio in Denmark Street. I think we realised we had to move fast, because there was an undercurrent of all these people coming up, who were going to start bands. You could feel something was going to happen. When we advertised for a guitarist, Mick Jones turned up, just to see what was going on. There were other bands like that coming up, the Hammersmith Gorillas, the Count Bishops. They were mainly pub rock, and we didn't want to get into that really, but something was bubbling.

"Did You No Wrong"—those were the songs that we did already, a few cover versions. People thought we did it because we were into the songs, but we just didn't have our own numbers. A number called "Through My Eyes." "Psychotic Reaction," we used to do that.

6 NOVEMBER 1975	**St Martin's School of Art, London**

Adam Ant They all came in together, the Pistols. John had really baggy ripped-up pinstripe trousers with braces and a T-shirt saying something like, "Rock 'n' Roll" written on it with "I Hate" painted over it. He looked fantastic. They all came in together and they were really little, they must have been fifteen or sixteen some of them. Jonesy was tiny, he had denims, white cap-sleeve T-shirt, baseball boots, looked like a young Pete Townshend. A white Les Paul Junior, wanted to borrow our equipment, so we lent it to him and it wasn't loud enough so they went off round the corner and got an old Fender. Matlock had splattered trousers and white patent Sex boots with red laces, he had these trousers and a light pink leather top, a girl's thing with the two cowboys on it. Paul Cook looked like Rod Stewart, like a little mod really. John was picking his nose and eating sweets—it's something people don't remember much, he used to cough up big lumps of phlegm. I watched them play. I remember Malcolm standing at the front, orchestrating them, telling them where to stand. I'd met Malcolm before when he tried to sell me something when I went into Sex, and I didn't have the money. Viv was there. There weren't many there, maybe a dozen of their people, this was November 1975. Danny hated them, the whole band hated their guts because they couldn't play. In fact there was such a ruck that I left the day after. I went to rehearse with them the day after and had such a row that I had to leave. They did "Seventeen," "Anarchy in the UK," "No Lip," which was my favorite song, "Whatcha Gonna Do About It," with the lyrics changed, and I think that was it. Maybe not, they did a lot of covers. "Substitute," that was it. But I remember "Seventeen," and I do remember "I Hate You Baby," then he just lost interest in the whole thing. I remember him eating sweets, he'd pull them out and suck them and just spit them out, and it was the look—he just glazed, he looked at the audience. This was their first gig, they were very nervous and at the end of their gig Rotten slagged off Bazooka Joe as being a bunch of fucking cunts or whatever, and Danny leapt from the front row, got hold of John and pinned him against the back wall. He was going to beat his face off, and made him apologize.

John Lydon It was vile, they pulled the plug on us. I don't blame them, we were terrible.

Glen Matlock	Malcolm said, "You get it together. Get some gigs together." I went to the Central School of Art, Al McDowell, and Sebastian Conran, asked him if we could have a gig, and he asked if we'd done any, and I said, "No, it's our first one." He asked what was the name, and I said, the Sex Pistols, although we hadn't really decided. And Sebastian went, "Oh yes, wonderful! With a name like that, we have to book you." So that was that. Then in the meantime this gig at St Martin's came up. Al came along to it, and thought it was really funny... pandemonium. We were supporting a band called Bazooka Joe... all those snotty kids from Gospel Oak and all that. The idea was that we were going to use their equipment, but they wouldn't let us use it at the last minute. So we had to go back to Denmark Street and trundle all the equipment through the crowds. Pushing a big bass amp isn't exactly fun. Then we set up and played for about twenty minutes and they pulled the plug on us. Although everybody enjoyed it, you know.
Steve Jones	It was fucking wild. I was so nervous I took a Mandrax. It was packed, it seemed like millions of people at the time, with Bazooka Joe, and when we started playing the Mandrax was hitting me, and I cranked the amp up. It was a 100-watt amp in a little room with no stage, and it was great. Everyone was looking at us, you could tell there was a buzz. Then they pulled the plug on us after about five songs, but the next gig, all that crowd was there again.

7 NOVEMBER 1975   **Central School Of Art, Holborn, London**

Glen Matlock	That was a very good one, one of the best gigs we did. It was only our second gig, though. We supported Roogalator. They'd already booked them, and it was supposed to be a double headline, but we went on first. Paul Ryan, who booked it, asked if he could borrow our bass amp. No, that's alright. Do you mind if I borrow a lead? Er, okay. Do you mind if I borrow your guitar...? The one in those pictures. Steve was playing the guitar that used to belong to Sylvain from the New York Dolls. Malcolm had brought some stuff back, because he hadn't got paid... bands starting out don't normally have that. As good as new Fender twin. Steve had purloined the amps, but I bought the cabinet.
Al McDowell	It went down really well, actually. There were lots of people, but it was really energetic. It wasn't like a huge revelation, it just seemed very direct. It was very addictive, I remember there was some kind of mood which came from them that I can still feel, which is something to do with John's contact with the audience. Everyone else seemed pretty much like a rock band. Obviously he was making it very direct and confrontational. Also the entourage, like Helen, and Malcolm, that group of people were over there, with their mohair sweaters and stuff. Everyone immediately, from my memory, was dancing wildly. Again, I don't think it was shock-horror revelation, it was just very direct dance music. The people in the Central were really into rock'n'roll, it was a whole rock revival thing going on, and it fitted in with that.

NOVEMBER 1975   **St. Albans College of Art**

Shanne Hasler	I was on a Foundation Course at St. Albans, in my second year, and it was around Halloween in 1975. A band just turned up and played, we didn't know who they were. We hardly even bothered watching them, but we were dancing because they were so terrible. We thought they were a piss-take of a 1960s group. Apparently one of them was crying afterwards because it was so bad. They were terrible. Very slow, very amateurish. A youth club group. But really posey as well. I suppose because they were from London.

21 NOVEMBER 1975   **Frognal, London**

27 NOVEMBER 1975   **Queen Elizabeth College, Kensington, London**

5 DECEMBER 1975   **Chelsea School of Art, Chelsea, London**
        Photos: Mick Rock
        Review: Kate Phillips, *NME*

Viv Albertine	I went to the gig at Chelsea School of Art. I completely caught the atmosphere immediately, it didn't need any explaining. It was a matter of attitude, and fuck everything else. I can't remember the music or anything. It was just something I understood, and that was it. It was like a soulmate, or a kindred spirit, and that was it really. It was about half full. Rory introduced

me to Malcolm—he was very charming, polite, not snobby or anything, which he never really was, I liked that. That's all I really remember. Mick wouldn't go, I remember that. He'd heard of them, they were QT Jones and the Sex Pistols then, I think. He wouldn't go because he was getting a group together and they were considered rivals, which they always were. So I told him about it the next day, said it was great.

Roger Armstrong — Ted Carroll and I remember seeing Chelsea Art College, very very early. Malcolm rang us up and said, "Come and see my new band." It must have been one of the first couple of gigs, there were maybe fifty people in the hall. They were a total mess, but it was fun. Johnny just slagged the audience off, basically, and the audience slagged him off and threw things at him, and that encouraged him... All this for forty or fifty people. But it was that college-kid level, it wasn't even on the level of playing the Hope and Anchor. It wasn't as if they were playing to people who would throw bottles and glasses at the slightest encouragement.

9 DECEMBER 1975   Ravensbourne College, Chislehurst, Kent

10 DECEMBER 1975   Fairholt House, London Polytechnic, London

Paul Cook — When we'd do colleges, we'd turn up supporting somebody. By then John handled himself so well on stage. He had everyone in stitches. We supported Shabby Tiger once. I think they were a sort of Scandinavian rock band, they all had long hair and leopard-skin leotards, bleached hair... We just laughed at them.

23 JANUARY 1976   Watford College, Watford

12 FEBRUARY 1976   Marquee Club, Soho, London
Review: Neil Spencer, *NME*

Neil Spencer — Tony Tyler and Kate Phillips had met the Pistols at some event or other, and Malcolm had invited Tony down to see them at the Marquee. They were supporting Eddie and the Hot Rods. Tony called me up, invited me down with him. We arrived at the Marquee, and the guy at the door said, "You better get in there quick, there's a riot going on." We walked into the Marquee and a chair sailed through the air, across the room in front of me, before I saw anything else. There were only about twenty or thirty people in there. And there they were, playing away. Complete brats. Instantly, it was a very powerful memory. I wrote the review, Tony wrote the headline, "Don't look over your shoulder, but the Sex Pistols are coming." We had quite a long chat, but I didn't tape it. "We are into chaos." They all said that. I think Malcolm had told them to say that. "We're not into music, we're into chaos."

Nils Stevenson — I saw them at the Marquee, and it was so great. I thought it was the best thing I'd ever seen, and after that it was me bugging him. Originally he asked me to co-manage them, this has always been a bone of contention. But once I saw them play I decided I definitely wanted to do it, and I don't really remember what arrangement we made. It was a bit like Iggy when he played at King's Cross, it was fantastic, so exciting.

I thought the Pistols had a similar quality. The band were all over the place, not playing very well, not being sure of what songs they were playing, and the chaos, and Rotten saying, "I've always wanted to watch this group play." He just walked offstage with this long microphone lead, sits in the audience, and sings along when he wants to, and throws Jordan across the floor, throws chairs about. I knew I just had to be involved.

Vic Godard — We saw the Sex Pistols virtually by accident. We were just walking past the Marquee one night and heard this noise coming out. We went in there and saw Jordan on the stage and Johnny Rotten in the audience, throwing chairs about. We thought that was really good. They were brilliant, absolutely fantastic.

TV Smith — I'd picked up an *NME* and seen what must have been one of the first Sex Pistols reviews, and how Rotten had been throwing chairs around, and I thought, "Shit, he's got there before me." That was exactly what we wanted. The only thing that came near it was Iggy's *Raw Power*. That kind of feel on that album. Something that wasn't to do with authority, that got to what we were feeling. If music doesn't correspond to what people are really feeling, it's nothing.

14 FEBRUARY 1976	**Andrew Logan's Party, Butler's Wharf, London**
	Pictures: Joe Stevens
	Film: Derek Jarman
	Press: *Sunday Times*

Jordan

The first time I remember Malcolm being really excited, we did that Andrew Logan thing, and Malcolm came rushing up to me saying, "The *NME* are here!" He was really excited. It's funny to think of it now. "The *NME* are actually here. Do something, Jords!" He wanted them to get a bit of outrageous publicity. He said, "Take your clothes off, girl." And I said, "No, I'm not going to." He said, "Go on, we haven't got much time." I said I'd do it if John said so. "I'll do it if John rips them off!" Which is what happened. I jumped onstage and John ripped my clothes off. And that was all for publicity, Malcolm asked me to do it and I did it, after a bit of persuading. It was funny, actually, he broke the zip on the back of this polo-neck leotard, and a pair of Manolo Blahnik shoes!

Derek Jarman

I remember Jordan coming to ask me to bring my camera up, because the band was playing. I didn't know who they were at that stage, I don't think any of us did. I went up and they were on the stage Andrew had constructed for Sebastiane, so it had all the marble up, and all the remains of the Sebastiane set. Obviously I can't remember what they were singing because it was all completely new, and it was a high-energy racket. There were about ten or fifteen people there, and Jordan and Vivienne in the front row were egging them on and gobbing at them and pretending to have battles with them, and Johnny turning his back and singing mostly to the wall rather than to us. I remember having to be careful with the camera even with that small number of people there, because it was all over the place. Jordan was rushing around wrestling with people. It all happened late one afternoon.

Steve Severin

The strangest one was when they played at Andrew Logan's house, which was where that Chelsea lot finally did come face to face with it. I think that shook them up more than they wanted. They wanted something arty and new, but they weren't quite prepared for it, and some of the anger from the stage was definitely directed at them. I think they wanted to embrace the Pistols, and the Pistols weren't having any of it. Malcolm probably wanted them to, so it was in the New York blueprint.

| 19 FEBRUARY 1976 | **Hertfordshire College of Art and Design, St. Albans** |
| | Pictures: Ray Stevenson |

| 20 FEBRUARY 1976 | **College of Higher Education, High Wycombe** |

Glen Matlock

That was a total abortion. We supported Screaming Lord Sutch. Steve's mate, Jim, one of their mates from school, he was trying to do the sound, pissed out of his head, and he didn't know anything about sound at all, he wasn't invited to do it. Johnny smashed every mike on the stage, so there was nothing to even sing into. But it was Screaming Lord Sutch's PA and all the other guys in the band were going ape-shit, and Johnny just totally denied that he'd done it. But everybody had seen him do it. "No I didn't." And Lord Sutch just burst out laughing, at the barefaced cheek of it all.

Richard Boon

It was a horrible students union college thing, a terrible DJ who really wanted to be Mike Read, and there were all these louts who couldn't relate to the Sex Pistols at all. They were very disappointed, they were sitting along the front of the stage with their backs to the stage, signaling to their mates, and Johnny crept along the front of the stage and tousled their hair. One of their mates from the back came running and picked Johnny up and threw him on the floor, and started piling in. Tis was during "No Fun"—this throng of thrashing people—and Johnny kept on singing and crawled out from this melee and crept back onstage and the number ended. It also ended the show—the DJ came on and said, "Oh, well, boys and girls, in the *NME* they say we're not into music, we're into chaos, and I think we know what they mean." So of course we got chatting and back in Reading, Howard and Peter were saying, "Yes, yes, we can do it." They'd been planning to form a group, to do something for a while.

| 21 FEBRUARY 1976 | **Welwyn Garden City** |

Pete Shelley	We saw them at High Wycombe, and the day after they were playing again, and so we went to that one as well. They were good. First of all we were struck that they were no better than we were, so it gave us a bit more because there's always that thing—there was then and to a vast extent now—that a lot of people don't get anything together because the level of competence is getting higher and higher all the time, which leaves people nothing to hold onto. They were college gigs, so heads of the bills were Mr Big and Screaming Lord Sutch, so it was still in that yawning gap, going for a night out drinking Newcastle Brown. At one of the gigs they had a brick put through their van window, so there was antagonism at that early stage, it was a rough noise, it wasn't refined, pruned. On the second one John had flu, he had to keep going off to puke up, and come back on. It was a bit chaotic.
Howard Devoto	[Pete Shelley and I] were reading *NME* in the bar together, when we read the "Don't Look Over Your Shoulders" article, which he pointed out to me, and the fact that they played a Stooges song and said, we're not into music, we're into chaos—oh, that's interesting. And off we went down to London. I think I spoke to Neil Spencer. I remember one of the reasons we went down was I could borrow a car that weekend, and we thought, let's go down and see if they're playing. Richard [Boon] was at Reading University, and we called in and picked him up, and I called the *NME* from Reading, and got put on to Neil Spencer, who told me they were managed by this bloke called Malcolm who's got a Sex shop on the Kings Road, and he didn't know whether they were playing or not. So we drove in from Reading and along the Kings Road thinking we were looking for a dildo emporium, and we found the shop with SEX on it. Went in. As I remember Jordan was there and she said Malcolm would be back shortly, so we came back later and Malcolm was there, and we saw them twice that weekend.
	High Wycombe and Welwyn Garden City, both college gigs. I think at Welwyn, Screaming Lord Sutch was the main attraction, and I remember John smashing their microphone down and stalking off the stage. I think he said he was going to be sick, and went and threw up in the toilets. When he came back there was some argy bargy over whether they could borrow Screaming Lord Sutch's gold microphone. At one of them they were the middle of three bands, and like in the picture of the Electric Circus, there was Siouxsie and the little contingent at the front, and a few people around the back, but everyone else was in the bar. That's my memory of one of them. At the other there was more of an audience. I wrote down a few jolly remarks—"How are you, chuckies? Having fun, chuckies? Because we are!" Various things about stiffs. He was certainly being very abusive and moody. I remember his shoes, and his ratty red sweater. We thought they were fantastic. We really did. It was, "We will go and do something like this in Manchester."

23 MARCH 1976 The Nashville—the first time Dave Goodman worked with the group

Dave Goodman	Albion phoned up one night, and the van was still loaded up, to do a gig at the Nashville. Fifteen quid, just a young band, their first gig or something, they're called the Sex Pistols. They were support band to the 101ers, and they were using our PA as well, a typical Albion con. They turned up late, didn't do a sound check, but they were nice enough guys, except for John who was a bit stand offish. I loved them, and I went up to Malcolm, asked if they had any more gigs, and he said, "You're the first person who's offered us any help."
	We did another one there, where it was their own gig, all Malcolm's art-school people came along in their Roxy Music gear. I think in all we did five or six gigs at the Nashville, then we moved over to the 100 Club. That first night at the Nashville was when Strummer went crazy for the Pistols, kicked our monitors in, and left the 101ers a few days later to get the Clash together. We had to go down and kidnap Mickey Foote from the squat and hold him to ransom to get the speakers replaced.
Joe Strummer	One day the Sex Pistols were supporting us at the Nashville, and that was when I first saw them. I walked through the corridor, and we'd done our sound check and in came these Sex Pistols people, I remember looking at them as they went past: Rotten, Matlock, Cook, Jones, McLaren, and coming up the rear was Sidney, wearing a gold lam... Elvis Presley jacket, and I thought groups in those days didn't talk to each other, it was extremely cut-throat. You fought for gigs, but I thought I'd talk to them, and I said to Sid, that's a nice jacket you've got there, mate. He looked at me and went, yeah, it is, I got it down at Kensington market. We were

humans, talking. Then I walked out onstage while they were getting their sound check together and I heard Malcolm going to John, do you want those kind of shoes that Steve's got, or the kind that Paul's got? What sort of sweater do you want, and I thought, blimey, they've got a manager, and he's offering them clothes! To me it was incredible. The rest of my group didn't think much of all this, but I sat out in the audience, there can't have been more than forty people in the whole boozer, they did their set, and that was it for me. The difference was, we played Route 66 to the drunks at the bar, going, please like us. But here was this quartet who were standing there going, we don't give a toss what you think, you pricks, this is what we like to play, and this is the way we're gonna play it. Regardless of whether you like it or not. That was the difference. [Lydon] pulled out this huge snot rag and blew his nose into it, and he went, if you haven't guessed already, we're the Sex Pistols. Really, come on, you know, and they blasted into Substitute, or Submission, or something. They were doing Stepping Stone, which we did occasionally, but they were light years different from us. They were on another planet in another century, it took my head off. I understood that this was serious stuff, they honestly didn't give a shit. John was really thin, and kept blowing his nose between numbers. That's almost all he'd do between numbers. The audience were shocked.

Graham Lewis   The Nashville was really funny. Someone took me. People were expecting pub rock, and they got this group that was playing really funny versions of Small Faces songs which I had in my collection. The singer kept asking people questions, and they weren't used to that. The person who took me was embarrassed. It was hilarious, a great clash of culture. It was confrontation: you won't like this, you wouldn't remember it anyway, because its by the Small Faces, and you've got no culture.

25 MARCH 1976   Hertfordshire College of Art and Design, St. Albans

30 MARCH 1976   100 Club, Oxford Street, London, supporting Plummet Airlines

Glen Matlock   I remember doing the first gig at the 100 Club, and he was out of his box. He sounded abysmal. The band was all right, but he was singing the right words to the wrong songs. And I went up to him and said, John, "You're acting like a cunt, get it together." And this was in the middle of a song, in front of a crowd at the 100 Club. He says, "Do you wanna fight?" And I said, "Not particularly, I'm playing the bass, we're doing a gig." And he stormed off the stage, and up the stairs, and Malcolm went after him and he was outside waiting for a bus to go home. We're still playing. Malcolm made him go back and apologize to us. Which he did.

Berlin   The first time I saw them was their first gig at the 100 Club. I missed the one at Ravensbourne Art College. The Pistols were incredible. If you take it that you've been used to Alice Cooper, David Bowie, Marc Bolan and all that, I can remember in detail walking down the steps of the 100 Club and just noise, basically. I can remember who was there—there was Paul Getty, Vivienne, Malcolm, Helen the midget, Siouxsie, Steve, Debbi, Tracey, Sharon, all these people who were the Bromley contingent. I remember Johnny crouching on the stage, wearing a red jumper with a white collar, safety pins, jeans, orange hair, and screaming. I said to Steve, "Where is this energy coming from?" It was a totally different thing, aggressive, violent, and at that point it didn't incite the audience as much. People were just standing there.

3 APRIL 1976   The Nashville, West Kensington, London

Alan Jones   I still think their very best performance was the first time at the Nashville. It was a little club atmosphere, everyone knew each other. I remember John sauntering on and going, "Oh hi Debbi, hi Alan, hi!" It sounds a bit elitist but it was nice. That was the one I took Caroline [Coon] along to, which was why she started promoting it quite heavily.

4 APRIL 1976   El Paradise Strip Club, Soho, London
Photograph Ray Stevenson
Reviewed in *Melody Maker*, 8 April 1976

Jonh Ingham   It was like a strip club. You pay your money, turn left and walk in, and you're in a place that's the size of a good-size living room. There's rows of seats, and a stage up there that couldn't have been more than ten feet wide and maybe six feet deep, with a mirror behind it. People are all standing around. The early Pistols crowd were there. Jordan and what's-her-name from Modettes. Viv Albertine. Caroline was there. The Arrows pop group were there. A strange assortment of people. And Ray Stevenson walked in and started setting up umbrella strobes. I started getting really cynical at that point, I'm thinking, "What is this shit?"

They came on, and John's wearing this ripped red sweater, and his hair and his Ben Franklin glasses, and I liked him immediately. They looked funny. There was some stuff between the songs where John was trying to be Johnny Rotten, it was very funny to me. It was like a comic book. It wasn't the madman we all saw nine months later at all. He was saying, "You'd better like what I'm doing because otherwise I'm just wasting my time"—and that had me grinning from ear to ear. All the songs kind of sounded the same, but they were clearly different. The thing about them all sounding the same was just from people who didn't listen. While a lot of the songs were similar, some really worked as pop songs, and others were like, well, it'll be over in two minutes. That was apparent while it was happening, it wasn't something you thought about afterwards.

Joe Stevens   When they played the strip joint in Soho, they did three short sets, about fifteen minutes apiece. Ray Stevenson had his strobes set up, and they were radio strobes, so he had them in the back of the band and they'd all go off when he hit the shutter. And his lights were the only lights they had for the show. So if he chose not to take any pictures during one number, you didn't see the band. I had trouble focusing, because I couldn't see the band. How do you focus on darkness?

23 APRIL 1976   **Nashville, West Kensington, London**
                      Pictures Joe Stevens, Kate Simon
                      NME letter from Neil Tennant

Jonh Ingham   I'm watching the Pistols playing, from the back, and they're not being very good. It was kind of disappointing after everything up to that point. Suddenly Vivienne is slapping this girl's face. I'm at the back, the stage is down there, and she's in the front row, off to the side, and going, whack! whack! whack! Slapping this girl. And this guy, who is getting the worst from Malcolm, is her boyfriend, standing about six feet away. He comes barreling over and grabs Vivienne. Whether Malcolm has watched the whole thing, I don't know. The next thing this guy is ten feet away across the stage, with Malcolm about a foot behind him, fists flying out. The classic photograph. And John, with this look of glee, dives off the stage and starts throwing a few punches as well. Steve came forward and started pulling them away, apart from each other. Steve tried to break it up. Then of course it was complete melee. They went on to finish. Vivienne said afterwards to Caroline that she was bored and decided to liven things up. She just slapped this girl for no reason at all. It was extremely electrifying, I'll say that.

Paul Cook   That's when all the publicity got hold of it, and the violence started creeping in. I don't know what caused that. I think everyone was just ready to go, and we were the catalyst. People just wanted to go mad, but we didn't instigate it.

24 APRIL 1976   **Jonh Ingham Sex Pistols interview in *Sounds***

Jonh Ingham   I'd made an arrangement with Malcolm to meet the Pistols. The first one was midday. He wanted to meet in Denmark Street. At that time I didn't know about the studio where Glen and Steve were living, or the Glitterbest office. Malcolm tells me to meet him at twelve-thirty, I went up there at exactly twelve-thirty, and he's standing there with Nils, outside Keith Prowse or one of those places. Malcolm says, "Where have you been, you're late, they've gone already. They came at twelve, waited twenty minutes, and they've gone." Yeah, right. So we made another appointment. Let's meet at seven-thirty. Again, its outside, in Denmark Street, so I show up at seven-twenty. He's standing there and Paul and Steve and Glen are there, and he's going, "You're late again." I say, "No, I'm early." He says, "We were just about to leave." And I say, "You know, fuck off. You're winding me up." And he laughs, and I've passed a test. At this point, I had a beard. I'd had a mustache and I really hated shaving, and I'd decided that I'd let it grow until my twenty-fifth birthday and then shave it all off. So I had about six weeks of growth, way past designer stubble. We go to that awful pub down at the corner of Cambridge Circus there. John's down there with a couple of girls. So we're walking down there, I'm talking with Paul and Steve and Glen, we're talking about bands. They were questioning me as much as I was questioning them, and clearly what I actually thought was not the point of the conversation. I remember a couple of names mentioned where I was not particularly plus or minus, but I said minus because I knew that was the right answer. That kind of stuff.

All this is in that first interview, almost exactly as it happened. Through this, I'm getting on very well with Steve, which is odd, because in many ways we're completely opposite. Paul's a nice guy, he's very normal, and we're having a nice time. The interview starts, and Malcolm is sitting there, and he'll answer questions that are directed at them if he thinks it will serve his cause better. I can't remember everything we said, but it's all on paper. And all the time, John's sitting there, very politely bored. And they're talking about him like he's not there. I get the story about how they call him Rotten because of his teeth. And I'd got from the first interview with Malcolm the story about the jukebox, and the wire coat-hanger for the microphone. They're talking about John, and how he doesn't like rock, so on. And John's sitting there, he's quite intimidating, but I'm not going to be intimidated. And finally I ask, "Why are you doing this?" And they're telling me why he's doing it, but finally I turn to him and look him in the eye and say, "Okay, I've heard it from everyone else—why are you doing it?" And it's like a snap edit, one frame he's normal, and the next frame, the kilowatts are on. There's no transition at all. "Because I hate shit." And he rants on and on, I hate this and I hate that, glaring at me. I look at Malcolm and he has this expression like, "Well, he's out of control, isn't he?" He's got a nervous look on his face, you know. "Don't look at me, it's not me, it's him."

I just cracked up laughing. This boy was incredible, you know, he really amused me. He's going, "I hate hippies." I'm finding myself defending myself to this kid, going, "I'm not a hippy, I've never been a hippy, I just haven't shaved." From the first sentence, I was absolutely sold. I admired the man, instantly. At the same time, as with Malcolm, I just kept looking at this guy, these awful clothes—I mean, I loved the style of it, it was cool, but I'm looking at these two girls with John, and thinking, why are you turned on by this guy? Not really knowing anything about him, at this stage, not knowing "I don't like sex," all that shit. Clearly there was a very sexual atmosphere between these people, these two girls and John. It made me wonder, what is there about this guy, that you're so turned on by him?

29 APRIL 1976   **Nashville, West Kensington, London**

John Lydon   I remember a fight with Paul, but it wasn't really a fight. The Nashville. I decided to quit that night. Someone mentioned my quitting, you know? They'd decided that I was an arsehole again, that time came back. As it kept on recurring. Over nothing at all, I suppose. It was actually highly enjoyable, and after the gig it was a huge laugh. What kept winding me up all the time was that I kept feeling left out of things. I didn't ever feel part of the band.

5 MAY 1976   **Babalu Disco, Finchley Road, London**
          Pictures: Ray Stevenson (color)
          Advertised on Capital Radio
          Ted Polhemus account in *BOOM*

11 MAY 1976   **100 Club, Oxford Street, London**

Ray Stevenson   There was a sudden point when I realised how good they were, but I can't remember when it was. It was probably the 100 Club, that telepathy, tension thing, where Rotten would be slagging off the audience, and Steve and Paul would be doing something, and they would just go into a number at the perfect moment. Rotten's control. I was seeing them very much as amateurs, and to imagine this bozo kid from Finsbury Park, with no schooling, no history of music at all, was phenomenal.

15 MAY 1976   **Recording sessions, Chris Spedding**
          Three tracks recorded: "Problems" / "No Feelings" / "Pretty Vacant"
          These were first released on a bootleg 7" before being included on the official 2002 Virgin release, *SEXBOX*

Ray Stevenson   It was the band's first time in the studio, a learning process for them. Spedding didn't inspire me with a great deal of confidence. They went in for demo tapes, and that was what came out, decent sound on everything, and no playing about.

| 17 MAY 1976 | **Screen on the Green Cinema, Islington, London—CANCELED** |

| 18 MAY 1976 | **100 Club, Oxford Street, London** |

Jonh Ingham

There was the 100 Club gig a few weeks after that, every Tuesday through May, June. They were supporting, and they were just playing, it was very fresh and new, and nine tenths of the audience would probably be for the headlining band. At that stage we're talking about fifty people. A hundred would be a good gig. I must have known Sid by this point. I was most friendly with Glen and Paul, and Steve to a slightly lesser level. You could talk to John, but you couldn't call yourself a friend. I went because it was interesting, and there was the feeling of being in at the beginning of something new. I was never bored watching it.

| 19 MAY 1976 | **Northallerton, Yorkshire** |

Glen Matlock

We'd had a little bit of press by then. That girl Pauline turned up, from Penetration, with her boyfriend. They'd traveled quite a long way. They used to come to a lot of gigs. She was a nice girl too, had a great voice. Anyway we got there, it was this little market town, and it was like a chicken-in-a-basket place. And this bloke, I'm not kidding, with a Tom Jones tux, gets up and goes, "All right ladies and gentlemen, they've come all the way from London tonight, please put your hands together, here for you in cabaret, the Sex Pistols." And we were like, "What?" That was the first one, then I think we went to Whitby Bay, and we couldn't find anywhere to stay, they took one look at us... Anyway, we played this place, and they kept telling us to turn it down, they came up about three times, and in the end we were just larking about, pretending we were miming kind of thing, like you'd do on the Hughie Green show. And this bloke comes up and says, "No lads, its no good, we'll pay you what you're due, but we just can't hear the bingo in the other room." So we played about fifteen minutes of that gig.

Pauline Murray

We found they were playing this place in Northallerton, which is nowheresville near Harrogate, and it was literally like a row of garages, and the end one was a night club. The people in there were like your regular crowd. No stairs, just a few tables around, small PA columns. They came on and it was like nothing we'd seen before, it was so funny. The reaction of the people was amazing. They were totally manic, mad.

| 20 MAY 1976 | **Penthouse, Scarborough** |

John Lydon

We were so intensely disliked, there was no real audience for us outside of the 100 Club, that was it. Anywhere else you were taking your life in your hands. We'd go up north and we'd be lucky to return. We played all sorts of weird places like Scarborough and Barnsley. A teddy-boy pub, of all places, in the middle of nowhere.

Paul Cook

We did a poxy little tour up there very early on, in early 1976, we played places like Grimsby, Preston, maybe Manchester, and in Wales as well, where that Welsh crowd came from. People used to hear about it and come along. Not thousands of them at first... it was great. Pretty depressing though, up North, because there wasn't anything to do after the gigs. We had this old van, and we had to read the contour lines on the map because we couldn't go up high hills!

| 21 MAY 1976 | **Middlesborough Town Hall, Middlesborough** |

| 25 MAY 1976 | **100 Club, Oxford Street, London** |

| 30 MAY 1976 | **Reading University, Reading** |

Richard Boon

I booked them to play at the art department in Reading—supported by Harry Kipper of the Kipper Kids. They went down pretty well with the Fine Art department! Hardly anyone came to see them, but those that did really liked them.

| 4 JUNE 1976 | **Lesser Free Trade Hall, Manchester** |

Howard Devoto

I said to Malcolm, "Do you want to come and play at my college, if I can get you in there?" And he said yes. He said, "If you can set it up, we'll do it." So I must have tried to persuade the Students Union to put them on, but they wouldn't go for it. Not because of their reputation, just that they'd never heard of them. There was very little in the press. So I started looking round for a venue, and someone told me about this little hall above the Free Trade Hall, and I phoned them up, got it for £25 or something, and meanwhile, like on this ticket, we were planning to play ourselves, on the 4th of June 1976, but we hadn't got it together. We got about a hundred, which wasn't bad at all. I remember the band being very pleased. John wasn't at all attacking at that one, he uttered a few kind words. By that time I would have been to a few gigs, I was aware of differences in the audience reaction.

Morrissey   There was a whisper. There was a certain glut of Manchester people who knew about these things. I eavesdropped, I got a ticket for 50p, a small white ragged thing which someone had sat behind a typewriter for days, typing out these individual tickets, and the first Sex Pistols appearance was quite difficult, there weren't any instructions. Being northern, we didn't know how to react, but for the second appearance we had been instructed by the music press—we stood up, we went to the front, things like that. The first appearance, people were very rigid. There was a support group on that had come from Blackburn or somewhere like that, and their hair swept off the stage, it was dreadful. As I recall people were unwilling to respond to the Sex Pistols, the audience was very slim anyway, it was a front-parlor affair. If somebody spoke three rows back you could hear what they said, and join in. No, the audience was very sparse. And yet later, of course, everybody was there. But they weren't.

Tony Wilson   I got a letter and a cassette from a guy called Howard Trafford, and he said this is a really wonderful group just started up in London, they're coming to Manchester on June 2nd, Lesser Free Trade Hall, and that of course was the Sex Pistols. So I began a conversation with Howard. We went on preparing *So It Goes* to be a quick moving, groovy, fast TV show, that didn't have too much respect for the music because the music was pretty shitty. It wasn't until I sat in that concert hall with about thirty seven people, between thirty and forty people that first night. The second time, six weeks later when the Buzzcocks did their first gig and Slaughter and the Dogs were on the bill, there were about a thousand people, but the first night, I didn't know what the fuck was going on, until they played "Stepping Stone." As soon as they did that, it was clear that they were deeply and remarkably and fabulously exciting.

15 JUNE 1976   Assembly Hall, Walthamstow, London
Wobble Nick Kent incident

17 JUNE 1976   Assembly Hall, Walthamstow, London
Midsummer Music Festival Benefit supporting Kilburn and the High Roads and the Stranglers

Tony Wilson   I went back to Granada and said we absolutely must put them on the show, and the researcher, Malcolm Clark, was asked to check them out with me. We went to Walthamstow Assembly Hall, and that again was a completely non-attended gig, maybe eighty people, of whom forty were a large, single line semicircle, just out of gobbing range.

29 JUNE 1976   100 Club, Oxford St, London
Recorded by Caroline Coon—note this includes a short instrumental called "Flowers of Romance," included on *SEXBOX*

Dave Goodman   They'd jam a bit when they got onstage, making sure everything was working, and it turned into something they called Flowers of Romance, after Sid's first band. They'd be stoned, we turned them on to dope. They would have got into it anyway, but we had the supply.

3 JULY 1976   Pier Pavilion, Hastings

Poly Styrene   On my nineteenth birthday I saw the Sex Pistols on Hastings Pier. I just saw this tacky sign with "Sex Pistols" written all over it. The name was like a Freudian joke. They were just incredibly young and fresh looking. It's a question of peer pressure, isn't it? You seen other people your own age doing things and after that you get all sorts of things together to compete. I liked the way they were writing about their surroundings: it was definitely a change in consciousness.

4 JULY 1976   Black Swan, Sheffield, supported by the Clash in their first public show

6 JULY 1976	**100 Club, Oxford Street, London, supported by the Damned in their first public show**
9 JULY 1976	**Lyceum Ballroom, the Strand, London, supporting Pretty Things and Supercharge**

Jonh Ingham — The next thing was the Lyceum, the Pretty Things thing. What was really strange was that it seemed such an amazingly unimportant gig. They're third or fourth on the bill to the Pretty Things at the Lyceum. I mean, come on. And they were so absolutely petrified before, backstage. Steve couldn't talk, he couldn't utter a word, he had the look of death on his face. To them, it was extremely important. It was the first time they'd played in a big space. John was really nervous. I found that strange. It hadn't occurred to me that for them, they wanted to win people over. Perhaps they were scared by the sheer physical size of the joint. That was the night that John stubbed out cigarettes on the back of his hand while he was singing. I remember talking about that in the review. It frightened me. By that point we were rolling joints, and I think Louise's was in full swing by then, so "We don't take drugs" was just publicity by then. He had the most manic look in his eye when he did it. It was back to the Iggy thing in a way: you couldn't predict this person.

10 JULY 1976   **The Sundown, Charing Cross Road, London**
First set ends after thirty minutes and the second set is canceled

Jonh Ingham — Whatever gig I saw between the Lyceum and Manchester, there was a quantum leap in ability from previously. Up until this point, they were getting better at it, but it was still the same kind of noise. They were getting better at being the same thing. But suddenly there was this major step up in musical ability. Glen was phenomenal, the bass playing was tremendous. Paul was right on the beat. In one night, suddenly they were all just there. Suddenly you knew that this was a really great band.

13–30 JULY 1976   **Recording Sessions, Dave Goodman**
"Pretty Vacant" / "Seventeen" / "Satellite" / "No Feelings" / "I Wanna Be Me" / "Submission" / "Anarchy in the UK"—two versions, first issued on 1966 *No Future* LP, most now on CD version of *Spunk*

Dave Goodman — We recorded all the first stuff in Denmark Street, over two weeks. They'd play live, maybe four or five takes of each song, then overdubs. They needed some good tapes. I heard the Spedding tapes just after they came out of the studio, and they didn't happen. They sounded like rough mixes, guitars not loud enough. I said I could do better with my four-track, so they said, "Do it then." I think we overdid it with the guitar overdubs, but they worked.

20 JULY 1976   **Lesser Free Trade Hall, Manchester**

Linder — I remember going into the Lesser Free Trade Hall and I just knew that something strange was going to happen. I just knew it. These people looked so separate and apart and so different. Not threatening at all, just fascinating, me longing as usual for something different. Exotic, and these strange leather trousers and mohair jumpers. It was just so strange... Johnny was wearing this big mohair jumper that seemed to be growing all the time, the fluff getting longer, and arms growing out like an octopus. It was a shimmery night. All this energy and light.

Jonh Ingham — The next time, in Manchester, was about two weeks later, it was a next step-up again. It was light years ahead of what we'd just seen. It was amazing. That was the first night they did "Anarchy," and that was just monstrous. It was so cool, and there was no warning. They hadn't talked about it. The first we knew about it was when they were on stage.

31 JULY 1976   **Jonh Ingham review in *Sounds* of the Free Trade Hall show on the 20th**

7 AUGUST 1976   **Caroline Coon cover story in *Melody Maker*, "Punk Rock: Crucial or Phoney?"**

10 AUGUST 1976   **100 Club, Oxford Street, London, supported by the Vibrators**

Mark Perry — August, at the 100 Club. They were brilliant. I remember I was wearing this beautiful satin jacket, and it got ripped to shreds. It was hanging off me, and I was in heaven. This was it, I'm really into it. Johnny Rotten kicked me in the shoulder, I was in the front row. Come to think of it, they weren't as good as young bands that start now, because bands know how to do it better now. But then, the sound was rather hollow, amateurish, but it was exciting. And the sneering, and the audience put-downs, and the gobbing. We were pogoing and smashing into each other.

14 AUGUST 1976 **Barbarellas, Birmingham, attended by Polydor A&R man Chris Parry**

19 AUGUST 1976 **Village Inn, Runton, Norfolk**

21 AUGUST 1976 **Boat Club, Nottingham**

29 AUGUST 1976 **Screen on the Green Cinema, Islington, London**

Roger Armstrong

I remember distinctly the Screen on the Green, the first of those. The Buzzcocks and the Clash getting no fair crack of the whip on the PA whatsoever. Miserable little sound like a transistor radio, then the Sex Pistols came on and suddenly they switched the PA on. I think the others had been going through the monitors. I thought it was so funny, these people putting something new together, and here's the old tricks. That was the night Johnny knocked his tooth out on the microphone.

Nils Stevenson

It was great. The most memorable thing about it was Steve always threw up before he went onstage, always without fail, because he was so nervous. So he opened one of Roger (Austin)'s filing cabinets. But the funny thing was, the next time, he remembered where he'd done it the last time and did exactly the same thing again. He could be quite piggish sometimes.

31 AUGUST 1976 **100 Club, Oxford Street, London, supported by the Clash**

1 SEPTEMBER 1976 **Recording of Granada TV *So It Goes***

2 SEPTEMBER 1976 **Nags Head, High Wycombe**

3 SEPTEMBER 1976 **Club De Chalet Du Lac, Paris, France**

Jordan

Yeah, me and Vivienne went together. It was a scream. We got wined and dined by Jean Charles Castel de Bergac. Nice man. If you can imagine me and Viv turning up at Gatwick, at the wrong terminal, miles away, not a hope, couldn't get on the Metro, didn't know what we were doing, where we were going. Nobody knew we were turning up, it was supposed to be a surprise. It was really exciting. And going to discos—Malcolm and Vivienne and the Sex Pistols and I went to a really straight disco. They were jiving, and we were, too! Me and Malcolm dancing together, I remember that.

Glen Matlock

We went to France quite early on as well. It was a scream, that gig. Madness. It was free to get in. This new club was opening, and nothing is free in Paris. So practically the whole town turned out for this new thing. It was jam packed. And they'd only finished painting the place that morning. They had to carry all the chairs outside in the afternoon to get them to dry, and they weren't, and there's women in white dresses getting up and they've got black chair marks all over them. They weren't too happy. And they had this new glass floor, and I was kind of pogoing, just sort of stomping, and the janitor of the place is going, "Oh, *sacre bleu!* The floor, *monsieur*," and I'm trying to play and he's tugging my trouser leg, because it's glass, with lights underneath. The more he did it, the more I did it, you know.

Nils Stevenson

It was so refreshing, that trip, playing this fantastic place that was absolutely packed. It was a riot to get in, and the punters had no idea what the group was actually like, and they were absolutely devastated, really pissed off, when the group played. But it was marvelous to get out, and everyone got very close again, the whole group was very close for the whole trip. It was marvelous. Billy Idol drove his van over, and the Bromley people slept in the van. It was fucking great. But the group kept Siouxsie and all those people at arms length, it had got a bit elitist in that way already. By Paris the group had got a bit full of themselves and they were keeping the crazy fans at arms length... I think perhaps Steve and Paul were embarrassed by the way Siouxsie looked. John would open up to them a lot more.

4 SEPTEMBER 1976   **Granada Television, *So It Goes*: the Sex Pistols' first UK TV appearance**

Tony Wilson   We decided to make a virtue out of our last show, with three unsigned bands. McLaren gave me the T-shirt that day, they behaved pretty badly. They had a row with Clive James. They had drunk quite a bit. They were meant to do three-and-a-half minutes, they agreed that and rehearsed it, and there were five minutes left, and they just kept playing for seven minutes and kicked their equipment apart. Two days later the director edited it down to three-and-a-half minutes. He did a good job, but someone threw away the original take, which was a shame. The audience was dumbfounded, as they came offstage there was complete silence except for the footsteps of [producer] Chris Pye coming down the stairs from the box to try and hit somebody. Everybody was wound up. The next day I was in trouble at Granada, there was bad feeling.

Pete Shelley   We almost had a fight in the hospitality room there. It was almost like a village hall. There was a band called Gentlemen, and I got into an argument with the guitarist. He was going, "You can't play your instruments," and I was going, "Well, so what?" He was getting really irate because he'd been learning his craft for years and all these people coming along and not playing the game, not only playing badly, but making money out of playing badly, and using that as part of the selling point. One of the Pistols' roadies had to step in and separate us.

11 SEPTEMBER 1976   **The Royal Ballroom, Whitby**

12 SEPTEMBER 1976   **Fordgreen Ballroom, Leeds**

13 SEPTEMBER 1976   **Quaintways, Chester**

15 SEPTEMBER 1976   **Lodestar, Blackburn**

41   Late 1975. Contact sheet from Peter Christopherson. Taken adjacent to the band's studio space
        at 5 Denmark Street, these photographs are the earliest formal portraits of the Sex Pistols.
        Peter Christopherson was a member of the design collective Hipgnosis.

42   15 December, 1975. The earliest known Sex Pistols gig poster, for Rosie's Restaurant at Central
        School of Art and Design, London.

43   19 February, 1976. Hertfordshire College of Art and Design, St. Albans.

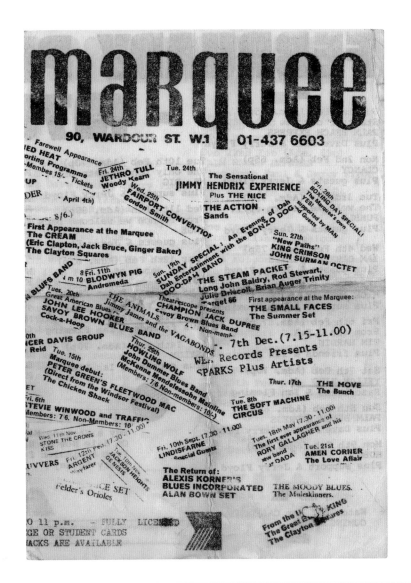

marquee

90, WARDOUR ST. W.1 01-437 6603

...Farewell Appearance
...ED HEAT
...orting Programme
...Members 15/- Tickets
...UP
...DER   (April 4th)

Fri. 24th
JETHRO TULL
Woody Kearn
Wed. 25th
FAIRPORT CONVENTION
Gordon Smith

Tue. 24th
The Sensational
JIMMY HENDRIX EXPERIENCE
Plus THE NICE
THE ACTION
Sands

Fri. 26th
BOXING DAY SPECIAL!
The Marquee's own
YES!
supported by MAN

...8/6.)
...First Appearance at the Marquee
The CREAM
(Eric Clapton, Jack Bruce, Ginger Baker)
The Clayton Squares

Sun. 19th
SUNDAY SPECIAL: An Evening of Dah
Dah Entertainment with the BONZO DOG
DOO-DAH BAND
Theatrescope presents
CHAMPION JACK DUPREE
Savoy Brown Blues Band
4. Non-members

Sun. 27th
"New Paths"
KING CRIMSON
JOHN SURMAN OCTET

8 Fri. 11th
BLODWYN PIG
4 m 10   Andromeda

...BLUES BAND

Tues. 20th
THE ANIMALS
Great American Blues Jimmy James and the VAGABONDS
JOHN LEE HOOKER
SAVOY BROWN BLUES BAND
Cock-a-Hoop

THE STEAM PACKET
Long John Baldry, Rod Stewart,
Julie Driscoll, Brian Auger Trinity
...arget 66

First appearance at the Marquee:
THE SMALL FACES
The Summer Set

...th
...NCER DAVIS GROUP
...Reid   Tue. 15th
Marquee debut:
PETER GREEN'S FLEETWOOD MAC
(Direct from the Windsor Festival)
The Chicken Shack

Thur. 29th
HOWLING WOLF
John Dummer Blues Band
McKenna Mendelssohn Mainline
(Members: 7/6 Non-members: 10/-)

..7th Dec. (7.15-11.00)
W.. Records Presents
SPARKS Plus Artists

...Fri. 6th
STEVIE WINWOOD and TRAFFIC
Members: 7/6. Non-members: 10.00)

Thur. 17th
THE MOVE
The Bunch

Tue. 8th
THE SOFT MACHINE
CIRCUS

...al Wed. 11th Nov
STONE THE CROWS
KISS

Fri. 10th Sept. (7.30-11.00)
LINDISFARNE
Special guests

Tues. 18th May (7.30-11.00)
The first ever appearance of
RORY GALLAGHER and his
new band
...QADA

Tue. 21st
AMEN CORNER
The Love Affair

...UVVERS   Fri. 12th Feb
ARGENT
Wayfarer

...10th Nov
JACKSON HEIGHTS
GENESIS

Felder's Orioles
...CE SET

The Return of:
ALEXIS KORNER'S
BLUES INCORPORATED
ALAN BOWN SET

THE MOODY BLUES.
The Muleskinners.

...O 11 p.m. – FULLY LICENSED
...GE OR STUDENT CARDS
...ACKS ARE AVAILABLE

From the U.. KING
The Great B.. atures
The Clayton ...

FEBRUARY PROGRAMME - 1976 -

Sun 1st Feb (Adm. 65p)
Start of our new residency...
PALM BEACH EXPRESS
Plus Dave Paul & Jerry Floyd

Mon 2nd Feb (Adm. 65p)
CLANCY
Plus guests & Jerry Floyd

Tue 3rd Feb (Adm. 75p)
The welcome return of...
FUMBLE
Plus guests & Jerry Floyd

Wed 4th Feb (Adm. 75p)
IAN CARR'S NUCLEUS
Plus guests & Jerry Floyd

Thurs 5th Feb (Adm. 65p)
MICK ABRAHAM
Plus support & Ian Fleming

Fri 6th Feb (Adm. 70p)
From the U.S.A.
TIM HARDIN
Plus friends & Ian Fleming

Sat 7th Feb (Adm. 70p)
YELLOW BIRD
Razorbacks & Ian Fleming

Sun 8th Feb (Adm. 65p)
PALM BEACH EXPRESS
Plus Dave Paul & Jerry Floyd

Mon 9th Feb (Adm. 60p)
HOBO
Plus support & Jerry Floyd

Tue 10th Feb (Adm. 70p)
The only London date of...
MR. BIG
Plus support & Jerry Floyd

Wed 11th Feb (Adm. 80p)
From France we welcome back
ANGE
Plus guests & Jerry Floyd

Thur 12th Feb (Adm. 65p)
London debut of ...
STARS
Plus support & Ian Fleming

Fri 13th Feb (Adm. 70p)
DANA GILLESPIE
Plus friends & Ian Fleming

Sat 14th Feb (Adm. 70p)
ASYLUM
Plus support & Ian Fleming

Sun 15th Feb (Adm. 65p)
PALM BEACH EXPRESS
Plus Dave Paul & Jerry Floyd

Mon 16th Feb (Adm. 80p)
~~SAVOY BROWN~~ ROB SAMAPPLE PIE
Plus guests & Jerry Floyd

Tue 17th Feb (Adm. 75p)
NUTZ
Plus guests & Jerry Floyd

Wed 18th Feb (Adm. 65p)
KILBURN & THE HIGH ROAD
Plus support & Jerry Floyd

Thur 19th Feb (Adm. 70p)
NATIONAL FLAG FLU.
Cock Sparrow & Ian Fleming

Fri 20th Feb (Adm. 75p)
The welcome return of...
BACKDOOR
Plus friends & Ian Fleming

Sat 21st Feb (Adm. 70p)
BEARDED LADY
Plus support & Ian Fleming

Sun 22nd Feb (Adm. 65p)
PALM BEACH EXPRESS
Plus Dave Paul & Jerry Floyd

Mon 23rd Feb (Adm. 65p)
STRIFE
Plus support & Jerry Floyd

Tue 24th Feb (Adm. 80p)
From Holland we welcome
TRACE THE ENID
Plus support & Jerry Floyd

Wed 25th Feb (Adm. 75p)
GONZALEZ
Plus friends & Jerry Floyd

Thur 26th Feb (Adm. 70p)
MIKE HERON'S REPUTATION
Plus support & Ian Fleming

Fri 27th Feb (Adm. 70p)
DRUID
Plus guests & Ian Fleming

Sat 28th Feb (Adm. 70p)
Return by public demand
GIGGLES
Plus support & Ian Fleming

Sun 29th Feb (Adm. 65p)
PALM BEACH EXPRESS
Plus Dave Paul & Jerry Floyd

SAVE MONEY
Buy a Marquee Membership Card
On Sale Now At Only 60p
Free Admission For Members On
Every Sunday

Watch out for CALEDONIA-
COMING SOON!

Mon 8th & Tue 9th March
Come and say 'Goodbye'
FAREWELL CONCERT
PINK FAIRIES

All Programmes are subject to alteration and the Management cannot be held responsible
for non appearance of artistes.

Photo: Joseph Stevens ©1978

44   12 February, 1976. Program for the Sex Pistols live at the Marquee, London.

45   **ABOVE:** 14 February, 1976. Sex Pistols at Andrew Logan's Party, Butler's Wharf, London. **BELOW:** 19 February, 1976. Hertfordshire College of Art and Design, St. Albans.

46   20 March, 1976. The Sex Pistols perform at the Nashville Rooms, London.

47   **ABOVE:** 30 March, 1976. The Sex Pistols at the 100 Club. **BELOW:** 4 April, 1976. The Sex Pistols at El Paradise Club.

48   April 1976. The first offset-printed Sex Pistols handout featuring a bio of the band.

49   **ABOVE LEFT:** 4 April, 1976. Flyer for the Sex Pistols gig at El Paradise Club, designed by Helen Wellington-Lloyd. The Sex Pistols' performance was supported by Ted Carroll's Rock On Disco. **ABOVE RIGHT & BELOW:** 29 April, 1976. Flyer for the Sex Pistols live at the Nashville Rooms, with notes on reverse by Malcolm McLaren.

SEX PISTOLS

Teenagers from Londons Shepherds Bush and Finsbury Park:
       'We hate everything.'
The Sex Pistols are....
                    John Rotten   Vocals
                    Steve Jones   Guitar
                    Glenn Matlock Bass
                    Paul Cook   Drums
The boys met at the shop 'SEX' in Chelsea's Worlds End in
October '75. Enthused and spurred on by the shop owner,
Malcolm Mclaren, they became the Sex Pistols.
       November found them gatecrashing college gigs
throughout London and it's suburbs, causing a furore
wherever they went.
       After being banned from the Marquee club in
February '76 and sell-outs at other gigs, the group
created a precedent by starting their own rock venue at
the El Paradise club in Soho on April 4th.
       Their own numbers include :

                    Pretty Vacant
                    Submission
                     Only Seventeen
                    Problems
                     No feelings
     Along with their own versions of 'The Who's'
'Substitute' and some lesser known Small Faces songs.
The Sex Pistols spontaneity and honesty threatens all
the highly packaged pop of the past.

Sole representation and management:
 Malcolm McLaren,
  93 Bell Street,
   London, N.W.1.
01-673-0855
01-723-7982

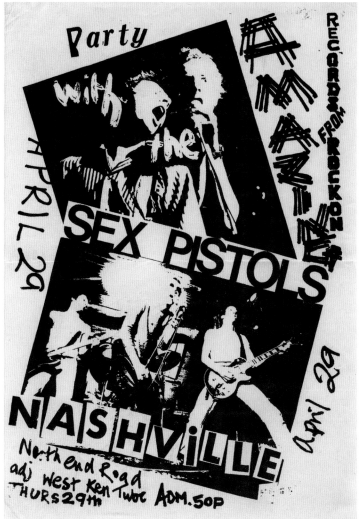

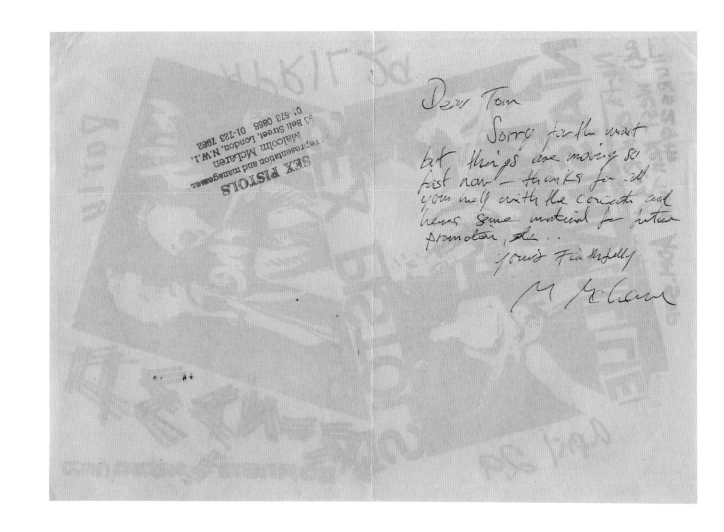

SEX PISTOLS

THE 100 CLUB

LONDON'S PREMIER JAZZ CENTRE

100 OXFORD STREET, LONDON, W.1

Manager: ROGER HORTON   Telephone: 01-636-0933

The average members' price is between 80p and £1.50 depending on the day of the week and the quality of the artiste performing. Admission for guests is usually 20p to 50p dearer. All British and Overseas Students and Nurses may attend any session at members' rates.

Club Calendar for May and June 1976

Patrons do not require membership to attend the 100 Club. Membership (which costs £1 per year) is beneficial however in that substantial reductions in admittance prices are offered to members and a current programme is posted to each member every month. If therefore you intend to patronise us regularly (and we certainly hope that you will) membership becomes very worthwhile.

ALL SESSIONS TILL 11.00 p.m. unless otherwise stated

MAY

Saturday	1st	7.30 to 1 a.m. ALEX WELSH AND HIS BAND and IAN BELL'S JAZZBAND
Sunday	2nd	GENE ALLAN'S JAZZMEN (All members admitted free this evening. Others 80p)
Monday	3rd	7.30 to Midnight THE LOUIS MAHOLO BAND
Tuesday	4th	Rock Special THE FUNKIES plus SILENT SISTER
Wednesday	5th	7.30 to Midnight Special Presentation SOPRANO SUMMIT, featuring the American saxophonists BOB WILBER and KENNY DAVERN
Thursday	6th	7.30 to 1 a.m. SOUL NITE with CAPITAL RADIO'S SOUL D.J. GREG EDWARDS plus RONNIE'S SOUL SOUND
Friday	7th	7.30 to Midnight THE NEW ERA JAZZ BAND
Saturday	8th	7.30 to 1 a.m. HARRY STRUTTERS HOT RHYTHM ORCHESTRA plus STEVE LANE'S SOUTHERN STOMPERS
Sunday	9th	THE GENE ALLAN JAZZMEN (All members admitted free this evening. Others 80p)
Monday	10th	7.30 to Midnight EL SKID, featuring ELTON DEAN and ALAN SKIDMORE plus THE DICK MORRISSEY/TERRY SMITH BAND
Tuesday	11th	Rock Special SEX PISTOLS and KRAKATOA
Wednesday	12th	KEN COLYER'S ALL STAR JAZZMEN
Thursday	13th	7.30 to 1 a.m. SOUL NITE with CAPITAL RADIO'S SOUL D.J. GREG EDWARDS plus RONNIE'S SOUL SOUND
Friday	14th	7.30 to Midnight MR. ACKER BILK AND HIS PARAMOUNT JAZZ BAND plus THE NEVILLE DICKIE TRIO
Saturday	15th	7.30 to 1 a.m. MONTY SUNSHINE'S JAZZ BAND and THE GEORGIA JAZZ BAND
Sunday	16th	THE GENE ALLAN JAZZMEN (All members admitted free this evening. Others 80p)

Saturday	19th	At press time we are awaiting confirmation of an appearance by STEPHAN GRAPPELLI AND THE DIZ DISLEY TRIO plus THE GEORGIA JAZZ BAND. See Musical Press or 'phone Club nearer to date. If Stephan Grappelli is unable to appear our bill will be THE AVON CITIES plus THE GEORGIA JAZZ BAND
Sunday	20th	THE GENE ALLAN JAZZMEN (All members admitted free this evening. Others 80p)
Monday	21st	The attraction has not been finalised for this date. See Musical Press or 'phone Club nearer to date
Tuesday	22nd	The Legendary American Blues Man SNOOKY PRIOR
Wednesday	23rd	KEN COLYER'S ALL STAR JAZZ MEN
Thursday	24th	7.30 to 1 a.m. SOUL NITE with CAPITAL RADIO'S SOUL D.J. GREG EDWARDS plus RONNIE'S SOUL SOUND
Friday and Saturday	25th 26th	The American Jazz Cornettist RUBY BRAFF with THE LENNIE FELIX TRIO
Sunday	27th	THE GENE ALLAN JAZZMEN (All members admitted free this evening. Others 80p)
Monday	28th	The attraction has not been finalised for this date. See Musical Press or 'phone Club nearer to date
Tuesday	29th	Rock Special ROOGALATOR + SEX PISTOLS
Wednesday	30th	THE BLACK BOTTOM STOMPERS

JULY

A few of the attractions at the beginning of the month

Thursday	1st	SOUL NITE (as every Thursday)
Friday	2nd	7.30 to Midnight THE LONDON VINTAGE JAZZ ORCHESTRA
Saturday	3rd	7.30 to 1 a.m. MAX COLLIE'S RHYTHM ACES and BILL BRUNSKILL'S JAZZ MEN
Sunday	4th	THE GENE ALLAN JAZZMEN (All members admitted free this evening. Others 80p)
Wednesday	7th	KEN COLYER'S ALL STAR JAZZ MEN

TUESDAY JULY 27th
EDDIE "GUITAR" BURNS

Printed in England by Mapro Publishing Services Ltd., 7 The Quay, St. Ives, Huntingdon, Cambs. Tel: St. Ives (0480) 64623.

If you wish to join the 100 Club fill in this form, detach from the calendar, and post it, together with a remittance of £1.

To MUSICAL ENTERPRISES LTD., 100 OXFORD ST., LONDON, W.1.

I wish to join the 100 Club and enclose the membership subscription of £1 for one year's membership from date of joining. (S.A.E. please.)

Name ....

Address ....

....

Monday	17th	7.30 to Midnight THE STAN TRACEY QUARTET
Tuesday	18th	See Musical Press for details.
Wednesday	19th	7.30 to Midnight THE LONDON JAZZ BIG BAND with RAY CRANE, AL FAIRWEATHER, COLIN SMITH (Tpts), WILLIE GARNETT, MALCOLM EVERSON, AL GAY, PHIL DAY, BRUCE TURNER (Saxes), MIKE HOGH, TONY MILLINER, JOHN PICARD (Tbns), STAN GREIG (Pno), HARVEY WESTON (Bass) and LENNIE HASTINGS (Drs),
Thursday	20th	7.30 to 1 a.m. SOUL NITE with CAPITAL RADIO'S SOUL D.J. GREG EDWARDS plus RONNIE'S SOUL SOUND
Friday	21st	7.30 to Midnight THE ORIGINAL CRANE RIVER JAZZ BAND with MONTY SUNSHINE, SONNY MORRIS, KEN COLYER, etc.
Saturday	22nd	7.30 to 1 a.m. THE AVON CITIES and THE ORIGINAL EAST SIDE STOMPERS
Sunday	23rd	THE GENE ALLAN JAZZMEN (All members admitted free this evening. Others 80p)
Monday	24th	7.30 to Midnight THE NEW KEITH TIPPETT BAND
Tuesday	25th	Rock Special SEX PISTOLS
Wednesday	26th	KEN COLYER'S ALL STAR JAZZ MEN
Thursday	27th	7.30 to 1 a.m. SOUL NITE with CAPITAL RADIO'S SOUL D.J. GREG EDWARDS plus RONNIE'S SOUL SOUND
Friday	28th	7.30 to Midnight THE BLACK BOTTOM STOMPERS
Saturday	29th	7.30 to 1 a.m. ROY KIRBY'S PARAGON JAZZ BAND plus THE SHEFFIELD BOTTOM STOMPERS
Sunday	30th	THE GENE ALLAN JAZZMEN (All members admitted free this evening. Others 80p)
Monday	31st	7.30 to 1 a.m. A Tribute to PHIL SEAMAN, with THE HARRY SOUTH BIG BAND with GEORGIE FAME THE STAN TRACEY QUARTET with special guest RONNIE SCOTT THE JOHN STEVENS/GEOFF CLYNE GROUP with KENNY WHEELER and RAY WARLEIGH And many other top Jazz personalities.

JUNE

Tuesday	1st	British Blues Festival JO ANN KELLY ORIGINAL BRETT MARVIN THUNDERBOLTS GORDON SMITH, and other guests.
Wednesday	2nd	KEN COLYER'S ALL STAR JAZZ MEN
Thursday	3rd	7.30 to 1 a.m. SOUL NITE with CAPITAL RADIO'S SOUL D.J. GREG EDWARDS plus RONNIE'S SOUL SOUND

FRIDAY JUNE 4th & SATURDAY JUNE 5th

SPECIAL PRESENTATION

'ECHOES OF ELLINGTON'

Due to the illness of Brooks Kerr, changes have been made to the line up of guest stars previously advertised.
We are now able to proudly present
THREE famous Ex-Ellingtonians

RUSSELL PROCOPE
WILD BILL DAVIS
SAM WOODYARD

playing the Music of The Duke with

CHRIS BARBER'S JAZZ & BLUES BAND

Tickets for both dates now on sale: Members £1.75. Guests £2.50

Sunday	6th	THE GENE ALLAN JAZZMEN (All members admitted free this evening. Others 80p)
Monday and Tuesday	7th 8th	The attractions have not been finalised for these dates. See Musical Press or 'phone Club nearer to dates
Wednesday	9th	Legendary American Jazz Pianist ART HODES
Thursday	10th	7.30 to 1 a.m. SOUL NITE with CAPITAL RADIO'S SOUL D.J. GREG EDWARDS plus RONNIE'S SOUL SOUND
Friday	11th	Return Visit of THE LEGENDS OF JAZZ featuring ANDREW BLAKENEY, LOUIS NELSON, JOE THOMAS, ALTON PURNELL, ED GARLAND and BARRY MARTYN
Saturday	12th	7.30 to 1 a.m. BILL BRUNSKILL'S JAZZ MEN plus THE NEW ERA JAZZ BAND
Sunday	13th	MIKE WESTBROOK'S BRASS BAND with PHIL MINTON, DAVE CHAMBERS, KATE BARNARD and PAUL RUTHERFORD
Monday and Tuesday	14th 15th	The attractions have not been finalised for these dates. See Musical Press or 'phone Club nearer to dates
Wednesday	16th	KEN COLYER'S ALL STAR JAZZ MEN
Thursday	17th	7.30 to 1 a.m. SOUL NITE with CAPITAL RADIO'S SOUL D.J. GREG EDWARDS plus RONNIE'S SOUL SOUND
Friday	18th	7.30 to 1 a.m. GEORGE MELLY AND THE FEETWARMERS

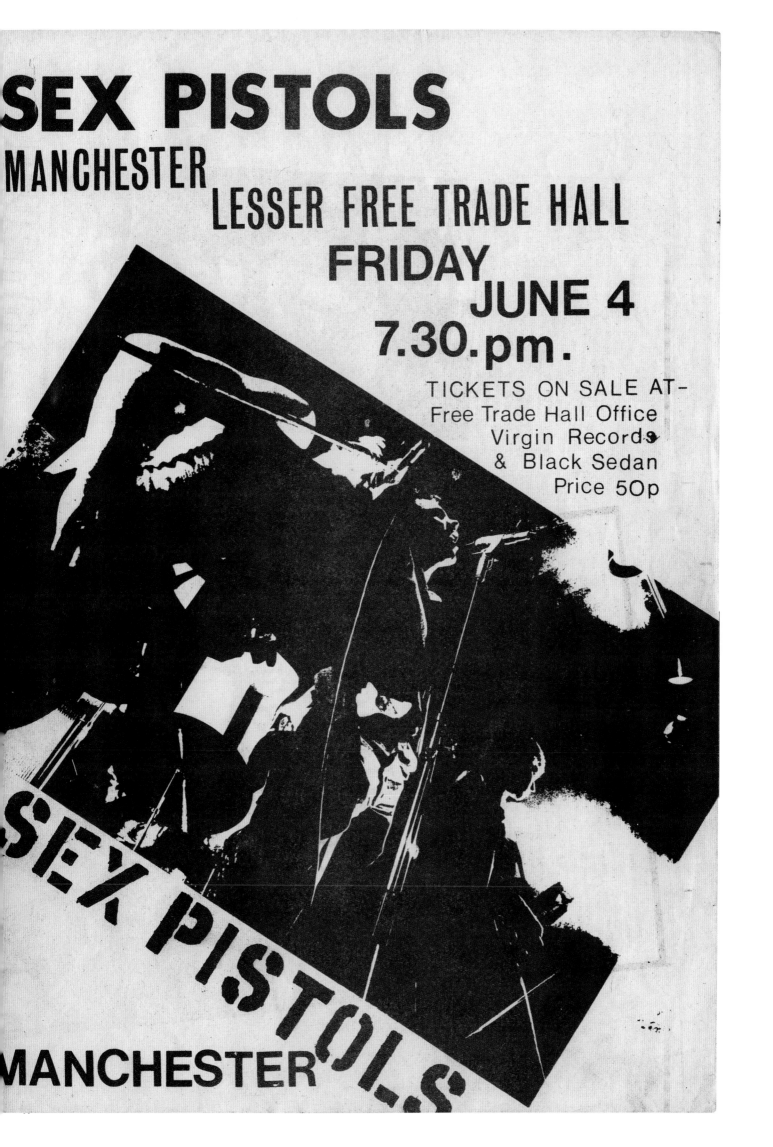

SEX PISTOLS

TUES 15th

100 CLUB

100 OXFORD ST, W1

sartorial
correctness

Sex Pistols

and a CASt (PLAStER)

7.30 till LAtE. bars

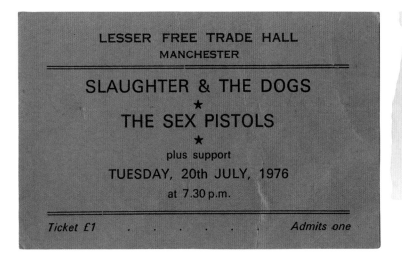

LESSER FREE TRADE HALL
MANCHESTER

SLAUGHTER & THE DOGS
*
THE SEX PISTOLS
*
plus support
TUESDAY, 20th JULY, 1976
at 7.30 p.m.

Ticket £1 . . . . . . Admits one

Manchester Lesser Free Trade Hall

Friday 4th June 1076

THE SEX PISTOLS   (23)

+
BUZZCOCKS

7.30pm   Admit One   50p.

B.I.T.S.U.
PAID - 4 JUN 1976
CHEQUE No.
R.E.FINANCE

EL PARADISE club

BREWER ST W1
SUNDAY APRIL 4TH
7PM-2AM

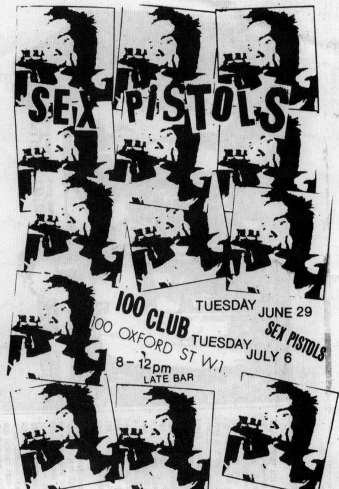

SEX PISTOLS

100 CLUB   TUESDAY JUNE 29
100 OXFORD ST W.1   TUESDAY SEX PISTOLS
8-12pm   JULY 6
LATE BAR

SEX PISTOLS

100 CLUB
TUESDAY'S IN MAY
11, 18 & 25
100 OXFORD ST.

Party
with
the
SEX PISTOLS
APRIL 29
NASHVILLE

North End Road
W14 West Ken
THURS 29th   ADM. 50p

April 29

SEX PISTOLS
SEX PISTOLS
SEX PISTOLS
SEX PISTOLS
SEX PISTOLS
SEX PISTOLS
SEX PISTOLS
SEX PISTOLS
SEX PISTOLS
SEX PISTOLS
SEX PISTOLS
SEX PISTOLS
SEX PISTOLS
SEX PISTOLS
SEX PISTOLS
SEX PISTOLS
SEX PISTOLS
SEX PISTOLS
SEX PISTOLS

SEX PISTOLS

TUES 15th

100 CLUB

100 OXFORD ST, W1

sartorial
correctness

Sex Pistols

and a CAST (PLASTER)

7.30 till LATE. bars

SEX PISTOLS
I.V. boxing MATCH ALI v DUNN
100 CLUB

SEX PISTOLS PARTY
TUESDAY MAY 25
100 OXFORD ST.
What you gonna do ab
LATE BAR, TIL MIDNIGHT Nite Party
Dogwatch PROBLEMS
+ SUPPORT TED CARROLL'S rock on disco
Creation, Stooges, Dolls, Teenage

61   19 August, 1976. Poster for a Sex Pistols gig at West Runton Pavilion.

62–63   July 1976. Front and back covers of the first Sex Pistols press kit assembly.

64   29 August, 1976. Flyer for the Sex Pistols at the Screen on the Green.

65   29 August, 1976. Silk-screened poster for the Screen on the Green performance.

A MID-NITE SPECIAL

MIDNITE TILL DAWN
"ON STAGE" REFRESHMENTS AVAILABLE!

SEX PISTOLS
CLASH
AND BUZZCOCKS

SUNDAY AUG THE SCREEN 29th
ON Islington Green

FROM- "SEX" KINGS RD. CHELSEA 351 0764
TICKETS £1 OR BOX OFFICE SCREEN ON THE GREEN 226 3520

SuB·Mission

ANARCHY IN THE U.K.

I wanna Be ME

no feelings

SEVENTEEN

problems

SATELLITE

pretty vacant

SeX PisTOLs

100 CLUB
100 OXFORD ST.

TUESDAY AUG 31ST

8 – 12pm
LATE BAR

LONDON'S MOST NOTORIOUS BAND!

SEX PISTOLS

INAUGURATION DU NOUVEAU
CLUB DU CHÂLET DU LAC
VENDREDI 3 SEPT
BOIS DE VINCENNES 75012 PARIS

PiSToLS in PRiSOn

Chelmsford maximum security prison isn't no council tenancy, but it is in
the suburbs, right next to some office buildings and a service station on the
corner (quick getaway). The prisoners are in for ~~three years~~ three years and up.
~~To while away the hours~~ To while away the hours they can join inter-prison
weightlifting, join the film society for 11p a week (mostly recent releases),
rent a colour tv for 3p a week, and see rock bands once a month.

Any band that cares to can play, ~~except~~ except for Hawkwind. Everyone was
on acid—

"Uh, you mean Hawkwind?"

i.e., they won't be asked back

No, I mean the prisoners. Anyway, Hawkwind started yelling 'Kill! Kill!'
and there was a minor riot. So no encores for them. Tonight it's the Pistols.
Most of the lads will be digging them behind a variety of chemicals. *the group came in the van*

It was Paul's last day at the brewery, so he came down separately, ~~walk in~~
walking through the front door, talk to the screw sitting behind an inch thick sheet of glass,
walk through a noisy, dull grey sliding door into a small, dull grey room
with a low ceiling, table with chair at each end, the door slides shut, instant
claustrophobia, the metal grey door in front noisily slides open, walk into a
puke green room and sit under the bulletin board—'Charlie Smith is having a
leaving party (at his request) after 28 years of service. We are presenting
him with a silver cup'—to wait for a screw to take you into the prison's
innards. Upstairs in the mess, the band wait for Paul, sitting at a table
devouring sandwiches and tea. John has dressed for the occasion: NO FUTURE
FUTURE FUTURE down the front of his shirt, ANARCHY dripping across the back.
Through the barred windows, across the courtyard, a cell block, the rows of
windows criss-crossed with three sets of bars, turns golden in the afternoon
sun. At a table at the other end of the room a group of screws have afternoon
tea, all in blue i uniforms with large, thick silver chains hanging from their
belt, looping to their knee and ending in a fistful of keys. It really needs
Godard, camera slowly tracking from one end of the room to the other, from
Pistols to Police, to get the full effect.

Screw (incredulous): 'Is that the pop group?'

Other Screw (superior sneer): 'Well. They're supposed to be.'

The small theatre echoes a lot. There is a backdrop behind the equipment,
a cityscape with lots of billboards, in between the Coke and Cinzano ads the
simple messages POT and LSD. The band warm up with a diamond hard 'Wham Bam
Thank You Maam', then a few of their own. When the sound check finishes
everyone except sound wizards Dave and Kim have to go backstage, and the
audience are let in.

They run. Long hair, short hair, young, middle aged, their clothes a jumble
of jackets, sweaters, slippers, boots. Six blacks stroll in; five of them walk
out after ten minutes. Some guys have sewn flares into their levis.

"God, there won't be any girls in the audience," says Steve.

"That's alright," jeers Nils, "You'll still be able to play."

They walk on one by one. Steve gets a few wolf whistles, John gets a lot.
He welcomes them with a greeting from the Queen (cheers and whistles) and a
message from the recently released Ron, who would have loved to come, but he's
been banned. Dead silence.

John enunciates 'Anarchy' very clearly. There is wild applause. 'I Wanna
Be Me' gets a little less approval, the third tune a little less, and so on.
And they are playing great. In the short breaks between songs John taunts them.
You're like a bunch of fucking statues! I bet you've all got a good case of
piles! Move!

"We're not allowed to."

I don't care—tear the fucking place apart!

The audience loves it, yelling back with no hesitation. They even warm to

AND WHERE WAS MALCOLM?

some of the songs; 'Sub Mission', 'No Fun', 'Stepping Stone', 'Problems',
'Liar', all get heavy cheers and whistles. Steve is exploring clean country,
lots of clear, precise notes. Middles and ends have been altered, tidied up.
John is enunciating what he considers the important lyrics very clealry.
Paul and Glen hammer it all home mercilessly. A beat for the feet.

"We try to keep it down to five chords a song," Steve confesses afterwards.

In 'New York' he breaks two strings. While new ones are strung the xxxxxx
audience want John to tell a joke. "No, you tell me one."

"Okay," replies the Captain. He sits in the Captain's Seat, front row centre.
He is big, tanned, middle-aged. He always sits in the Captain's Seat. "There
was this guy, see, and he didn't have a dick. So when he got home at night he
gave his wife a good bollocking!" Laughs.

"Fuckin' 'ell! That's twenty years old!" John's choice of a first word cracks
the place apart.

As the intro to 'Seventeen' winds up Paul leans back, both arms in the air.
Only instead of crashing down into his skins he just keeps on going back over
backwards, stool and all. "Pissed!" yells John, pointing an accusing finger at
the culprit lying on the floor helpless with laughter. "Sorry," he waves when
he finally regains his seat.

The prison hippie—long hair, flares, beads, bare feet, ultra glazed eyes—
throws his denim coat on stage. John stands on it, then ignores it. The owner
asks for it back. With great effort John lands it three feet short. With a
nervous look around the hippie gets up and grabs his jacket. During the last
song reprise of 'Anarchy' he leaps to his feet and starts xxxxxx dancing.
Nobody stops him. Afterwards, two of the cons say that the first couple of
times he did that he got beaten on. The pipes just bent on his head.

As they walk off there's dead silence. For five minutes it's quiet, then a
sudden eruption of applause and yells for more. After the encore there is
another eruption. The longer the band play, the longer they're out of their
cells. "Go on," says a screw. "Give them another one." John refuses. "I'm
selfish," he smiles. It is 7.45.

The cons leave, some wringing their ears. Three stack chairs while the band
pack equipment. "Jesus," says one, surveying the stage. "We were going to try
and scive some clothes off you lot, but you're all dressed in rags!" They help
load the van; three guards stand and watch, the Alsatian at their feet period-
ically howling. One guy xx sits in the front of the van, talking to the band.
A joke is made about hiding in the van on the way out.

"No thanks. I'm out in a month."

"Not if we can help it," a young guard says with a jokey xxx smile.

The van crosses the courtyard to the exit gate. It opens noisily, the van
rolls in, the gate closes behind it, then after a minute the front one rolls
back. It's a few seconds before the shock sinks in: traffic, people walking
about, lights, noise.

"That was really strange," says John, "Not having any girls in the audience."

Terry
19/9/76

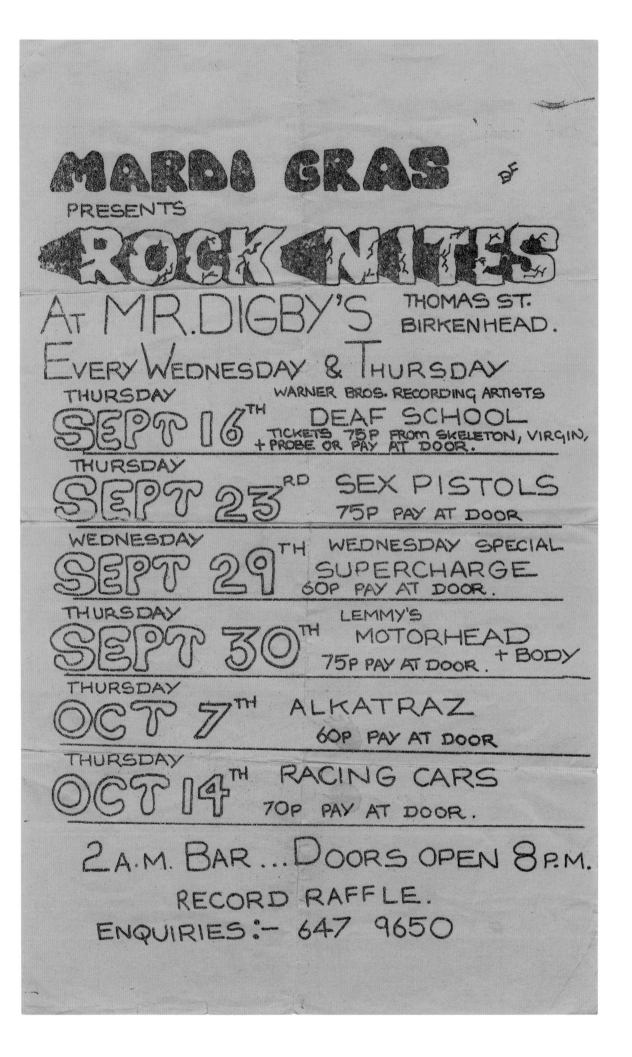

MARDI GRAS DF
PRESENTS
ROCK NITES
AT MR. DIGBY'S THOMAS ST. BIRKENHEAD.
EVERY WEDNESDAY & THURSDAY

THURSDAY WARNER BROS. RECORDING ARTISTS
SEPT 16TH DEAF SCHOOL
TICKETS 75P FROM SKELETON, VIRGIN,
+ PROBE OR PAY AT DOOR.

THURSDAY
SEPT 23RD SEX PISTOLS
75P PAY AT DOOR

WEDNESDAY WEDNESDAY SPECIAL
SEPT 29TH SUPERCHARGE
60P PAY AT DOOR.

THURSDAY LEMMY'S
SEPT 30TH MOTORHEAD
75P PAY AT DOOR. + BODY

THURSDAY
OCT 7TH ALKATRAZ
60P PAY AT DOOR

THURSDAY
OCT 14TH RACING CARS
70P PAY AT DOOR.

2 A.M. BAR ... DOORS OPEN 8 P.M.
RECORD RAFFLE.
ENQUIRIES :- 647 9650

9) 20 Sept, 100 Club. I have been to visit Pat in hospital, so arrive after the first band, Subway Sect, have started. Feeling worn (it has been a long day, mostly spent waiting for Malcolm) I head straight for the bar and thus miss actually seeing them. They sound good though, a bit Velvet Underground and doomy but quite together. Jamie is at the bar, even though he said earlier he felt to ill to come. Much recognising is going on and many greetings. As always, I feel out of place, restless and inclined to drink. To and fro I go. Andy and Mark are by the door, where it is fairly cool (inside it bears comparison to the pits of hell) discussing Lowry, whose massive exhibition they have just seen. Mark wonders that I don't like Lowry and there ensues a somewhat philosophical discussion of taste and fashion. To prove there are no bad feelings, Mark starts handing out Inghams Prison gig leaflets. Suzie and the Banshees play, or rather, perform....a sort of monologue, very out of tune/time....a bizarre reflection on the Lords Prayer and other great lyrics. Amazing. Clash then, very fast and efficient but somehow lacking in character and purpose. Malcolm blames this on Bernards management and I think he is right. Clash will make it once they split with him, if they can follow the ideas already inherent in their music....lovely songs, Londons burning etc....but play as if they really meant it. Just now they play like the punk band that can play its instruments better than the Sex Pistols and that it is exactly what they sound like. Dumb to push that angle. More standing around chatting. I have managed to develop a relationship with the bar staff and thus get served readily, even when there are no glasses and no change either.
Enter the Sex Pistols. The temperature is now well into the hundreds. We sweat, just standing. The band and the pogo dancers are enveloped in steam, perspiration dropping in pools. Anarchy to start, great, then a slackening off towards the middle of the set , people stop dancing, perhaps with exhaustion. I remember the last time I was down her watching them play, their first time. A vivid contrast. Four months ago it was.
I manage to get a seat to stand on, they play fantastic, a knock out. The audience is full of grinning, sated idiots, good feeling, a success. Anarchy again for encore... the kids scream the words back at them. Dave goes mad with the PA, letting loose into screaming feedback. Even John looks pleased.
Before I ev n know where I am again, the club is clear, but for a few wanderers and the acres of broken glass and tables. The band all look very red-faced and tired. John and Jamie a pair of ill matched twins in their matching macs. Much muttering with the french band, not wanting to play now everyone has left. And so out to the cool night.

SEX PISTOLS

24 ROCHFORT HOUSE,
GROVE STREET,
DEPTFORD,
LONDON,ENGLAND.
SE8 3LX.

Dear John,
I meet Mary Harron the other day in London's Marquee Club.She seemed very interested in my mag-'Sniffin'Glue and Other Rock'n'Roll Habits For Punks!'(copy enclosed)
and she asked me to writea piece on London's most exciting band,the Sex Pistols.I enclose my article and hope you'll print it,even though I don't really like your mag,perhaps
my piece will liven it up a bit.
Mary did ask me to include photos but I'm affraid I couldn't get'em together
before the 18th,which she said was the deadline.You/ll,and all those NYC punks,will
have to guess what they look like.They look like a bunch of morons if you wanna know.
Cheers,
Mark P.

Mark P.

THE VERY BORED SEX PISTOLS.
The Pistols story starts in about/1975.in a
King's Road boutique-'The Sex Shop',owned by ex-art student,Malcolm McClaren.Steve Jones,
Glen Matlock and Paul Cook used to hang around in the shop.They got chatting with Malcolm
and told him they had a band and wanted to do something,he agreed to become the manager.
A guy called Johnny Rotten was the finishing touch,he was noticed leaning over the shop's
juke-box,"looking bored"and he became the singer.The band as such,Johnny Rotten-vocals,
Steve Jones-guitar,Glen Matlock-bass and Paul Cook-drums,havn't got much going for'em
but with Malcolm and the shop behind them they are a killa act.
The first gig they played was in an art college
in South London,that was in January.Since then,they've started a whole new scene-the
clothes,the music and the atitude.The own songs are real good-'Sub Mission','No Feelings',
'Problems','Pretty Vacant','I Love You,You Big Dummy',and the best of all'Anarchy In the
U.K'.They also do great versions of'No Fun','Substitute'and'Steppin'Stone'.You always have
loads of Pistols Lookalikes in the audience,including me,I don't care,it's a gas.They've
had trouble,loads of it,like when they smashed some of the Hot Rods(the Pistols'rivals)gear
for that they got banned from the Marquee Club,then there was the time they attacked the
audience at the Nashville,and were banned,at Dingwalls Dance Hall they got banned for
throwing a glass at the Ramones,which they didn't even do.....'cause I know who did.It's
things like this that have made the Pistols but the music's still there,it's a real
agressive sound.The band are always moving and so's the audience.....they're the biggest
gas since the Who's club days.At a gig the other week I confronted Rotten-

MP-Do you like shocking your audience?
Rotten-Yes.
MP-Would you be dissapointed if the audiences became unshockable?
Rotten-Well...I think that was a stupid questions and you were stupid to ask it!
MP-Alright,What makes you fight write the songs?
Rotten-The audience....
MP-You gonna continue writing in the same vein?
Rotten-It's what the audience wants.
MP-Suppose the audience gets bored with they way you write?
Rotten-Oh,man....
MP-Suppose you get bored with us asking stupid questions?
After that Rotten didn't seem very bothered.He's a
weird guy,I sometimes wonder how much hehas to do with the group.I mean who cares,they're
still more fucking exciting than anything from New York,I bet!
Pistols rule,O.K.
Mark P.

M: I'm Mary Harron from Punk magazine in New York.

J: Oh yeah, I've read that...or a bit of it. That's the one with
the bad spelling. Yeah, I like that, that's good.

M. I talked to Malcolm last week. ~~that~~ ~~McLaren, Pistol's manager~~
~~and~~ ~~(the shop called Sex)~~

J. I bet that was wonderful.

M. Ha ha ! I've got my tape recorder on,do you mind ?

J. Nooh, it's not illegal to have an tape recorder.

M. Cause i'm going to write a story about you.

J. Saying what a load of old cunts we are ? We like that.

M. How do you feel about the set ?

J. It wasn't a good one. We can do much better than that. We were in
Wolverhampton last night, and Dundee the night before. Fuckin'
travellin' around the back of a van is no fun. It fucks you up.

M. Is it hard playing in a city like this where you've never played
before ?

J. No, if they don't like it they can just fuck off. It's not hard, it's
good fun. I wouldn't have it any other way. If it wasn't fun I wouldn't
do it. We're Not Only In It For The Money, although it would be great
to be stinking rich .

M. It's gonna take a while.

J. Maybe. Who cares, really. Just as long as I have a bit of fun.

M. I think it's easier to get famous than it is to get rich.

J. Yeah, I mean just go out and rape somebody and you're famous....
course I could be a nice little angel like Rod Stewart.

M. Is he a real angel ?

J. I hate Rod Stewart. He's a cunt. And Elton John and all those
wanking bastards. Just a bunch of posers.

M. Did you ever like Rod Stewart, when he first came out ?

J. Never....I always thought he was an obnoxious little runt. Cocky
arrogant bigmouth.

M. Who do you like ?

J. Ooh, now you've got me stumped. (laughs) I don't know, y'know.
There's nothing to like, is there ? I haven't heard a good record in
years. I like that first Modern Lovers album. I don't like
~~Jonathan Richman's second album~~

2.

Jonathan Richman's second album. It really sounds like Tesco music -
supermarket background music. A little bit too...realistic.......
Oh I don't know, 'cause it's such a difficult life.

M. Do you rehearse much ?

J. Yeah. We've only been together a year. Yes, We do rehearse, contrary
to rumours. (Laughter) Do you believe, we genuinely enjoy doing it !
XXXXXXXXXXXXXXXXXXXXXXXXXXXXXXXXXXXXXXXXXXXX

M. Yeah, because I think you can play.

J. I can't play anything. Not even a tambourine.

M. Had you been in a band before - like at school ?

J. Never. Never. I was just bored stiff like the rest of 'em. So I decided
not to be bored anymore.

M. What were you doing before?
(Pause)
Is it printable ?

MJ.No. Slightly illegal, ha ha.

M. Is the record company really going to push you?

J. They'd fucking better. If they don't it'll be bollocks to them. I'm not
going to let them ruin me. I'm not going to let them turn us into a
bunch of fucking idiots . Top Of The Pops posers.

M. Has there been any pressure on you to change, once you'd got a record
contract ?

J. Not from inside the group, but outside , yeah. You know, no record
company would ix sign us up unless "We Changed Our Image" . EMI liked us
just the way we were, which is why we signed. They're a bit loony y'know.
They want to really have a laugh with us. It'll be good. Just want to go
mad with one group to see what it would be like.

(Note: This interview was recorded in October. Two months later
Hysteria in the press after Pistol's first TV appearance
(They said 'fuck' and looked obnoxious). Half the gigs on their tour were cancelled, and EMI was
thrown ~~EMI~~ into complete turmoil. Rumour has it that the powers at EMI
would love to let the Pistols go, but can't because they're not in breach
of contract. When I asked the press dept. to comment on management
relations with the Pistols the answer was "No comment".)

M. Have you got control over record sleeves?

J. I hope we have, yes. But once it gets into "Oh, you can't have that,
that's obscene" then I'm afraid somebody's gonna get a kick back.

M. What about posters ? What will they be like ?

J. You know, all nude boys and things. Things that annoy everyone.

M. What's the best gig you've done ?

J. How'm I supposed to answer that ?
Johnny makes one of his faces, eyes rolling maniacally .

3.

M. What other information can I think of...

J. At least you're not asking the usual stupid questions like what are
my favourite colours.

M. Do you get that ?

J. Uugh, all the time. You just have to tell 'em to fuck off.

M. I did want to ask you something . Do you think the anarchy thing has
been misrepresented ? (The Pistol's first single is called 'Anarchy in the U.K.')
'Chaos' and 'anarchy' are two of their slogans)

J. People are trying to make it out as a bit of a joke, but it's not a
joke. It's not political anarchy either. It's musical anarchy, which
is a different thing.

M. You're not interested in politics ?

J. No. It's stupid. Load of bollocks, politics. They're all fuckin' liars
anyway. It's musical anarchy. Just get rid of everything that's
boring and fucking farty and organised. As soon as it gets too
organised again then just split.

M. You think you could leave music and go off and do something else ? What
would you like to do later ?

J. Now what would be a really trendy thing to, say.

M. No, no, no. Don't give me a trendy thing to say.

J. Commit suicide.

M. Na, na, na.

J. No idea.

M. So it's not death attracted or anything ?

J. Ooh, has Nick Kent been talkin to you ?

M. I have talked to him.

J. He says I'm going to kill myself.

M. Why ?

J. He thinks I'm a loony. He doesn't Like Me.

M. Why doesn't he...oh yes, I remember.

(Some months back, Sid Vicious, a good friend of Johnny's , saw
Nick Kent, a rock writer, and photographer Mike Beal? at a Pistols'
concert. ~~they were doing nothing provocative, just standing there,~~
for no reason he attacked them with chains , lashing Kent
around the face
~~and ~~ ~~XXXXXXXX~~ . There have been some
brutal incidents in the short life of British punk rock.)

M. Have you enjoyed everything about being famous - or having some fame ?

J. No. I mean, that's a true answer, no. You ask a real fucking creep
"Yeah, its great. Far out man." No, I don't let people affect me like that.
I'd be stupid if I did.

4.

Backstage, we are surrounded by the Pistol's Liverpool fans. These are rather shy and sweet kids, underneath an ~~alarming~~ an alarming selection of rubber trousers, dyed hair black lipstick and stillettoes.

Voice; (Pointing to the fans) What do you think of this lot behind you ?

J. If they're really into it, that's fine. If not they make me sick.

M. Oh no, they're very into it.

J. Well then, that's fine. Better than wearing business suits. Although business suits could be good.

Voice: She's run out of questions.

M. Yeah, I have actually.

J. Don't matter though, does it ? At least you x talk like a human being. You don't have to be a real bastard. Fuckin' stupid, some of 'em.

~~MX.~~What do they do ?

J. They adopt an attitude. The super cool rock journalist: "Really, I'm a nice person, actually." Trying to make you like them. Boring.

M. Do you think they're nervous about meeting you ?

J. Yeah.

M. These kids wanted to meet you. They were the ones sitting around the bandstand.

J. Why didn't you move ?

Voice: Why didn't you dance ? Tell 'em Johnny.

J. Got leprosy ?

(The kids explain that because of their bizarre clothes, other members of the audience were hostile tb them.)

J. Long as you do what you want to do don't let some silly cunt interfere.

Fan: Some people charge around at you.

J. Charge back.

Fan: Do you have a special vendetta against anybody in the audience ?

J. Just the silly drunken pissheads.

Fan: It seemed like you were yellin' at someone in particular.

J. They're just stupid.

M. What goes through your head when you're singing ? What do you fell ?

J. It's like (Making Faces)

M. No, no cut the shit. (laughing)

R. I never understood why people are scared to go onto a stage, cause it doesn't take anything. You don't have to be drunk or ~~XXXXXX~~ out of your head. Just walk up there. That is if you like doing it.

M. Did you ever have nerves before you went on ?
R. The first time, yeah.

- 5 -

R. The first time, yeah...The first time I knew I wasn't gettin' it from a group. I thought - I'm goin' to do it. Then, 'cause I can't be entertained.

M. You can't be entertaining?

R. I can't be entertained by other bands, 'cause there aren't any really. They're just as new as we are.

M. So there's nobody whose music you -

R. I couldn't go out and have a good night listening to another band.

Silence

R. What's New York like, anyway?

M. It's really good.

R. The New York groups - they're very into proving how good they are. How intellectual. I don't like that. I think that's silly.

M. What don't you like about it?

R. You know, going on about social significance. -Blah blah- colours? Drowned by the background noise, of blaring disco next door.) This, that and the other.-

M. But people are always saying that you're music is socially significant.

R. Well, we don't, do we?! We want to be amateurs. Don't mouth your own philosophies, 'cause you just get laughed at.

M. When you're playing something like the 100 Club, do you get a strong feeling from the audience, do you feel they're a part of you?

R. Well, they are. They can get on stage any time they like, and they do. Just stand up against the wall with a microphone. It's good fun. Don't like the super stars - you know- "Look at the gods onstage! Get some hero-worship man!"

M. You wouldn't like that?

R. No, it's too bullshitty.

M. How do you feel about the possibility of that happening to you. Say you become a real fashion and people wanted to do big tours?

R. I'd do my best to stop it. 'Cause I like wandering about the audience's before I go on. Don't like "Oh, we're very mysterious fellows, what?"

M. The image of being bored, you know-you get this from the papers. - Is that something you did 'cause you were annoyed by the reporters who were asking you questions? Were you sending them up?

R. Of course. I took the piss so bad. It's so easy to sell someone a line.

M. Did you play in France ever?

R. It was really good, they loved us. They really loved us.

M. Do you think they understand what's going on?

6.

J. They just - "My God , what's that !" Ha ha. But they liked it. Instead of sitting down and thinking about it, they just knew they liked it and got up and danced, and done what they wanted which is how~~x~~ it should be. It's hard to get people to react like that when they've been dulled most of their lives.

M. What do you think are the things - when you're growing up - that are most dulling ?

J. School.

M. Did you hate it ?

J. Yes. I refused to let them educate me. I was at some Catholic school in London. Poxy.

M. Did they tr~~g~~ and throw you out ?

J. They did throw me out. Cause I attacked one of the teachers. Which I remember reading in your magazine about David Johansen.

M. Have you played any universities ?

J. We played Dundee University. We went down really well. I lost my voice and I couldn't speak, and they started throwin' bottles cause we wouldn't go ~~ox.~~ back on. That's a good reaction. They just went mad, they loved it. ~~XXXX XXXXXXXXXXXXX~~ It was great to see hundreds of people going mad, bouncing of the walls.

M. Do you find most of the time it's the reaction you get here in Liverpool ? (i.e a largely dead audience, a feww people dancing, a few people throwing insults.)

J. Maybe ...a lot of people got their backs stood up against it because of the press. They come just to be cynical. They think we're all stinking rich phonies "Oh its all a big con trick". We're all millionaires and middle class snotty little gits.

M. Is that true ? Are you not making any money ?

J. Can't you tell by my old Etonian accent?

M. No, I don't mean that.

J. No, we're not making no money at all yet. Maybe now we've signed up. ....Shit, we owe so much.

M. How do you afford the equipment?
JOHNNY LAUGHS.

M.No comment ?

J. They fall of lorries, y'know. (Translation - We rip it off.)

Fan. Is it easy to be nasty ?

J. Well you should know that yerself. No, if someones a real cunt, you tell them what they~~n~~are. Big deal. Its not meant maliciously. I just want them to be honest.

7.

M. But isn't that part of the performance ? I don't mean its a pose - wheergh! (Johnny is rolling his eyes at me and putinng on his Night Of The Living Dead look at the use of the word 'pose'. For all the new wave bands , this is the worst insult possible . Worse than 'trendy', even worse than 'intellectual'.)
ha ha! ergh! When you're on stage and there's some sha-sha-shadowy figure at the back of the room - no, no come on now - you can't really hate him like you can somebody you know. (I'm referring to his shouting at the audience.)

J. Why, do you think I do ?

M. No, I don't but -

J. Well what are you talking about ?

M. Well - I don't know ! The conversation is getting a little confused here.

J. Its good fun anyway.

M. Do you write all the lyrics ?

J. Yeah.

M. Have you ever improvised lyrics on stage ?

J. Sometimes, yeah. If we don't particularly want to do something for one night then I'll just make up whole new verses. Wonderful.

M. Is there a lot of improvisation with the musicians as well ?

J. Well there's gotta be. You can't be so strict. You'd bore yourself to death - like a lot of little robots. Morons.

M. When the equipment fucks up does that spur you on ?

J. No, it slows it down. Like when he broke his strings tonight I had a choice of either just standing there and telling 'em what big cunts they are for just sittingthere goin' "Gaahh" or just ignoring them and wait till it's fixed. I just couldn't be bothered to talk to them. Why should I. Make your own fun chappies !

M. How old are you ?

J. Twenty.

M. What sort of music did you used to like ?

J. Well God, there wasn't much to lile. What was there...there was Bowie, but the only album of his I really liked was Diamond Dogs. That was great. Grisly and awful. (laughs) Oh, I like Nico. I do like her. She just moans on and on. She's nice. That kind of stuff, I suppose. Not always. The Doors I like.

Fan: What do you think of people sittin ' around starin' at you.

J. They're stupid. They should stare at themselves. Just do something.

8

M. What's it like in the studios ?

J. It's really difficult in the studios. Cause the engineers are like -
   "We don't think much of you chaps !" They're not very helpful. It's a
   whole different world.

Voice: She's run out again Johnny. She's run out of questions.

J. It's the long pause.

M. The alternative is asking stupid questions, so I'm trying to think
   of a good one.

J. Come on then, stupid questions ! ...My favourite colour is metallic blue.
   I like walks in the park.

M. OK, improvise.

J. (lyrically) I like the sky at night...and the full moon. And all that
   bullshit. My favourite flower is poison ivy.

JOHNNY AND THE FANS DICBSS THE PROBLEMS OF WEARING RUBBER CLOTHES.

Fan: You just can't get it on or off.

Fan : Where did you get your jacket ?

J. At a jumble sale. I just cut it up a little to make it look good.
   (Johnny Rottens jacket is festooned with safety pins, nail scissors and
   other decorations - a fashion that has been much imitated.)

M. The people who go to the store SEX - is it just a fashion ?

J. It's not a fashion. It's nothing to do with Vogue. It's not really
   accepted by the huge trendy world outside.

M. But is there a split between those who go to SEX for sexual reasons,
   and those who are following the fashion ?

J. Well really, it's all sex. They're not being fashionable at all. I
   don't know really. I know what I like. Most people started off just trying
   to be trendy, and ended up perverts.

M. Really ?

J. Why not ? It's something to do, innit ?

M. Have you seen Patti Smith ?

J. Just a bunch of bullshit. Going on about (putting on whining voice)
   I don't like her.
   "Oh yeah, when I was in highschool". Two out of ten for effort...
   I used to hang around the hotel where she was staying. The last night
   they had to carry her up the stairs. I liked her for that. She was such
   a physical wreck.

M. Would most of you be on the dole if you weren't with the band ? (i.e. on
   welfare ~~because of massive unemployment in Britain that has hit the kids
   especially hard~~ Because of massive unemployment, thousands of English kids
   are on the dole .)

9

J. Everybody's on the dole. I'm on the dole for about another week. Why not ?
   Rob the fuckers. See, we're not very patriotic in England. Fuck that
   country.

M. What's wrong with it ?

J. What's right with it? Its run by a load of old fuckers...doesn't cater to
   nobody to no purpose.

M. What's its future ?

Chorus: Nothing.

J. No future.

M. Will it get worse ?

J. Yeah. We'll get food parcels flown over from America to feed the starving
   English. We'll end up like Pakistan....That's what I never understood about
   America. Everybody's so patriotic.

M. I thought England was supposed to be patriotic.

J. It is for all the old farts. "Mummy and Daddy". We're only patriotic to
   ourselves.

M. XXXXXXXXXXXXXXXXXXXXXXXXXXXXXXXXXXXXXXXXXXXXXXXXXbecause you've gotten hardX
   Look, in twenty years time, if you do have money , you're going to be a
   horrible rich old person !

J. I'll be one of the biggest cunts there is. That is , if I live till then.

M. I thought you had a survival instinct.

J. Who can tell ? Such a wonderful world we live in.

M. You must like some people though.

J. No I don't. I like nothing.

M. Aagh. Bullshit.

J. Honest. I'm being really profound. (Laughter)

M. Hehe - this is a kind of dumb question too - who do you admire the most ?
   LONG SILENCE

J. XXXXXXXXXXXX. Well, could you answer it ? You've probably met Gunga Din, or
   some far out Pakkie. Some Buddhist who gave you a profound philosophy of life.

M. Yes. Yes. And that's why I'm here today. Changed my life... I think this is -
   Johnny's batting his eyelids at me now.

J. Who do you want me to slag off ? The queen's an old cunt, how about that ?

M. OK If you had to make an enemies list of ten people , who would they be ?

Johnny Rotten and Chorus: The Queen! Princess Anne's horse! Max Bygraves...That
Tory leader - Margaret Thatcher Des O'Connor Hughie Templeton Hughie
Green Ena Sharples Paul McCartney David Hunter, Les McKeown , Woody Mick Jagger
                                                            McKeown Wood

---

10

Fan. Do you like anyone ?

Fan. Himself.

J. Yeah, I love myself. I've got to stop this. I'm getting all profound.

ANARCHY IN THE U.K.

PUNK special

100 CLUB
100 OXFORD ST.
Monday SEPTEMBER 20

SEX PISTOLS
CLASH
SUB WAY SECT
SUZIE AND THE BANSHEES
AND FROM FRANCE
STINKY TOYS
OPEN 7 PM LATE BAR
ADMISSION £1.50
(£1.00 NUB ETC.)

7PM LATE BAR

Sex Pistols

ANARCHY IN THE U.K.

Sex Pistols

Fri 8th October
Lafayette's,
WOLVERHAMPTON

Sat 9th October
The Cricket Ground,
NORTHAMPTON

Sex Pistols

ANARCHY IN THE U.K.

Sex Pistols

ANARCHY IN THE U.K.

Sex Pistols

Thur 14th October
Mr. Digby's
BIRKENHEAD

Fri 15th October
Erica's
LIVERPOOL

Sex Pistols

BALLROOM

HARBOURSIDE, TORQUAY.

CLUB ROCK NIGHT

TOP ROCK BANDS EVERY TUESDAY NIGHT

TUESDAY 21st SEP. **STRIFE** **60p. ON THE DOOR.**

TUESDAY 28th SEP. *Eddie and the Hotrods*

TUESDAY 5th OCT. **SEX PISTOLS**

TUESDAY 12th OCT.  **FIRST L.P. NOW IN THE SHOPS HEAR IT.**

DOORS OPEN 8pm. LICENSED BARS. ROCK DISCO.
ADVANCE TICKETS FROM 400 BOX OFFICE. FLOX RECORD CENTRE.
CASTLE RECORD SHOP. TORQUAY. OR SOUNDS RECORD CENTRE PAIGNTON.

84   6 July, 1976. Johnny Rotten.

85   December 1976. Johnny Rotten.

86   **ABOVE LEFT:** 20 September, 1976. A Sex Pistols poster by Jamie Reid for the 100 Club appearance with the Clash, Subway Sect, and Stinky Toys. **ABOVE RIGHT:** 8 & 9 October, 1976. A Sex Pistols poster for Lafayette's in Wolverhampton, and the Cricket Ground in Northampton. **BELOW LEFT:** Autumn 1976. Sex Pistols and "Anarchy in the UK" blank poster by Jamie Reid, using a Ray Stevenson photograph. **BELOW RIGHT:** 14 & 15 October, 1976. A Sex Pistols poster for Mr. Digby's in Birkenhead, and Eric's in Liverpool.

87   5 October, 1976. The Sex Pistols live at the 400 Ballroom, Torquay.

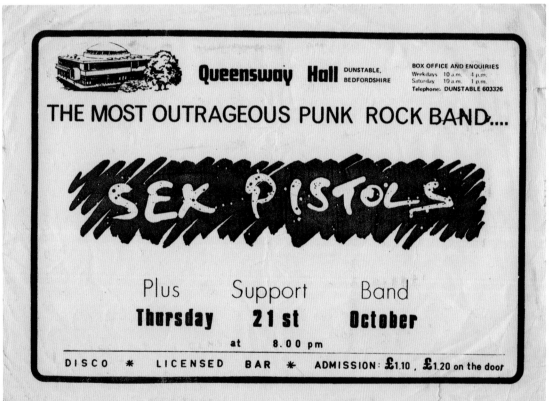

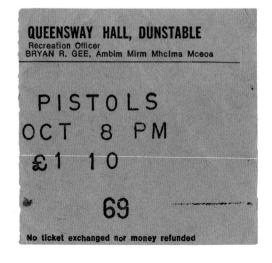

SEX PISTOLS

you can help to make
London's travel better.

The rock revolution

A STARTLING new pop
phenomenon has hit the
clubs and cellars of London.
The music revolution is violent and aggressive . . . and
it's called punk rock.
JOHN BLAKE provides a
guide for parents and fans,
in the first of a series on the
changing face of pop.

(See Page 6).

HA HA.

RED/cjr   2nd November 1976

Mr. Dennis Shepherd

Copy to: Mr. Frank Brunger ✓

SEX PISTOLS - SINGLES BAGS

This is to confirm that you have agreed the
undermentioned:-

1. That the bags should be produced on a thin
    cartridge paper which has already been
    approved by the factory/laboratory.

2. We shall print one side black, leaving the
    surface which is in contact with the record
    white. The outside, i.e. black, should be
    sealed and varnished in order to get the
    highest gloss possible.

Quantity required - 10,000.

R.E. DUNTON

88   **ABOVE:** 21 October, 1976. The Sex Pistols at Queensway Hall, Dunstable, designed by Jamie Reid.
      CENTER: 21 October, 1976. Alternate flyer for the Sex Pistols at Queensway Hall, Dunstable.
      BELOW: 21 October, 1976. Ticket stub for the Queensway Hall gig.

89   EMI Press folder for the Sex Pistols. Clipping for the Sex Pistols' "Anarchy in the UK."

90   2 November, 1976. Internal EMI memo about the Sex Pistols black picture sleeve.

91   "Anarchy in the UK" acetate, sides A and B, from Abbey Road Studios. The first ever acetate of
      the Sex Pistols cut by EMI. It has the "Bible quotation version" of "Anarchy in the UK," backed with
      David Goodman's "No Fun."

D.J. COPIES TO: *ADEFJPRS*

**TOP COPY
TO PROMOTION**

DATE: **1.11.76**

SIZE & SPEED	7" 45 r.p.m. SINGLE

E.M.I. RECORDS — PROMOTION DETAILS
(THE GRAMOPHONE COMPANY LTD.)

* 56992(P)

TRADEMARK **EMI**	RECORD NUMBER **EMI 2566**	RELEASE DATE **12 November 1976**

(A) TITLE	ARTISTE	(B) TITLE
ANARCHY IN THE U.K.	SEX PISTOLS	NO FUN

PUBLISHER	MUSIC BACKING BY	PUBLISHER
COPYRIGHT CONTROL		COPYRIGHT CONTROL
COMPOSER	LABEL CREDITS	COMPOSER
SEX PISTOLS		SEX PISTOLS
ARRANGER	COMPETITIVE VERSIONS BY	ARRANGER

SOURCE OF REPERTOIRE CODE: **27105**	MARKETING MANAGER'S CODE: **3**
MUSIC CLASSIFICATION CODE: **418**	T.P.M. CODE:

A & R DEPT. REMARKS ____ PRODUCED BY DAVE GOODMAN ____

(P) 1976 EMI RECORDS LTD

NB RUSH RELEASE ALSO SPECIAL SEMI-GLOSS, BLACK BAG WITH NO HOLE, ON 1ST 10,000

COPIES. ____ SIGNED *PVBurgot*

MARKETING MANAGER'S REMARKS ____ 150 EXTRA DJ'S

300 DISCO MAILOUT

Initial 10,000

____ SIGNED /

* IF "URGENT," "RUSH" OR "SPECIAL ATTENTION" MARK AT TOP AND DETAIL IN THE REMARK SPACES

PROMOTION USE ONLY

PRESS ADVERTISING	SPECIAL PROMOTION

10198 B

SEX PISTOLS

ON STAGE !!

at last !

LONDONS OUTRAGE !

SeX PiSTOLS

++ MONDAY 15 NOVEMBER ++ 7 P.M. TILL 11.00 P.M. ++

++ THE NOTRE DAME HALL ++ LEICESTER PLACE ++

++ LEICESTER SQUARE ++ ADMISSION £1.00 ++

KINGS RD. - JAN-FEB marconi awar   John Gry
CAFG.   Decan Box B2 Bernie with   Kurofred

Nove 6th 1975.   St. Martins .. "Bazoka Joe"   Brent Ford & Nylons   no-one there.
                                                                          Ian Dury
   " 7th   Central School of Art .   Brent Ford & Nylons   Solo Jets?
Bromley Contingent Northerners   Ravensbourne College of Art   N.E. POLY?   Stranglers
                    FOG?   Shanne
December   Bromley and St. Albans   Lord Sutch?
Bernie   Welwyn Garden City.   High Wycombe.   Ron
&   Watts
in   January 1976   Andrew Logan's party.
Paris   St. Albans.
??   February 14/2 15/2   First 100 Club

March   Marquee supporting Eddie & The Hotrods - first ban   Jordan
                              St. Albans   equipment.
April 4th   El Paradise   NE   first
                   Rollers (23rd) Ted Carroll DJ.   Poly.   press
April 23rd & 29th (30th) Nashville (29th was party)   gig may 6? Fight & ban
                   30th - Fight / ban 3rd
30/3 11/5 18/5 25/5 15/6 29/6 6/7 10/8 31/8 100 CLUB residency
                   Damned   Ace
July   Lyceum with Pretty Things. - awful!! no P.A.
                   Manchester   Slaughter & Dogs.
w/e 31 July June Manchester Lesser Free Trade Hall   2nd time Buzzcocks
         4th northern tour.
August 29th   Screen on the Green ("So It Goes" on Tele in dressing room)
                   Clash. Buzzcocks.   Sheep
September 3rd.   Paris, France - Chalet du Lac.

September 19th.   Chelmsford Prison

September 20th.   100 Club Punkfest. Clash. S. Seet Siouxsie. Stinky Toys
                                                              I.C.A.
        "   21st   Cardiff   Talk
             22nd   Swansea   Malcolm's
             23rd   Newport   clothes
             24th   Burton on Trent
             27th   Doncaster - OUTLOOK.

             E.M.I. SIGNING 8th October
October   10th   RECORDING LANSDOWNE STUDIOS DAVE GOODMAN   Anarchy
        "   12th   Dundee - College - went mad - loads   - weekend -
                    of encores.   mixed & ready.
             13th   Wolverhampton - Lafayette   - NO -
             15th   Liverpool - Erics   1st NOTRE DAME
             20th   Birmingham -
             21st   Dunstable - with the Jam . 80 people turned up.
             Queensway Hall .

             long recording w. Chris Thomas.   26/11.

Dec. 1st.

Nove 6th 1975.   St. Martins (Bazooka Joe)

    " 7th   Central School of Art (Roogalator) (Brentford & Nylons - 2nd time)

~~December~~   Ravensbourne College of Art
               Bromley and St. Albans, *Shanne*
               Central School of Art ~~eg~~ (Brentford & the Nylons) *John Grey, Shanne*
14/2 ~~January~~ 1976   Andrew Logan's party. *High Wycombe?*
   15/2   St. Albans *Shanne*
February   First 100 Club   (*Lord Sutch - High Wycombe*)?

~~March~~ *Feb* Marquee supporting Eddie & The Hotrods - first ban
St. Albans March 20 *Nashville* (with Viv Stanshall)
   → April 4th   El Paradise
           101'ers (Ted Carroll D.J.)   *N.E. Poly - Ian Drury, Stranglers*
April 23rd & 29th Nashville (2nd was party)
    30th?   *fight/ban* *banned somewhere here.*
30/3 11/5 18/5 25/5 15/6 29/6 6/7 10/8 31/8 100 CLUB residency
they *Middlesboro' - (Steve D.o.M. pockets.)*
July   Lyceum with Pretty Things. - *awful!! no P.A.*
June 4 }   *W. Clash*
w/e 31 July } Manchester Lesser Free Trade Hall. *W Buzzcocks, Slaughter & Dogs*
northern tour w. Nils
August 29th   Screen on the Green ("So It Goes" on Tele in dressing room)
          W. Clash, Buzzcocks
September 3rd. Paris, France - Chalet du Lac

September 19th. Chelmsford Prison (*Paul drunk*) *leaflet, letter (press kit)*

September 20th 100 Club Punkfest. *Clash, S. Seet, Siouxsie, Stinky Toys*

   "   21st   Cardiff }
       22nd Swansea }
       23rd   Newport }
       24th   Burton on Trent (*listen bootleg*)
       27th   Doncaster - *OUTLOOK*

          E.M.I. SIGNING 8th October
                         (w/e anarchy mixed h/
October   10th RECORDING LANSDOWNE STUDIOS DAVE GOODMAN *ready but not used.)*
   "   12th Dundee - *college, went mad, loads encores.*
      13th Wolverhampton - *Lafayette*
      15th Liverpool - *Eric's* ~~1st NOTRE DAME~~
      20th Birmingham
      21st Dunstable *Queensway Hall w. The Jam. 84 people*

Anarchy NOV 15th NOtre Dame
Release 26 Nov. (long recordings with Chris Thomas)

                                     B'ham
                                   ↑
100 Club supports 6/7. Damned 10/8 Vibrators 31/8 Clash E.S. Studs
                                     exciting: big grg
                                    & rest arranged

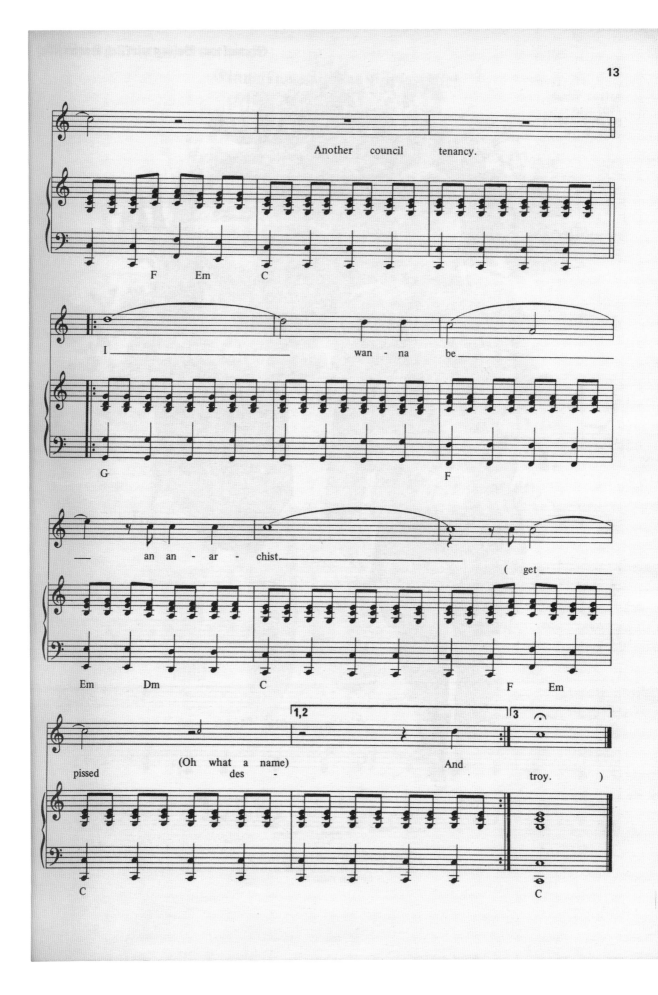

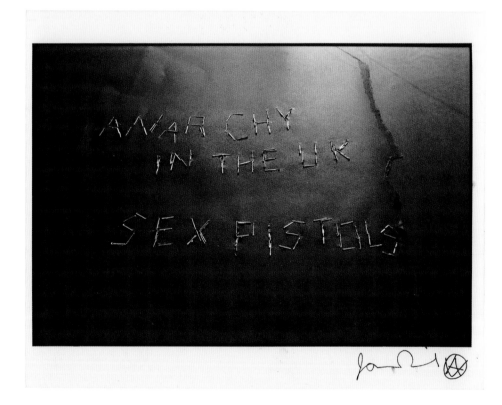

"MUSIC TALK"

SINGLES RELEASE INFORMATION

Weekly Releases for November 26th, 1976   Release 1186

Maxi single

DON LANG & his Frantic Five — WITCH DOCTOR / Cloud burst/6.5 Special — EMI 2555

Previously advised for 12th November
PLEASE NOTE REVISED 'B' SIDE

JIMMY YOUNG — MISS YOU / Unchained melody — EMI 2561

SEX PISTOLS — ANARCHY IN THE U.K. / I wanna be me — EMI 2566

You must *all* have heard of SEX PISTOLS by now! Newly signed to EMI and fresh from their many confrontations with the media (notably the BBC Nationwide team), the Pistols' first single has arrived. The A-side is the band's most popular stage number and is virtually their anthem. A nationwide tour is planned for December.
ANARCHY RULES O.K. U.K.

For sale 19th November

THE WURZELS — MORNING GLORY / Rock around the A38 — EMI 2568

The Wurzels' new big climber. Sown early November ready for sale to the public November 19th. Likes a lot of attention especially in the early stages to encourage it to climb. Special manure used by EMI for a rush release — should be in full bloom around Christmas. What a gem for all lovers of the land. Oh-arrr! Oh-arrr!

JACKIE LOMAX — PEACE OF MIND / Blue world — CL 15897

For sale as soon as received
STEVIE WONDER — I WISH / You and I — TMG 1054

PLEASE NOTE THAT THE THREE BIG BEAR SINGLES, BB1, BB2 & BB3, ADVISED FOR SALE ON NOVEMBER 12th, WILL NOW BE AVAILABLE FOR SALE ON NOVEMBER 19th.

STEREO
SIDE ONE

ANARCHY IN THE U.K.
(Sex Pistols)
℗ 1976 EMI Records

EMI11334A
45 R.P.M.

SEX PISTOLS

Produced by
Chris Thomas

All rights of the manufacturer and
of the owner of the record
work reserved. Unauthorised
public performance,
broadcasting and
copying of
this record
prohibited.

EMI-11334
Made in Australia.

E.M.I. (Australia) LIMITED
(Incorporated in N.S.W.)

45
R.P.M.

PLEASE NOTE THAT THE PRODUCER'S CREDIT FOR THE B-SIDE OF
THIS SINGLE "I WANNA BE ME" SHOULD BE DAVE GOODMAN AND NOT
CHRIS THOMAS.

104   **ABOVE:** Solid black picture sleeve from the first edition of "Anarchy in the UK." **BELOW:** EMI Australia's first edition of the Sex Pistols' "Anarchy in the UK," with producer's credit correction.

105   **ABOVE LEFT:** Original EMI Abbey Road Studios 7" reference acetate for the officially released "Anarchy in the UK" single. **ABOVE RIGHT:** Original packaging for the "Anarchy in the UK" film-clip reel made for EMI by Mike Mansfield. **CENTER LEFT:** Original white label T/P advance copy of the "Anarchy in the UK" single, sent to the radio DJ John Peel by EMI. **CENTER RIGHT:** "Anarchy in the UK" 7" with incorrect production credit to Chris Thomas. **BELOW LEFT:** First edition of "Anarchy In The UK." **BELOW RIGHT:** Second edition of "Anarchy in the UK" with correct production credit to Dave Goodman.

The Ramones, Chris Spedding & the B Vibrators and
The Talking Heads will <u>not</u> be supporting the Sex Pistols
on their forthcoming British tour.

They have been replaced by The Damned, Johnny Thunder _ex New York Dolls_ ^with^
~~and~~ the Heartbreakers ~~from New York~~, and the Clash.

A spokesman for Spedding & the B Vibrators claimed that
they were never booked for the tour in the first place.

" We never even met the Sex Pistols management" he
said. " We were considering joining the tour but Chris has
recording committments in December. Certainly we signed no
contracts for the tour."

Seymour Stein, managing direcktor of Sire, the lable both
The Ramones and The Talking Heads record for said" We were advised
by people at Phonogram to pull out of the tour. Things
just didn't seem to be together - and we weren't told the
truth on a number of occasions.

"For instance we were originally told that there were to
be 20 dates on the tour, and later we were told there were six.

" Everything seemed very loosely put together and it wasn't
something we wanted the bands to get involved in. Things were not
handled as professionally as we would have liked.

" we were all a little over-exuberant about this visit and
probably allowed ^things^ ~~it~~ to go on longer than we normally would have
done. But nothing ^positive^ was ever finally agreed about the tour." _the pull out has nothing to do with the Sex Pistols image_

Sex Pistols manager Malcolm McLaren said that he was 'very
upset'about the cancellations.

" I'm feeling pretty down about this" he said. " Some people
are saying that it's my fault, but Phonogram(who deal with the
Sire label in Britain) are just not an organised company."

_" I understand that ~~the Ramones~~ ^Sire^ did not consider
it viable to tour. And the Ramones were afraid of
playing with the Sex Pistols, because they thought the
Pistols had a violent image_

2

Full dates for the new line-up are: DerbyxKingsxHall

Norwich University of East Anglia December 3, Derby Kings

Hall 4, Newcastle City Hall 5, Leeds Polytechnic 8, Manchester

Electric Circus 9, Lancaster University 10, Liverpool Stadium 11,

Cardiff Top Rank 12, Bristol Colston Hall 13, Glasgow Appollo 15,

Dundee Caird Hall 16 , Sheffield City Hall 17, Southend Kursaal 18,

Guildford Civic Hall 19, Birmingham Town Hall 20.

ThexPistols wiil

The bands will also play together at the opening of the

N new Roxy Theatre in Harlesden on Boxing Day.

--ends--

LENNON: 212-586-6444
EDITH CHANG

RONNIE ANDERTON 041-248-4661

Neil Warnock---Bron-267-4499 Cowbell--John Jackson

Fred Bannister --253-5518

Alan Cowderoy--Phonogram 262-7788

Jake Riviera

Bernard

David Cork--Endale

Martin Cole/Ron Watts--Roxy

Managers: Liverpool Empire 051-709-1555

Manchester Free Trade Hall 061-834-0943

Paris Theatre

ABC Ardwick Gn Nth 273-1141

CIVIC HALL'S
Birmingham Town Hall - 021-354-4401

Edinburgh Usher Hall- 031-228-1938   DANNY O'DONOVAN

Hammersmith Palais 748-2812

New Victoria 828-2231/834-0671

Victoria Palace 834-1317

Talk Of The Town 734-5051

Hammersmith Odeon 748-4081

Notre Dame Hall--Guy Pierre 437-9363   637-5571
EG - 730-2162 (SPEDDING

Lee Childers

Seymour Stein

Danny Fields

FRANK BRUNGER

MALCOLM —— CONTRACTS SIGNED
SPEDDING

Directors
M. McLaren
S. Fisher

Registered Office,
23 Great Castle St,
London, W.1.

GLITTERBEST LTD

40 DRYDEN CHAMBERS
119 OXFORD ST
LONDON W.I.

01-734-1137
01-734-1138

(LWT) CWBL — UNI DTES, KURSAAL.   GOLDSMITH - THT TR GT IDEA

Notre Dame Hall — GUY PIERRE

NASHVILLE - LWT - £10/HD BNS ON BAR - STAFF SD WD WK OUT

SURTY - £1000 - MMc

'DRK SAVAGE - BRF BKR - WTD IT

EALING TECH. -3D 45, TN NO

LIV. EMPIRE ——

COWD. — PARANOID ABT SEX P.
    Mc PLOTTING 2 TAKE LIMELIGHT FM RAMNES

TALK OF TOWN
    BKD AS A GP — NAT. ASSMD MOR GP ATT.
        A MTR AUD.
    WN CM 2 FNLS BKG RCSD TT SX PSTLS
    ATTCT A YG AUD. LCNSD 2 SV DKS @ T&LS.
    LCSNG WD BE DIFF. 2 ENF.
    W/OUT EVN ASSESS GP ITSF IT WS RCSD TT CDT
    GO AHD BLS OF LCSG

    _____

COWBELL —— INT. IN SEX PISTOLS WLD WDE

    , V. SHKY. WN GT INV. - DLVG DN THRU DK TNNL
    & GTG 2 TE LTE

SGST CLSH & DMND
ADVSD ON ⎡ BST WYS
       ⎣ HW 2 GT WK PRMTS
    _____ XCHGE MST BE PT IN @ LST 2 MO PRIOR
             2 VST

                V. HARD - BLS RAMONES OF CONSID. INT.

LANCASTER UNI — BARRY LUCAS
    0524- 65201

MARTIN COLE — BON WATTS
L'ROXY'J
ENDALE — 021-236-7651
DAVID CORIS

Directors

M.McLAREN
S.FISHER

GLITTERBEST LTD

40 DRYDEN CHAMBERS
119 OXFORD ST
LONDON W.I.

Registered Office,
23 Great Castle St,
London, W.1.

OI-734-II37
OI-734-II38

7 - VILLAGE BOWL, BOURNEMOUTH
21 - FIESTA, PLYMOUTH
22 - TORQUAY

PROMO VIDEO
'ANARCHY'
US - AUGUST

DANNY O'DONOVAN - LIV. EMPIRE
HAM. PALAIS

HATE
KURSAAL
LIVERPOOL — EMP.

RAMONES

ANTHONY MORRIS - PHONO MD
WARNOCK - BRON — SAYG RMNES NT CMG

"WE GT IT 2 HPN" - 9/11/76
'BRN R MKG TGS DFCT BY SYG RMNS R NT CMG'

— 11/11/76
2 McC. - WL NT BE TRG
"I THT" IT GD IDEA IN ORDR 2 SL RCDS'

CPTC — JLY HO-HO ABT TR SDG MR & MR
- RDCLS - FLWD BY ITM ABT MST MSR BDS TNG DN ~~IBT~~
RQST 2 PLY PLE'BNFT IN BELFAST

WHO R ALSO

'RBSH, SYS M. MC 'WE DT ND TM, WN GT JNY TDR & TE HTBKRS, FM. NY'
RXY - 'IN HTSDN'

'HTBKRS — LEE CHILDERS - 212-595-7441

UA - BACKING DAMNED

ORGNLY ~~CNTCT~~ HD IDEA OF ~~BENDIS~~
NY DLS - SMPLY BCS I'D LVD 2 SEE TM - TY WR
SCH AN INSP. 4 TS YG BDS — THAU MAN
TA BUNDLE - IF NT DLS, RMNES - STEIN IN TWN

'ALL PLATRE' - CHS HLL - IN NYC - RN INTO IN BR

EQL BLLG — STEIN BST 2 CNVNCE RMNES 2 DO IT
     10:30AM SNDY – 'DEF. ON'
        FT PUE ON MM
      STEIN RG UP – PSD OFF ABT RMNES NT GTG PRPR BLG
COWD. MT W/ BANN. — SIRE/PHNO DISAT.
  BGNL/MMC
       BRON DG RMNES —
     HD 2 GT-AC/DC TR   WT R 2 HDLNE

BANN/BRON NT GTG DTES   MM – PKGE ALT OPN/HDLNG
     5 DAYS – 'SMTG GG ON - WE DDT KNW WT'
CWBLL FNE UP – DSPRTE 2 GT INV.
BANN – BRN CLG UP, SYG RMNES NT CMG
   MM – TK OUR STTD DG ITSF – WT 2 CWBLL
   CME BK 'WT 2 BK DTES BT NO1 WTS SX PSTLS'
MAN: MSC FCE GT DTE @ FREE TDE HLL DEC. 10 – BRN SYG ALL
LCL PRMTRS WTG DTES – GTG TM.
                  NO BRON DTES
MON EVE – HD SME DTES   CWBL GT 2 DTES
  TLX ST BY COWD. IN CLBRTN W/ BRON
  NT FND STEIN – WR DSGSTD W/ U
TXT – DT DO RMNES TR. FR NT VBLE. SX PSTLS GTG ALL PUBLCTY. PHONO
  DT WT 2 DO TR.
MMC TRBL SCMR   BRN – CDT GT WK PRMTS
                    COW – WD GT 2 " " BDS
'WT ZS TR 2 HPN' – STEIN – WL TLX A.MRS – SD FNE,   US
  GT CNFMTN.
½ HR LTR, COWD FND – 'SPKN 2 SYMR, TR'S OFF.'
       PHONO STL FNG –
MMC – "COWD PLTG PRNOIA OVR SX PSTLS — PLTG 2 TK LMLTE FM RMNES'

_____

JAKE RIW. – DMND MST BE 2D – BGR TN HTBKRS – 'PT MR BMS IN STS'
'WE PT OURSLS OUT 2 DO A TR & U GT AL TS SPRSTR SHT — IT MKS U FLLK
  TRWG IT IN & TR W/ BAD CO.'

_____

INT. – IMPTT 4 KDS WHN RD AL ABT NY BT NVR SN IT. ESTC 2
  GT CMPRSN OF WTS GG ON IN NY & WT G ON LDN. DDT WT
  IT 2 BE INCEST. LDN BDS TR. IT WS JST A GT WY 2 END TE YR.

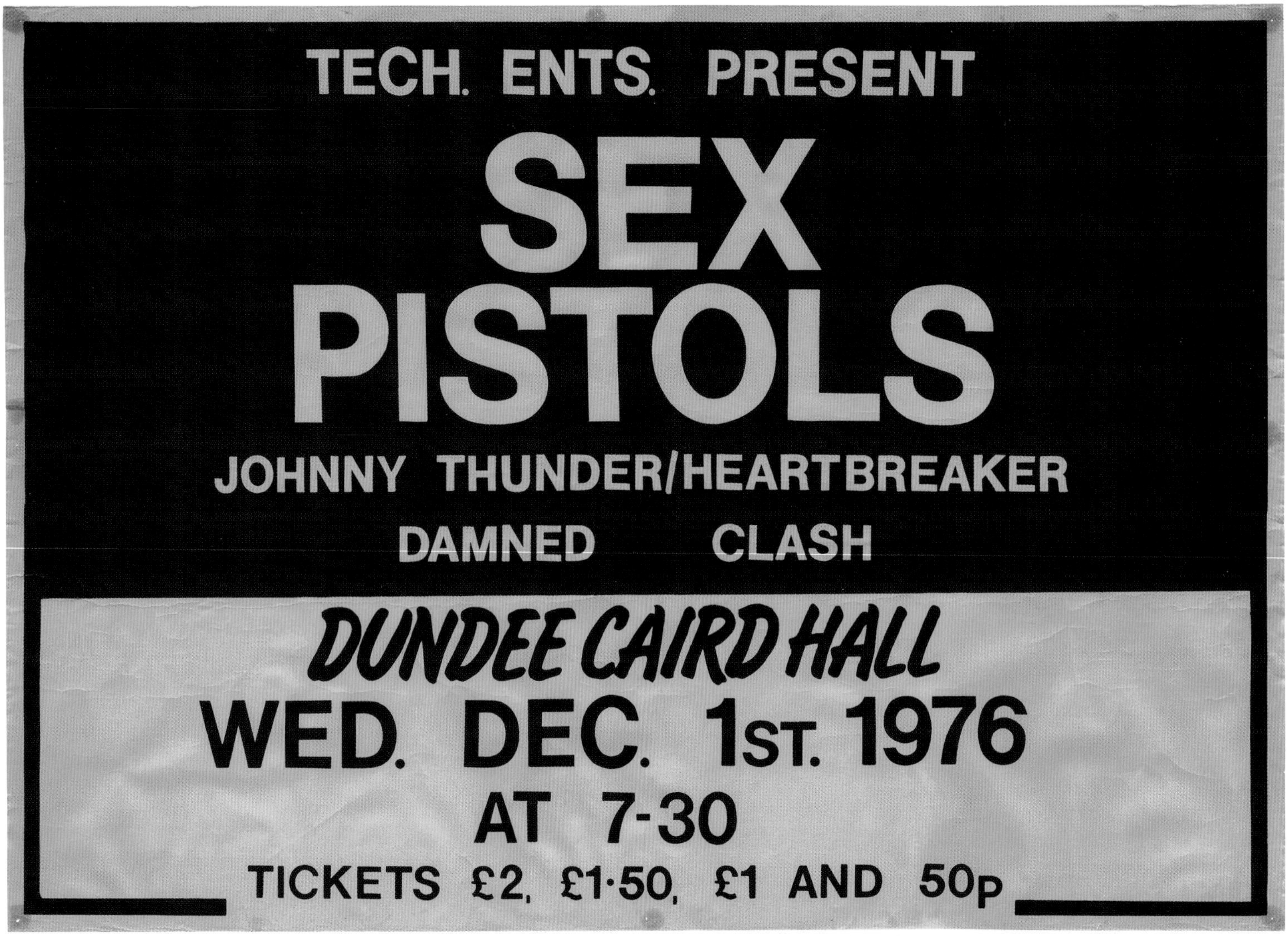

TECH. ENTS. PRESENT
SEX
PISTOLS
JOHNNY THUNDER/HEARTBREAKER
DAMNED
CLASH
DUNDEE CAIRD HALL
WED. DEC. 1ST. 1976
AT 7-30
TICKETS £2, £1·50, £1 AND 50p

106–107 December 1976. Jonh Ingham's manuscript for an article on the "Anarchy in the UK" tour.

108 3 December, 1976. Leee Black Childers' photograph of Bernie Rhodes, Johnny Rotten, and Paul Simonon on the "Anarchy in the UK" tour bus.

109–111 December 1976. Jonh Ingham's shorthand notes from the "Anarchy in the UK" tour.

112 1 December, 1976. Poster for a canceled show at Dundee Caird Hall.

113 9 December, 1976. "Anarchy in the UK" tour handbill for a gig at the Electric Circus, Manchester.

A NIGHT OF PUNK ROCK

on

THURSDAY, 9th DECEMBER

with

THE SEX PISTOLS
THE CLASH
THE DAMNED

AND

JOHNNY THUNDER'S HEARTBREAKER

**TICKETS AVAILABLE FROM THE ELECTRIC CIRCUS
AND VIRGIN RECORDS**

**ADVANCE TICKETS : £1.25
ON THE NIGHT : £1.50**

Printed by Electric (Modern) Printing Co. Ltd., Manchester

ANARCHY
THE ANSWER????

Does the Sex Pistols' "Anarchy in the UK" tour offer the real
answer to the needs of Youth? What is the meaning of this
latest controversial trend in the pop world? Oddly enough,
this group's own reported use of the word "antichrist"
indicates the answer.

This term describes the essence of the spirit of rebellion
against all that God stands for. Even though apparently just
a passing fad, therefore, such trends are clearly in part
fulfillment of Jesus' prophecy that before His return to earth,
wickedness would multiply beyond all previous limits.

The rise of such rampant evil is a direct result of national
rejection of God. Scripture warns that when this happens He
abandons men to vile affections, dishonouring their own bodies.
So great becomes the degeneration that, although fully aware
of God's righteous judgement that they who do such things
deserve to die, they not only do them themselves, but actually
approve and applaud others who practice them.

The iniquity of this day will culminate in the worst period
of judgement ever known in human history. When God arises in
wrath, the very ground we stand on will shake. The Bible says
it will be so terrifying that men will actually pass out at
the thought of the things which are coming.

But there is hope: not for the earth, but for individuals.
They who turn from their wicked ways, and experience the
amazing grace which transforms the heart will escape the wrath
to come. The power of Christ breaks unclean thoughts and
habits. Jesus is the friend of sinners: He died both to for-
give sin and to offer His life to overcome its tyranny. "The
vilest offender who truly believes, that moment from Jesus a
pardon receives."

Come and join us at the Elim Church, St Fagan's St, Caerphilly,
this Sunday at 6.30 pm (Tel: 88;007). Meet young people who
can testify further of the reality of God's power to break
the hold of sinful habits, and to satisfy without needing
modern trends.

15/12/76

114

ANARCHY IN THE UK TOUR
SeX PiSTOLS
DAMNED

AND FROM THE USA

JOHNNY THUNDERS & THE HEARTBREAKERS

(EX NEW YORK DOLLS)

With Special Guests

the CLASH

THE TOUR DATES

Fri	3 Dec	Norwich University	Mon	13	Colston Hall Bristol
Sat	4	Kings Hall Derby	Tue	14	Top Rank Cardiff
Sun	5	City Hall Newcastle on Tyne	Wed	15	Apollo Glasgow
Mon	6	Leeds Polytechnic	Thu	16	Caird Hall Dundee
Tue	7	Village Bowl Bournemouth	Fri	17	City Hall Sheffield
Wed	8		Sat	18	Kursaal Southend
Thu	9	Electric Circus Manchester	Sun	19	Guildford Civic Hall
Fri	10	Lancaster University	Mon	20	Birmingham Town Hall
Sat	11	Liverpool Stadium	Tue	21	Woods Centre Plymouth
Sun	12		Wed	22	The 400 Ballroom Torquay

TICKETS AVAILABLE FROM

Tue 21 Dec   Woods Centre Plymouth

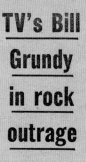

BILL GRUNDY: I'm told that the group have received £40,000 from a record company. Doesn't that seem… er… to be slightly opposed to their [deep breath] anti-materialistic view of life?

SEX PISTOL: No. The more the merrier.

BG: Really?

SP: Oh yeah.

BG: Well, tell me more then.

SP: We've fuckin' spent it, ain't we?

BG: I don't know, have you?

SP: Yeah, it's all gone.

BG: Really?

SP: Down the boozer.

BG: Really? Good Lord! Now, I want to know one thing.

SP: What?

BG: Are you serious or are you just making me, trying to make me laugh.

SP: No, it's gone. Gone.

BG: Really?

SP: Yeah.

BG: No, but I mean about what you're doing.

SP: Oh yeah.

BG: You are serious?

SP: Mmm.

BG: Beethoven, Mozart, Bach and Brahms have all died…

SP: They're all heroes of ours, ain't they.

BG: Really? What? What were you saying, sir?

SP: They're wonderful people.

BG: Are they?

SP: Oh yes! They really turn us on.

SP: Well, they're very…

BG: Well, suppose they turn other people on?

SP: [Mumbled] That's their tough shit.

BG: It's what?

SP: Nothing. A rude word. Next question.

BG: No, no. What was the rude word?

SP: Shit.

BG: Was it really? Good heavens. You frighten me to death.

SP: Oh, all right, Siegfried…

BG: What about you girls behind…?

SP: He's like your dad, isn't he, this geezer. Or your granddad.

BG: Are you er are you worried, or are you just enjoying yourself?

FAN: Enjoying myself.

BG: Are you?

FAN: Yeah.

BG: Ah, that's what I thought you were doing.

FAN: I've always wanted to meet you.

BG: Did you really?

FAN: Yeah.

BG: We'll meet afterwards, shall we?

[Laughter]

SP: You dirty sod. You dirty old man.

BG: Well, keep going chief, keep going. [Pause] Go on. You've got another five seconds. Say something outrageous.

SP: You dirty bastard.

BG: Go on, again.

SP: You dirty fucker.

BG: What a clever boy.

SP: What a fucking rotter.

[More laughter]

BG: [Turning to face camera] Well, that's it for tonight. The other rocker, Eammon, I'm saying nothing about him, will be back tomorrow. I'll be seeing you soon. [To the band] I hope I'm not seeing you again. From me though, goodnight.

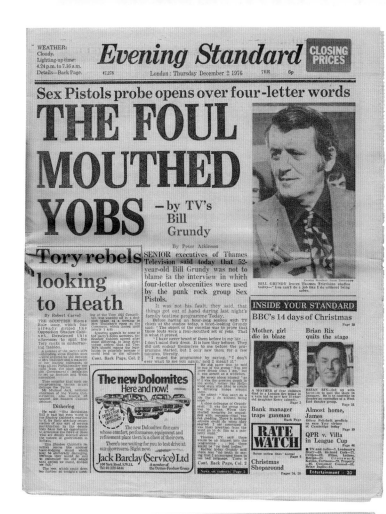

118   Transcription of the Sex Pistols' interview with Bill Grundy.

119   December 1976. British tabloid newspaper coverage of the band's televised interview with Bill Grundy.

EMI

EMI RECORDS 20 Manchester Square
London W1A 1ES

Telephone 01-486 4488
Telex 22643
Telegrams Emirecord London Telex
Cables Emirecord London W1

We do associate ourselves with the apology put out by Thames TV last night
following the Sex Pistols interview. We deplore this type of incident but
feel that in many cases the media deliberately provoke this act and that
may well have been the case with the interview on the Today programme.

The group are signed to EMI records and in no way does this incident affect
their relationship with us.

Rodney McGann

EMI Records Limited
Registered Office: Blyth Road, Hayes, Middlesex. Registered in England, No. 68172

member of the EMI Group of companies
international leaders in music,
electronics and leisure.

---

14 December, 1976

SEX PISTOLS - RESPONSE TO PRESS ENQUIRIES

(as agreed with Sir John Read)

1. We have made no long-term decision regarding the Sex Pistols.
    The position is still under review and we are watching the situation
    carefully. No further releases of the Sex Pistols records have yet
    been made.

2. Peter Cook and Dudley Moore

    The Chairman was asked last night (he believes by an Exchange
    Telegraph reporter) whether there was any truth in the story that
    EMI had recently banned a 'Dud and Pete' record.

    Sir John confirmed that this was absolutely true. The record in
    question contained expletives and language that were, in his view
    and those of others, totally unacceptable.

    This particular record was not being distributed by EMI (on behalf
    of Island) and was not being offered for sale in any of EMI's shops.

Sex Pistols
in James the full text
Herewith ok
JC

News from EMI

Comment on Content of Records by Sir John Read, Chairman

During the course of today's Annual General Meeting, Sir John Read, Chairman
of the EMI Group said:

"The EMI Group of companies operates internationally and has been engaged
in the recorded music business for over 75 years.

"During recent years in particular, the question of acceptable content of
records has become increasingly difficult to resolve - largely due to the
increasing degree of permissiveness accepted by Society as a whole, both in
the UK and overseas. Throughout its history as a recording company, EMI has
always sought to behave within contemporary limits of decency and good taste
- taking into account not only the traditional rigid conventions of one section
of Society, but also the increasingly liberal attitudes of other (perhaps
larger) sections of Society at any given time.

"Today, there is in EMI's experience not only an overwhelming sense of
permissiveness - as demonstrated by the content of books, newspapers and
magazines, as well as records and films - but also a good deal of questioning
by various sections of Society, both young and old, e.g. What is decent or
in good taste compared to the attitudes of, say, 20 or even 10 years ago?

"It is against this present-day social background that EMI has to make value
judgements about the content of records in particular. EMI has on a number of
occasions taken steps totally to ban individual records, and similarly to ban
record sleeves or posters or other promotional material which it believed
would be offensive.

"The Sex Pistols incident, which started with a disgraceful interview given
by this young pop group on Thames TV last week, has been followed by a vast
amount of newspaper coverage in the last few days.

Cont/...

"Sex Pistols is a pop group devoted to a new form of music known as 'punk rock'.
It was contracted for recording purposes by EMI Records Limited in October 1976
- an unknown group offering some promise, in the view of our recording executives,
like many other pop groups of different kinds that we have signed. In this
context, it must be remembered that the recording industry has signed many pop
groups, initially controversial, who have in the fullness of time become wholly
acceptable and contributed greatly to the development of modern music.

"Sex Pistols have acquired a reputation for aggressive behaviour
which they have certainly demonstrated in public. There is no excuse for this.
Our recording company's experience of working with the group, however, is
satisfactory.

"Sex Pistols is the only 'punk rock' group that EMI Records currently has under
direct recording contract and whether EMI does in fact release any more of their
records will have to be very carefully considered. I need hardly add that we
shall do everything we can to restrain their public behaviour, although this
is a matter over which we have no real control.

"Similarly, EMI will review its general guidelines regarding the content of pop
records. Who is to decide what is objectionable or unobjectionable to the public
at large today? When anyone sits down to consider seriously this problem, it will
be found that there are widely differing attitudes between people of all ages and
all walks of life as to what can be shown or spoken or sung.

"Our view within EMI is that we should seek to discourage records that are
likely to give offence to the majority of people. In this context, changing
public attitudes have to be taken into account.

"EMI should not set itself up as a public censor, but it does seek to encourage
restraint.

"The Board of EMI certainly takes seriously the need to do everything possible
to encourage the raising of standards in music and entertainment."

EMI 2566

ANARCHY IN THE UK!

ROCK GROUP START A 4-LETTER TV STORM

Viewers in big protest over shock outburst

Evening Standard
CLOSING PRICES

Sex Pistols inquiry over four-letter words

THE FOUL MOUTHED YOBS
— by TV's Bill Grundy

Four-letter Punk Rock group in TV storm

The bizarre face of Punk Rock

'Worthless, decidedly inferior, displeasing...'

The Punks— Rotten and proud of it!

RUBBISH MUST NOT BE DEPOSITED IN THIS AREA BY ORDER

Fury at filthy TV chat

NEWS ON CAMERA

Daily Mail

DRIVERS PAGE

DAILY EXPRESS

Obnoxious, arrogant, outrageous.. the new pop kings

WHO ARE THESE PUNKS?

Daily Mirror
BRITAIN'S BIGGEST DAILY SALE

TV's Bill Grundy in rock outrage

London's biggest evening sale

Evening News

THE RAGGED REBEL

THE FILTH AND THE FURY!

When the air turned blue..

Uproar as viewers jam phones

GRUNDY GOADED PUNK BOYS SAYS RECORD CHIEF

SEX PISTOLS

WHO ARE THESE PUNKS? PAGE NINE

News from EMI

6th January 1977

EMI AND THE SEX PISTOLS

EMI and the Sex Pistols group have mutually agreed to terminate
their recording contract.

EMI feels it is unable to promote this group's records
internationally in view of the adverse publicity which has
been generated over the last two months, although recent press
reports of the behaviour of the Sex Pistols appear to have
been exaggerated.

The termination of this contract with the Sex Pistols does
not in any way affect EMI's intention to remain active in all
areas of the music business.

* * *

Enquiries: Rachel Nelson
              Group Press Relations
              01-486 4488

* * *

From the Group Public Relations Department
EMI Limited
20 Manchester Square London W1A 1ES
01-486 4488

120 & 122   December 1976 – January 1977. EMI records fallout from the Bill Grundy interview.

121   Promotional "Anarchy in the UK" Sex Pistols flyer from EMI, highlighting British press reactions to the Bill Grundy interview.

123   **ABOVE:** October 1976. Vivienne Westwood.
BELOW: Spring/Summer 1977. Interior of the Seditionaries shop.

124   1978. Sex Pistols mug-shot flyer by John Tiberi.

125   March 1977. The Sex Pistols signing with A&M Records outside Buckingham Palace. Photo detourned by the Sex Pistols from the Glitterbest offices.

GOD
SAVE THE
QUEEN

There is no longer any association between A&M Records and

The Sex Pistols. Production of their single "God Save The

Queen", which had been tentatively scheduled for release

later this month, has been halted.

HARLEX LONDON 22233

ATTENTION STEVEN FISHER

AS WE INFORMED YOU AND YOUR CLIENTS THIS AFTERNOON AT APPROXIMETLY
3.00 PM A AND M RECORDS LIMITED RESCIND THE AGREEMENT BETWEEN
THEMSELVES AND THE SEX PISTOLS DATED 9 MARCH 1977. THIS ACTION
HAS BEEN TAKEN FOR THE REASONS EXPLAINED TO YOU AT THE
MEETING AND WE CONFIRM THAT DISCUSSION OVER THE FORM OF A
PRESS RELEASE TO THIS EFFECT HAS TAKEN PLACE BUT THAT YOUR
CLIENTS HAVE NOT PUT OUR CLIENT IN A POSITION WHERE A
STATEMENT FAVOURABLE TO YOUR CLIENTS IS AVAILABLE

ROBERT LEE

16.3.77 LP

SENT 17.53

23835 FRITEN G
HARLEX LONDON 222339

494, Whitton Avenue (West),
Greenford,
Middlesex.

Dated ..22nd..March..1977....

To: Glitterbest Limited ("the Manager")
23, Great Castle Street,
London, W.1.

and

Messrs. John Lydon,
Stephen Jones and
Paul Cook ("the group")

and

John Beverley

Dear Sirs,

I refer to an Agreement dated 20th September 1976
to which I was a party concerning the management of the
group (of which I was a member).

I am now writing to you to confirm that I have
resigned from the group as of February 11th 1977 and wish
to be released from all further obligations to the Manager
under the said Agreement and to the group and otherwise.

1.   In consideration of such release which you
all hereby agree to give me and in consideration of the
sum of Two thousand nine hundred and sixty-six pounds
ninety-eight pence now paid to me (the receipt of which
sum I hereby acknowledge) and of the further payment of
the sums mentioned below I hereby release the Manager and
all other members of the group from any and all claims
which I might have under the said Agreement and any other
agreements or documents to which I or the Manager or the
group were parties and I accept the said sums in full and
final settlement of any entitlement of fees royalties
earnings or benefits of any kind in any way relating to
the group or my services or the products thereof which
might otherwise be or become due to me.

2.   In consideration of my participation in a
recording session on the   third   day of March
1977 you hereby agree to pay me the sum of Twenty-five
pounds (£25) (receipt of which sum I hereby acknowledge)
in full consideration for my said participation.

3.   Notwithstanding the above I shall continue to
be entitled to one-quarter share of the net royalties
received by the group as composers of musical compositions
which I have co-written.

4.   I agree to treat the terms of this release
confidential and not to divulge any aspect thereof to
any person firm or company.

5.   I agree to sign any formal documents which
you may require to confirm the above arrangements.

               Yours faithfully,

               Glen Matlock
               Glen Matlock.

We agree and confirm the above.

. . . .
For and on behalf of Glitterbest Limited.

John Lydon . . . . .
John Lydon.

Stephen Jones
Stephen Jones

Paul Cook . . . . .
Paul Cook

John Beverley
John Beverley.

130

Directors

M.McLAREN
S.FISHER

Registered Office,
23 Great Castle St,
London, W.1.

GLITTERBEST LTD 40 DRYDEN CHAMBERS
II9 OXFORD ST
LONDON W.I.

OI-734-II37
OI-734-II38

16.5.77

Following the contracts with EMI and A&M the Sex Pistols have now signed
to Virgin Records for £45,000 over two years for releases in the U.K.
only. The Sex Pistols have also signed to Barclay Records for £26,000
over two years for France and Switzerland. A press conference and the
Sex Pistols own jubilee celebration will be announced shortly. The single
'God save the Queen' will be released 27 May.

MAILING

RIPPED ON AND
THEN CAPITALISM
ON THE PISTOLS.
IT NO GOOD LABOURING
THE POINT. OR
ROCK HAS GONE
STALE. THERE
U A BAND IN
THE FRONT LINE
TRYING TO DO
SOMETHING ABOUT
IT. AND THIS POSTER
'ONE CAN'T ALWAYS
BE POLITE, CAN ONE'
'TOES WILL GET
TRODDEN ON.

GOD SAVE
THE QUEEN

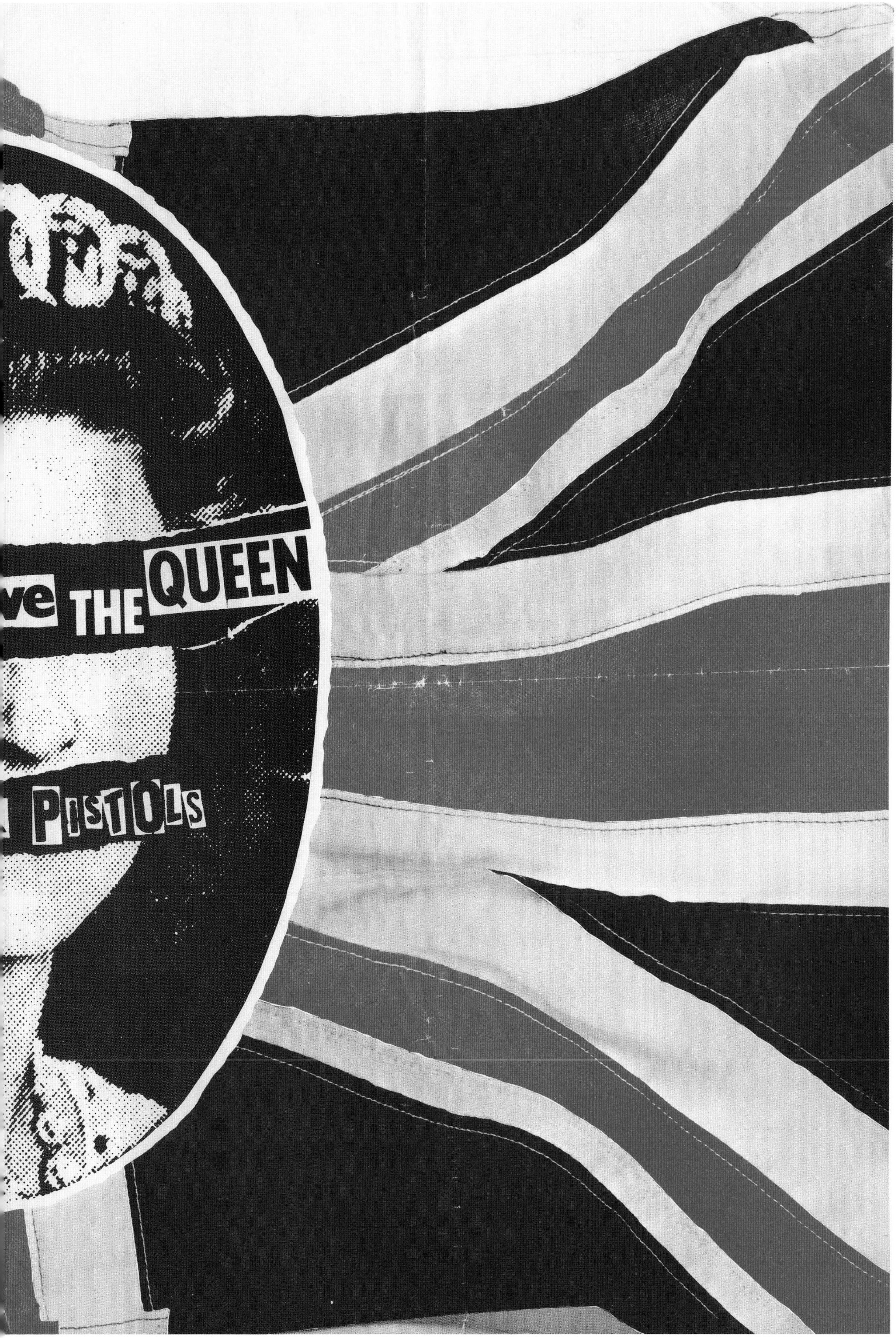
ve THE QUEEN
PISTOLS

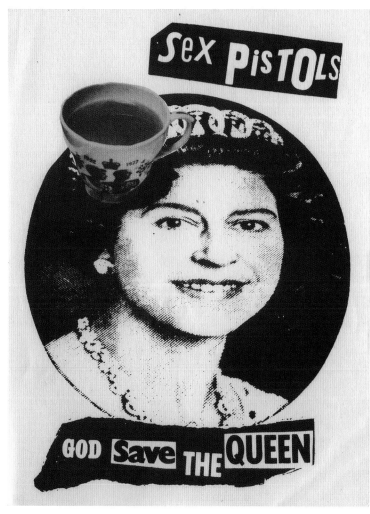

SeX PiSTOls

GOD Save THE QUEEN

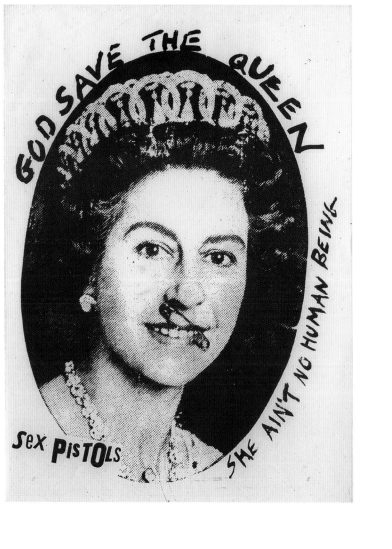

GOD SAVE THE QUEEN

SeX PiSTOls

SHE AIN'T NO HUMAN BEING

17 SEPTEMBER 1976	**H.M. Chelmsford Prison, Chelmsford**

Dave Goodman

It was the day Paul quit his job, so we had a big piss-up. Ingham came along, Malcolm didn't. We had some Thai grass before we went in there, and they let us in. It's a top security prison, and we were talking to this bloke who was coming up for parole. Hawkwind was the last band they'd had, passed acid out, played for ten hours. They let the guys in. The warders telling us, don't talk to anyone, people were passing us letters. This bloke Thor came in, six foot eight, muscles like you wouldn't believe, goes right to the front and sits down with his right-hand man. The band's really late coming on, they're getting wound up, and John comes on and yells, "Fucking wankers! The Queen sends her regards." The guards couldn't believe it. John changed the words of every song so it was directed at them. Very clever. After the first song, he goes, "If you don't like it, you can fucking go home. Stand up and dance. Where's the rules, let's have a riot." After the second number all the black guys got up, wanted to be taken back to the cells. Then Thor stripped off, threw all his clothes onstage. No one else would, and the guards said, "If you hit him over the head, you'd just break your truncheon." The guard said afterwards, "They'll be happy for a few weeks." They didn't get their riot.

Jonh Ingham

I reviewed it. The thing was, you weren't allowed to get up out of your seat. The number one guy was in there for murder, and he was huge, and he sat front row, center, and everybody else took their cues from him. So if he didn't like you, you were ready to be mincemeat. So for the first ten minutes, he was giving John all this lip, in between songs, and John just kept giving it right back to him, and the guy really got off on it, he thought it was really funny. So then it was cool. And they had maybe one band a month, so any entertainment is good, you know. Someone threw a shirt up on the stage, and John was swinging it, and dropped it right in front of him, and just stood there and leered at the guy. The guy had to get up out of his chair to get the shirt, and he was really nervous about it. Suddenly this guy who was clearly in there for drugs, long hair and all that, a total hippy, burst out of his seat and started raving, and the guards didn't do anything, so the whole place got verging on wild. It was very funny.

20 SEPTEMBER 1976	**100 Club, Oxford Street, London (Punk Festival)** Headlining, supported by the Clash, Subway Sect, Siouxsie and the Banshees, and the Suburban Studs

Marco Pirroni

They were supported by the Suburban Studs, who were dressed up like the guy from *Clockwork Orange*, and they had cardboard cutouts of the Bay City Rollers onstage. Even then I didn't understand why. I went by myself because no one else wanted to go. Everyone else I knew was really straight. No one was really interested. You couldn't hear anything, I never heard any of their songs till I saw them at Notre Dame Hall. The thing that impressed me most was that Johnny Rotten sang with his hands in his pockets. He was like, really bored. That was what stuck in my mind. They didn't get me thinking in a different way, I was already thinking that way, but I wasn't sure, it just confirmed my suspicions. It also made me think, "I could play better than that geezer."

21 SEPTEMBER 1976	**Top Rank, Cardiff, Wales**
22 SEPTEMBER 1976	**Stowaway, Newport, Wales**
23 SEPTEMBER 1976	**Bubbles, Swansea, Wales**
24 SEPTEMBER 1976	**76 Club, Burton-On-Trent, recorded in Good Sound**
27 SEPTEMBER 1976	**Outlook Club, Doncaster**
28 SEPTEMBER 1976	**The Place, Guildford**

29 SEPTEMBER 1976	**Strikes Club, Stoke**
30 SEPTEMBER 1976	**Cleopatra's, Derby**
1 OCTOBER 1976	**Didsbury College, Manchester**
2 OCTOBER 1976	**Priory Ballroom, Scunthorpe—CANCELED**
5 OCTOBER 1976	**400 Club, Torquay—CANCELED**
6 OCTOBER 1976	**Woods Centre, Plymouth—CANCELED**
7 OCTOBER 1976	**Winter Gardens, Penzance—CANCELED**
8 OCTOBER 1976	**Club Lafayette, Wolverhampton—CANCELED**
9 OCTOBER 1976	**The Cricket Ground, Northampton—CANCELED**

(Note: some of these venues were revisited later in 1976 and 1977)

9–11 OCTOBER 1976 **Recording sessions with Dave Goodman, Lansdowne and Wessex Studios**
"Anarchy in the UK" / "No Fun" / "Substitute" / "No Lip" / "Johnny B Goode/Road Runner" / "Whatcha Gonna Do About It" / "Through My Eyes"

Dave Goodman They were booked into the Deep Purple studio in Kingsway, by Polydor, but that never happened. They got sued by Lansdowne because they'd written slogans and stuff all over the walls, so we went up to Wessex. We did the "Anarchy" that was on *Swindle*, "No Fun," "Substitute," "No Lip," "Stepping Stone," "Whatcha Gonna Do About It," "Did You No Wrong."

EMI didn't want "Anarchy" anyway, they wanted a pop song. "I'm So Pretty," as they called it. Glen was going along with that, but "Anarchy" was the strongest and that was what it was going to be. We got money to do the single, and we did the whole set. I was called into EMI, and Mike Thorne had gone in there with Glen and done their own mix of my thing behind my back. They played me this acetate they had of his mix, and I just freaked. Next thing I heard they had Chris Thomas to produce.

9 OCTOBER 1976 **Jonh Ingham: *Welcome to the ? Rock Special*—four-page spread in *Sounds***

Jonh Ingham I did three interviews with Sid, and he was saying the most horrendously violent stuff. But to put it into a piece... I just recoiled from it, instinctively. Also it could have jeopardized his court thing. All that, "I don't remember the summer of love, I was too busy playing with my Action Man." The other thing about Sid is that he had an incredible sense of humor, and he would try these things on, just to see what your response would be, in the form of a joke. No one ever got that. The sneer thing. This was in the days before, I think, a lot of the drugs.

12 OCTOBER 197 **Technical College, Dundee, Scotland**

Glen Matlock That was quite good actually. Steve and Kim and Dave drove up with the gear, and we went up on the sleeper. It was great, going over the Tay, first thing in the morning. And we checked into this hotel, the best hotel I'd ever been in up until then. They had all this fish, six different selections of fresh fish for breakfast. Same for lunch. Malcolm hadn't thought about extras at the hotel. And of course we were starving, I tucked into kippers for breakfast, smoked haddock, and that went on for a day or two, and then Malcolm got the extras bill, and that was the end of extras in the hotel. Frankie Vaughan was staying in the hotel, there were all these women hanging out for him. We did the gig at the university or the art college, and he just got pelted with glass. But they wanted an encore! I think they wanted to get us out so they could pelt us some more, but we were hiding behind the door. I was talking to a couple of blokes after, they were saying, "Great gig," and I said, "Why did everybody sling stuff at us?" They said, "We thought that's what you're supposed to do, we thought you'd like that." With Scottish accents. They really thought that was de rigeur, you know.

13 OCTOBER 1976 **Lafayette Club, Wolverhampton**

14 OCTOBER 1976	**Mr Digby's, Birkenhead**

15 OCTOBER 1976	**Eric's, Liverpool**

Jayne Casey

Eric's was like a door opening. It took off instantly. It was great when the Sex Pistols played. It's just a blur, really... It wasn't so much that they were the greatest thing you'd ever seen, as much as everything that surrounded it. It was the feeling that something was happening, and that was the most exciting thing you'd ever experienced. The bands were just a part of that. People were coming together. We went and talked to them afterwards.

Mary Harron

There was something electrifying about the mythology that the Sex Pistols had already brought with them. They were chaotic, which I liked, I thought they were very good, and they had this big guitar sound, Steve Jones was very good, and Glen Matlock. It was wild, whereas everything had been much more proficient in New York. Much more controlled. There was a sense of chaos, and the New York scene was not about chaos, it was anarchy, nihilism. But the Sex Pistols created a sense of—what the fuck is happening? John Lydon being really insulting to the audience, which I thought was really funny. Very obnoxious. I went backstage. It wasn't that difficult, they weren't that well known, and I brought all these kids with me, who wanted to meet the Sex Pistols, I just thought, "Oh well, its all supposed to be about the kids, they should meet the fans." They sat with me. The band were very amused that I was coming to interview them, they were good-humoredly determined to give me a bad time—except for Lydon, who was very nice to me, I think because I was mature-ish, young, and nice to him. The thing is, I was a girl, and I didn't come on heavy. I didn't try to be rude. It was a wonderful interview. I was very impressed. The single biggest thing that converted me to English punk was talking to John Lydon. Incredibly intelligent and honest and clear-sighted. It had politics. American punk had no politics.

17 OCTOBER 1976	**Dave Goodman recordings sessions continue at Wessex Studios**

20 OCTOBER 1976	**Bogarts, Birmingham**

21 OCTOBER 1976	**Queensway Hall, Dunstable, supported by the Jam**

12 NOVEMBER 1976	**Appearance on BBC TV's "Young Nation" segment of *Nationwide***

    Malcolm McLaren and Johnny Rotten interviewed by Maggie Norden, live in studio miming of "Anarchy in the UK" with selected fans—later included in *Sex Pistols #1* promo film

15 NOVEMBER 1976	**Notre Dame Hall, Leicester Place, London**

    Filmed by LWT for *The London Weekend Show*—tx 28.11/76
    Photographs by Ian Dickson and Jonh Ingham

Nils Stevenson

Glen stuck his bass through the only legitimate piece of equipment. I was egging him on, actually. On the side of the stage. I jut thought it was marvelous to see Glen going mad, it was brilliant. He was playing up to the role, I think. He stuck his bass right through this amp and he looked really happy for about a minute then he sort of went, "Oh fuck," when he realized what he'd done. It was the first time he'd really let go in an angry way. Steve was always such a wanton character, and what's so special about him is he does exactly what he wants to do the second he wants to do it. It's quite remarkable to be able to do that. But to see Glen letting go like that was absolutely marvelous.

19 NOVEMBER 1976	**Hendon Polytechnic, London**

Vic Godard

I liked "God Save the Queen." I remember the first time they did that on stage. It was some college in Hendon, and he was reading the words off a sheet of paper. It was pretty shambolic, they'd obviously only just worked the song out. It was a riff with John singing over it.

20 NOVEMBER 1976	**Palace Theatre Manchester—CANCELED**

21 NOVEMBER 1976	**Talk of the Town, London—CANCELED**

26 NOVEMBER 1976	**Release of "Anarchy in the U.K." single, EMI 2766**

| 28 NOVEMBER 1976 | **LWT screen *London Weekend Show*, a Punk Rock Special** |

| 29 NOVEMBER 1976 | **Lanchester Polytechnic, Coventry** |

Roadent There was Lanchester Polytechnic where the Clash supported the Pistols and they refused to pay us because they thought "White Riot" was racist, and that "God Save the Queen" was right wing, so we were a bunch of National Front fascists. The Clash played "White Riot" and the students sort of went, "What's this?" And then the Pistols did "God Save the Queen," which was called "No Future" then, I think it was only the second time it had been performed live, and the students heard, "God Save the Queen," and they called an emergency general meeting of the union and by order of the committee they decided not to pay these right wing fascists.

| 1 DECEMBER 1976 | **Appearance on Thames TV early evening programme, *Today*, interviewed by Bill Grundy** |

Steve Jones I was fucking paralytic. They put us in this hospitality room with this fridge with six bottles of wine in there. I downed at least two, I know that. And he was drunk out of his mind too, Grundy. I wasn't wound up to give him a hard time, no one was going to do that, but he started coating us out, so when drunk, the obvious thing to do is to have a go, you know? That was hilarious. It was one of the best feelings, the next day, when you saw the paper. You thought, "Fucking hell, this is great." We came out of Denmark Street and there's all these guys there from the daily papers, following us down Oxford Street to Dryden Chambers. From that day on, it was different, before that it was just music, and the next day it was the media. After that, musically it became a nightmare.

Paul Cook I was just sitting there, I didn't hardly talk at all. I didn't know it was going out live, people swearing and that, I just thought we were having a laugh. I just thought everyone was taking the piss and it wouldn't have been shown. Steve was mad, ever since he was young he was looking for adventure and excitement, breaking the law to have a laugh. He started the Grundy thing. If the press were there and they wanted a story, he would always do something to please them. A real exhibitionist. Which is funny because he's quite shy by himself. He was the main troublemaker. He thrived on it. Even on tour he used to steal off the bands we were supporting, anything. He'd always complain about Malcolm—he'd say, "Malcolm is always going on about anarchy, but whenever I do anything, he always tells me off!" He don't want to know.

The whole thing had blown up, and that was it, press banging on the door. We were rehearsing that day in Harlesden, we went from rehearsal to the studio and went out after the interview with Grundy, Malcolm got us into the car and off. We just went home, woke up in the morning and there's all these press banging on the door. We were still half asleep, walking down Oxford Street, all these press chasing us along to the office—"What's happening?"—people were pointing at us down the road. We couldn't believe it, we were away then. There was never any blueprint, as people believe that Malcolm sat down and planned it in advance.

| 2 DECEMBER 1976 | **Sex Pistols headlines in Daily Mirror, "The Filth and the Fury."** |

Leee Black Childers The next morning, Jerry Nolan—who never sleeps, he's like a bat—he woke me up at about six or seven in the morning, and covered my bed with newspapers. Our reaction was what Jerry said when he threw all these papers all over the bed. "How are we gonna top that?" It was only later when we went into our rehearsal at the Rainbow, and we began to talk with the Clash and people like that, that we realised we were in the middle of a much more dangerous controversy than that. The idea was then, how are we going to get through that, at least as far as we were concerned? Malcolm loved it. He didn't care if we ever played, but we'd been hauled all the way from New York and we wanted to play. Malcolm was in glory, the more days he could sustain these headlines, the happier he was, because that was all he needed. By the time we were at rehearsal, the first day, he was crowing to me, anyway. I did detect moments of weakness as all the shows were being canceled, that kind of stuff, but I wasn't so sure myself, because although I'd managed David Bowie and Iggy and Mott the Hoople and Dana Gillespie and all of them, I'd always done it with Tony Defries, who knew what to do. I knew the physical necessities of managing a group, but I didn't have that extra little trick that Tony could do, and Malcolm could do. My concern was, are we going to play? Malcolm by that time was saying, "It doesn't matter if we never play." Now I see that it wouldn't have mattered, but at the time I was wondering where the next hamburger was coming from.

Anarchy Tour

3 DECEMBER 1976 **Norwich University, Norwich—CANCELED**

4 DECEMBER 1976 **Kings Hall, Derby—CANCELED**

Nils Stevenson The tour started pretty soon after that, and it was madness, they just couldn't play anywhere, it was ridiculous. Me and Mickey Foote were setting up this PA, pulling the bins out of the truck and setting them up, knowing that we weren't going to play. Sure enough we'd be told, "Sorry boys, its off," and we'd pack it all up and back to the bloody hotel, nothing to eat or anything, and off the next day. It was miserable.

No one ever thought about getting the roadies anything to eat, it was a mess. The group used to just sit around, giggle a lot, and they were traveling in style for the first time, they had one of those big buses, so the group were alright about it. We were getting tons of press, so you felt something was happening. That's when Malcolm was doing very well. He stuck to his guns when the civic authorities insisted that the group play, and Bernie really wanted them to do it. Because the Clash weren't getting any publicity out of the tour, the Pistols were.

5 DECEMBER 1976 **City Hall, Newcastle—CANCELED**

6 DECEMBER 1976 **Leeds Polytechnic, Leeds**

Pauline Murray We went to Leeds, just after the Bill Grundy thing, they'd been banned everywhere, we went up to the hotel, bands everywhere: Heartbreakers, Clash, Pistols, they'd taken over a whole floor, more or less. It was the time when all the newspapers were looking for the scam, the phone was ringing. Steve Jones would pick it up and tell them to fuck off. They didn't know where the next gig was because everywhere had banned them, the tour was all banned in various places. It was like a whole big party, a big laugh. They couldn't give a shit, it was madness. I don't think anyone stopped to think what was happening. It had got slicker, really. They were into the bondage clothes by then, it was in bigger places, Leeds University or somewhere like that,. It had gone up a step, and there didn't seem to be as much feeling for the audience. People were turning up then, to see this thing they'd read about. There was spitting starting to happen. I think they felt that as well.

Ray Stevenson Rather like school holidays, with guitars instead of a bucket and spade. "Whoopee, we're all going to Derby, Leeds, etcetera!" Leaving London there was a feeling that we were escaping from all that pressure, not realizing that it was waiting for us up there as well. EMI were being funny, so it was away from the EMI situation. All we could do was check into motels, and drink. I wasn't aware of any drugs on the tour.

You couldn't go out anywhere because you'd be accosted, so you were locked up with loads of alcohol. I didn't do the whole tour, but when I came back I found myself drinking in the afternoon on my own. It was terrible. I still had my BBC job at that point. I did the first bit and the last bit, but missed the Wales thing, which was a real shame. There were only so many pictures I could take of them drinking. There was nothing else to do.

7 DECEMBER 1976 **Village Bowl, Bournemouth—CANCELED**

9 DECEMBER 1976 **Electric Circus, Manchester**

Morrissey Well, silly me turned up at something like ten o'clock in the day, there was a lot of people I wanted to see, and I wanted to see them in the day as much as the night time. That was very important, so I sat in the venue all day, and nothing was happening, but when it did happen, it was worth being there. John Lydon walked in, Howard Devoto walked in, and John said to Howard, "Is this a rough area?" And Howard said, "Yes, round here everybody walks around in their underpants," which I didn't think was funny, but the place erupted. It was a good quip for the time, I think. The positioning of the Electric Circus was important in that you had to risk something in order to join in. If it was a genteel and easy area, it would have been too easy. You had to risk something, even if it was your own safety.

Richard Boon   I thought the Sex Pistols were really sloppy on the Anarchy tour, and the Clash were really vibrant. They were under mounting pressure, and the whole tour was fraught with media–induced problems. They were still good, but Steve Jones was a rock star, acting in a very old-fashioned manner, and with John the playfulness had gone. Some of the sharpness was still there, he was still engaging, but something had happened, life was being made very hard for them. Life became heavy. But it was still a very vibrant package.

10 December 1976   **Lancaster University, Lancaster—CANCELED**

11 December 1976   **Stadium, Liverpool—CANCELED**

Tony Wilson   I resigned at Granada over the Anarchy tour because Roger Eagle rang me from Liverpool. I'd had a documentary I was making on the Pistols canceled on the morning I was to start shooting it, by Granada, because my producer Linda MacDougal had read Ronald Butt attacking them, and called Granada and said, "Don't give Wilson his crew." This was after Grundy, things are going around in the press. The next day Roger Eagle rang me to say the police had been down to Eric's and said, "If you put this group on, you will not get your license next time it comes up." So I prepared for the *What's On* show that week, What's Not On is the Sex Pistols, and I then got a memo from Linda MacDougal saying, "There will be no mention of the Sex Pistols in this program." And I walked out.

11 DECEMBER 1976   **Recording session at EMI Studios, Manchester Square, with Mike Thorne**
"No Future" / "Liar" / "Problems" / "No Feelings"—all now available on *SEXBOX*

13 DECEMBER 1976   **Colston Hall, Bristol—CANCELED**

14 DECEMBER 1976   **Top Rank, Cardiff, Wales—CANCELED**

14 DECEMBER 1976   **Castle Cinema, Caerphilly, Wales**
The scenes around the venue filmed by HTV for their early evening news. The show was witnessed by Brian Case, who later wrote a report for *The Observer* (30.1.77: Mad About Punk)

15 DECEMBER 1976   **Apollo, Glasgow, Scotland—CANCELED**
The Sex Pistols are banned from entering the city

16 DECEMBER 1976   **Caird Hall, Dundee, Scotland—CANCELED**

17 DECEMBER 1976   **City Hall, Sheffield—CANCELED**

18 DECEMBER 1976   **Kursaal, Southend—CANCELED**

19 DECEMBER 1976   **Civic Hall, Guildford—CANCELED**

19 DECEMBER 1976   **Electric Circus, Manchester, copies of *Anarchy in the UK* magazine go on sale**

20 DECEMBER 1976   **Town Hall, Birmingham—CANCELED**

20 DECEMBER 1976   **Winter Gardens, Cleethorpes—CANCELED**

21 DECEMBER 1976   **Rainbow theatre London—CANCELED**

21 DECEMBER 1976   **Woods Centre, Plymouth**

Sophie Richmond   Plymouth was kind of drecky, everybody pissed in the hotel, being wild.

22 DECEMBER 1976   **400 Ballroom, Torquay—CANCELED**

22 DECEMBER 1976   **Woods Centre, Plymouth, supported by the Clash, the Heartbreakers, and Wire**

23 DECEMBER 1976   **Paignton, Penelope's Ballroom—CANCELED**

26 DECEMBER 1976	**The Roxy, London—CANCELED**

27 DECEMBER 1976 **Sex Pistols record with Chris Thomas at Wessex Studios**
Late December 1976, Seditionaries opens at 430 Kings Road

4 JANUARY 1977 **Sex Pistols pass through Heathrow Airport—press headlines ensue**

5 JANUARY 1977 **Paradiso Club, Amsterdam, Holland**

6 JANUARY 1977 **Art Centre, Rotterdam, Holland**
EMI announce that they have terminated the Sex Pistols' contract

7 JANUARY 1977 **Paradiso Club, Amsterdam, Holland**

Dave Goodman That was with the Heartbreakers supporting. I think that was when Glen walked offstage, refused to do an encore. That was about the end of the band with Glen.

Sophie Richmond They didn't rehearse, they couldn't bear to be in the same room together half the time, it was a real effort in the spring of 1977 to get them to go to Denmark Street, try to write new songs. This is projection, but Glen could write tunes, and they couldn't. They could produce words and chords, but they couldn't write tunes, like "Submission," so they were finished as a creative unit once he'd gone.

Berlin / Jersey

Steve Jones We got banned from Jersey, they wouldn't let us in there, because of the reputation. They wouldn't let us out of the airport. They called up the hotel and told them not to book us. We got out of there to a bar somewhere, then came back again. In Berlin we just went there for a week after Sid had that fight with whats-his-name down the Speakeasy, and no-one wanted to know us. It was fucking boring. Sid and Boogie had a car crash... went into another car. It was boring, that time, the image took over.

12 JANUARY 1977 **Johnny Rotten arrested in London and charged with possession of amphetamine**

17–20 JANUARY 1977 **Recording sessions with Dave Goodman at Gooseberry Studios**
"No Future" / "Problems" / "Pretty Vacant" / "Liar" / "EMI" / "New York"—these were included on the original *Spunk / No Future* 1977 bootlegs and are now collected on the *Never Mind The Bollocks* box

19 JANUARY 1977 **Malcolm McLaren meets A&M boss Derek Green for potential signing of Sex Pistols to A&M**

21 JANUARY 1977 **EMI make termination of Sex Pistols contract official: Glitterbest gets £30,000 from the record company with EMI Music giving another £10,000 for publishing contract**

24–26 JANUARY 1977 **More recording with Dave Goodman at Gooseberry Studios**

27 JANUARY 1977 **Meeting with Warner Brothers Records. The tension between Johnny Rotten and Glen Matlock come to a head**

EARLY FEBRUARY 1977 **Glen Matlock leaves the group "by mutual consent"**

John Tiberi It didn't make sense to me, getting rid of Glen, but everybody said they didn't like him, and that was it. The obvious thing was class.

11 FEBRUARY 1977 **Sid Vicious auditions for the Sex Pistols at Denmark Street rehearsal room**

13 FEBRUARY 1977 **Malcolm McLaren flies to LA to meet A&M US head Jerry Moss**
Radio interview with Rodney Bingenheimer for KROQ Radio. This was Sid Vicious' first official act as a Sex Pistol. Part of the interview was included in *Sex Pistols #1*

24 FEBRUARY 1977	**Glen Matlock's departure becomes official**

3 MARCH 1977	**Recording session at Wessex Studios with Chris Thomas**

"No Future" / "I Did You No Wrong" / "Pretty Vacant"

9 MARCH 1977	**Sex Pistols sign with A&M for £150,000**

10 MARCH 1977	**A&M signing outside Buckingham Palace**

Paul Cook   The best fight we had in the band was in the Daimler, going to sign the A&M contract at Buckingham Palace. The Daimler turned up at Denmark Street about nine o'clock in the morning, and John and Sid were in there already. I don't know how they managed to get them up that early. They were in bad moods, looking really wrecked. Steve got up in a bad mood, and the row started then, there was a big free-for-all in the back of the Daimler. It was so funny. Sid's legs nearly got broken, because Sid's legs were up on the seat and Steve fell on them.

It was just one of those early morning things. It was really funny. I think Sid was drunk when he turned up in the morning, then we went on to a press conference at that sleazy hotel in Piccadilly, everyone was drinking. Then we went to do another interview somewhere else and they got slowly worse and worse, and that was it. That wasn't the reason we got thrown off A&M, it was to do with the fight down the Speakeasy, I should imagine. I'm not sure. I don't know who signed us even, because we didn't really meet anybody. Malcolm was getting on with all that.

11 MARCH 1977	**Sid Vicious, Johnny Rotten, and Jah Wobble get into an altercation at the Speakeasy**

Sid picks a fight with BBC DJ and TV presenter Bob Harris, whose sound engineer, George Nicholson, receives a head wound that requires fourteen stitches.

Jah Wobble   We'd go down to the Speakeasy and there were all these old rock types who'd had their noses put out of joint, it was a bit like we did by the Blitz scene, "Oh it's not like the old days." They'd get a bit paranoid and comments would be passed, then glasses would be passed, if you know what I mean. Really pathetic, people who were old enough to know better, really. Harris felt really threatened by this, because I think deep in their hearts they felt they weren't very valid, these people.

16 MARCH 1977	**Sex Pistols dropped by A&M**

John Tiberi   It was just so cliched, after Sid's other trouble at the 100 Club, with the beer glass. But it put the kybosh on the whole A&M thing. All Malcolm's plans were scuppered. This time round it wasn't funny. This is the time of that interview that ended up in the *Swindle*, with the cheque. A lot of it was heartfelt: "What the fuck are you doing, you're supposed to be making hit records, and these people keep giving me money." He was beginning to act desperate. The calendar wasn't on our side, for the Queen thing. July was the big day.

21 MARCH 1977	**Notre Dame Hall, Leicester Square, London**

Sid Vicious' first show with the Sex Pistols. Filmed by NBC TV.

23 MARCH 1977	**Sex Pistols fly to Jersey—they are told to leave after twenty-four hours on the island**

John Tiberi   It was felt that the group should be out of the way, occupied. Jamie [Reid] took them to Jersey, I can't imagine why. I had something else to do. Sid didn't have a passport or something like that. But they were only gone twenty-four hours, I had to get them from Gatwick. It was a disaster: the police followed them, they got word from the airline, Jamie was freaked out. We went to the pub.

25 MARCH 1977	**Sex Pistols fly to Berlin for a holiday**

John Tiberi   I think it was a stroke of genius, packing them off to Berlin. Rotten was a precocious little shit, really. Trying to think of what this little shit wanted to do. We stayed at the Kempinski. I must have told them to wait in the cab while I sorted it out. There was nothing much to do except to entertain the bastards. Got in touch with the record company, who were a bunch of boring German bastards. "Yes, we have the record." I think it was EMI, actually. Hired a VW and bombed around Berlin, around the wall, in fact, all around these towers. Sid was a real tosser for not having a passport. If he had, we would have gone over. But I couldn't imagine leaving him behind. It was fun, though; I must say I really enjoyed that.

The band loved it, they didn't have a stage to play on, but they had fun. Getting into fights with film crews. It had got out of balance, as far as John and Sid was concerned, the whole thing was getting very top-heavy, it was all up there. It was removed, but it did connect with Malcolm pushing in rehearsals to write some new songs. The only one really interested in it was John. He found East German TV in the hotel room, he was knocked out by that. He was a grammar school boy, another Glen, really.

3 APRIL 1977 **Screen on the Green Cinema, Islington, London**
Filmed by Don Letts
Photographs by Jon Savage

Paul Cook For me, that was one of the best times of the band, when Sid had just joined. People thought he couldn't play, but he put another dimension to it. We were really tight, because we had rehearsed a lot to get him to learn the songs.

Siouxsie About the time of the second Screen on the Green, I thought it was finished, and when Sid joined, it became very stylized, and Rotten's sneer—I just thought, "They don't mean it." The audience weren't the same bunch of stupid hippies anymore, and there was this, "You can't be a fan of ours now because you've got a band of your own" kind of attitude.

Shanne Hasler I saw the Screen on the Green, and off Leicester Square. The audience was full of people in dog collars, trying to strangulate each other. The humor had gone out of it, it was commercialized, aggressive. Macho.

Marco Pirroni The last time I saw them was the Screen on the Green gig, and by that time Sid was playing bass, and he was hopeless, it was horrible. Rotten, or Lydon, used to have a real presence, a command over the audience, and the audience didn't care, they were just chucking cans at him, and at Sid. Sid didn't know what to do. They commanded no respect.

21 APRIL 1977 **Recording sessions with Chris Thomas at Wessex Studios**
"Problems" / "No Feelings" / "Liar" / "Seventeeten" / "Satellite" / "Submission" / "New York" / "EMI" / "Holidays in the Sun"

Paul Cook Chris Thomas was good, I thought. Professional. He seemed to know what we wanted to sound like, anyway. There was a bit of tension sometimes, but I thought it sounded great, I still do, a lot of it. Me and Steve would go in and do the guitar and drum parts, which is pretty unorthodox, its usually bass and drums, but we knew the songs so well we could do it without the bass. And we got them done quickly. The studio thing was alright really. John and Chris Thomas fell out sometimes, but that was just normal, really.

13 MAY 1977 **Sex Pistols sign with Virgin Records for £15,000**

Al Clark You'd have to ask Simon Draper for the details, but there was a discussion, before EMI. Then it all started again immediately after A&M. I think within weeks of that, "God Save the Queen" was on the release schedule. It was by no means a unanimous decision that the Pistols should be signed to Virgin. There was a lot of opposition from people who felt it was more trouble than it was worth. On the other hand, Virgin had been founded on its sparky defiance of the rules, had lost that, and signing the Sex Pistols was a good way to revive that spirit in the company, albeit in rather different circumstances.

16 MAY 1977 **Recording sessions with Chris Thomas at Wessex Studios**

23 MAY 1977 **Filming at the Marquee, Julien Temple promo for "God Save the Queen"**

Al Clark	They did some filming at the Marquee one morning, and John just sat there smoking, on his own, and Steve and Paul chatted, and Sid hadn't turned up. I left before he had turned up. It was clearly destined to burn brightly and briefly. It was going a bit. It's very tiring to be that much at the heart of things, and waiting for you do do the next thing. Particularly as they didn't choose seclusion.

26 MAY 1977 **Paris showing of *Sex Pistols #1*, a twenty minute promo film assembled by John Tiberi and Julien Temple**

John Tiberi	I had to get hold of footage, I was getting Sid out of hospital. They didn't need very much looking after. Sid's rehearsing. Malcolm's visiting companies. Perhaps Malcolm had started thinking about *Who Killed Bambi*. Anyway, Malcolm asked me to get hold of these bits of footage from the Anarchy tour, to make a show reel. I don't know where he got the idea of selling the band as a visual act. We were always very aware of this potential of the group, to get fired from record companies, and on TV. It was a new direction. That's why I was there, knocking on the door. I was very motivated by the Angry Brigade, I thought that was fantastic.

It was all re-filmed. It was very early days in video technology. The only place we could get the Grundy programme was from a guy who had recorded it. It was a promoter who did all the country and western gigs, and Sophie had rung him up to get him to record it. He was a competitor to Copeland. A different market. It was Philips format. But Julien did the re-filming, he shot the video image onto film and edited it into chronological order at the film school, overnight, and showed a cutting copy the following night. It was very stirring stuff, propaganda-oriented. |

27 MAY 1977 **Release of "God Save the Queen"/ "Did You No Wrong," Virgin VS184**
Difficulties in getting single out for distribution

John Tiberi	I remember a Capital Radio phone-in request show that got a special dispensation from the IBA to play the record, and then take comments. It was rather trite. I didn't think it was a particularly great Sex Pistols song. And I think Virgin was a mistake. They had them worked out wrong. It seems a shortsighted way of looking at the group to see them having to meet deadlines. The whole media thing of the Jubilee, it was a chance to take a crack at the power of the media. It was a semi-political, agit-prop statement, trying to get the name on buses, and they wouldn't have it. How can we sneak it in? No safety pin, either, thinking that people who knew would know.

The group wanted to be a pop group. They were a pain in the arse. They had no reason to be snooty about Glen, they had all the same ideas. I played a part in what happened, but I don't think anybody directed what happened. Malcolm did take the driving seat, and did the job, but if that thing had come out three months earlier, as it was going to with A&M, it would have been a very powerful statement, and it might never have come out with EMI. Not at all. We're forgetting the great groundswell that was happening in the music industry, saying, "Fuck Number One." Anti-chart. The chart with no Number One. The chart that said, "It isn't important anymore." It's grandiose to talk about how it affected the media. What was important was how it affected the music business. |

7 JUNE 1977 **Queen Elizabeth River Boat, River Thames, London**

Steve Jones	It was a stunt, that's all really.
John Lydon	It was really tedious. It was like patting yourself on the back, playing to a captive audience who have to pretend they like you, one way or another. Selfish rubbish is what that was. I enjoyed it, I don't know why, but something worked. I remember the power cut out, and I think Paul had to keep on playing. And there was a fight. That guy who used to run the Screen on the Green, Roger, got into a fight with someone.

My brother got arrested. I remember when we had got off the boat and Malcolm was on the boat, going, "There he is, that's Johnny Rotten!" to the police! He wanted me nicked. And I slipped away magnificently! That was how they got my brother, because he was me. Yes, we all got away. Damned if I was going to be beaten up in the cells for publicity. Fuck that! |

Alan Jones	The day of the boat party was the day I said, enough is enough. I was on the boat and Vivienne was hanging over the side having a piss through her trousers. I said, "Why don't you take them off?" She said, "Oh no, I can't be bothered." They were white muslin ones, and for the rest of the day she had piss-stained trousers on. And as soon as we got surrounded by the police, and the ensuing hysteria when we docked, and everyone was being filed off and being hit, and running off in all directions, and filed into the vans, and I stepped back and looked and I thought, "This is it. I don't want to know any more."
Jah Wobble	That was a laugh. I think I started the row, as it happens. All I remember is we'd come off and Vivienne Westwood and McLaren yelling "Fascists!" at the police, and all the duckers and divers like myself who'd been at it hammer and nails on the boat, just slipped away, and they all got nicked. I was just standing having a drink and some geezer barged me, I said, "Watch where you're fucking going," and he said something back and pushed me again, so I chinned him. I wanted to put him in the water. And it was all off, it was a good fight. McLaren come up to me and said, "Let's hijack the boat." I said, "Fuck off, that's piracy, that is, you silly cunt. You do it, Malcolm, you're the manager."
John Tiberi	For what there was, it was a very simple setup. There was an Australian film crew, and when they floated past the Houses of Parliament, we struck up. The police were brought on the boat to stop a fight. There was no fight at all when they got there. The captain obviously wanted the trip stopped, so the boat docked, there was SPG on the quayside. The boat was emptied, I stayed with the group, got the group off. Let them take care of it all. It was only on the film I saw Branson arguing, Malcolm getting arrested. The SPG were a lot more active then. The people on the boat just wanted it over, I didn't know it was going to get that violent. The idea is not to end up in the nick, although that was a personal decision, it was always my first instinct. It would appear from the film that they picked on Malcolm. Vivienne did a Boadicea number, started getting the police to attack her. They were both having their martyrdom.
Al Clark	I think there was an element in the decision to take them on, that Virgin could handle it where the others couldn't. One of the reasons was that when Malcolm came up with a scheme as outrageous as taking a boat trip down the river on Jubilee day with "God Save the Queen" hanging off the side of the boat, and playing "Anarchy in the UK" as they passed the houses of parliament and all that stuff. I just said, "Fine. You have your guest list, we'll have ours, it'll be fifty each," and it was organized. The bouncers were two builders who used to work at Virgin. The boat was hired under some preposterous disguise.
Dennis Morris	I remember it being fun. I was taking loads of pictures, everyone was having a good time, and the point I remember was when we actually docked, and then everybody had to make up their own minds about what to do. I think the situation was manipulated to get press out of it. Up to that point it was quite a good trip, but something had to be done to make it more than just going up and down the river. And just before the boat went in to dock, suddenly these launches were there, I suppose McLaren had this ace up his sleeve. He always had a failsafe, it wouldn't have been enough for the boat to go up and down the river. There had to be something like that. He did something to create that whole thing.

9 JUNE 1977 **BBC chart places "God Save the Queen" at #2**

John Varnom	It seemed clear that the music business was disapproving. In all probability, the British Market Research Bureau juggled the national chart positions so that "God Save the Queen" did not make number one. It was pipped by a Rod Stewart single. But Virgin's sales out of stock exceeded the sales figures of the Rod Stewart single. Richard even contacted the BPI directly over the discrepancy. He was very keen for a number one. The industry quite definitely was not. It wanted to bury the Sex Pistols.

Mick Brown, in Richard Branson's official biography:

Branson's suspicions that the chart had been fixed was lent weight by an anonymous phone call alleging that, in the week that the Sex Pistols might have been expected to reach number one, the BPI had issued an extraordinary secret directive to the BMRB, that all chart-return shops connected with record companies be dropped from the weekly census of best-selling records. Virgin, the store where most Sex Pistols were being sold, was struck off the list. A week later, the decision was reversed.

19 JUNE 1977   **Paul Cook and John Lydon attacked**

Paul Cook   I was walking along the Goldhawk Road with my girlfriend of the time, and these young teds, call them rockabillies now, three or four of them came up, and I had teddy boy shoes on, which was the order of the day. "Oy, what you got those shoes on for, punk?" "I like them, why?" And we walked on up to Shepherd's Bush green, them following us behind. I knew they were going to go for us so I turned round and had a go at them, and that was it. I just got a bit of a hiding. I got hit with some metal. It ended up in Shepherd's Bush station. I knew who it was, they were from round there. A couple of them got put away eventually, for other fights. It was a nasty period. People were frightened to go out. We were marked, everyone knew our faces. There weren't many punks around then. People think punks, leather jackets, chains, but then punks were normal kids with scruffy hair, macs on and stuff like that. More like flashers than anything else.

John Lydon   I was with Chris Thomas in a pub. "God Save the Queen" was in the charts, and as we left for his car in the car park, we were attacked by a gang of knife-wielding yobs, who were chanting, "we love our Queen, you bastard"—I mean, normally I'd say they were National Front, but a third of them at least were black. There was all sorts, just out for violence. I got some bad cuts from that. I got stabbed, and it severed two tendons, so this hand is fucked forever, and I'm left-handed. I can't close the fist properly. I'll never play guitar, there's no power to it. I jumped into the car and someone jumped in after me with a machete and cut me. I had on extremely thick leather trousers at the time, thank fucking God, because it would have ripped the muscle out and now I'd be a one-legged hoppity. And of course Malcolm thought that was hilarious.

Sophie Richmond   I was quite shocked to read—Steve attacked here, Paul attacked there, John, Jamie, the stuff in the Kings Road going on. Again, its like transgressing a barrier that you don't know is there, and this one was about the Royal Family, and no-one imagined that in Britain in 1977 anyone would give a shit about insulting the Queen.

Jah Wobble   I remember one nasty night, we went up the west end and this whole coachload of geezers saw us, it was Jubilee time, and it got very nasty. It was lynching time. John and me and John Gray and four or five others ended up in some restaurant, barricaded in. It was nasty. I think John felt that with Malcolm setting up all this publicity, he wasn't on the fucking streets, he was in limos and taxis, and John's on the streets. It was bitter.

Al Clark   The general climate of hostility and outrage towards the band—they may have behaved worse before they signed to Virgin, but the reaction to them was far more dramatic after they signed. It got into the Jubilee stuff, people's sense of patriotism was offended. For a few weeks the band seemed to me to be sitting targets for absolutely anybody with a grievance. I've never known so much national hatred focused on a pop group. It was the apex of eight months' worth of history that for the majority of people started with the Grundy appearance, and then the Jubilee happened. They had conveyed the image of being hard, indestructible, they became targets for the same sort of people who walked up to Robert Mitchum in bars in the fifties and wanted to try it on. They got treated as if they had no feelings, that their doctrine was being voiced back at them. And of course they didn't want to be treated as animals.

2 JULY 1977   **Release of second Virgin single, "Pretty Vacant" / "No Fun" (VS 184)**

5 JULY 1977   **Filming of promo video for "Pretty Vacant," directed by Mike Mansfield**

John Tiberi   I remember *Top of the Pops*, the idea was to catch Rotten's ego, and they did it. He had some leverage. We didn't have to do that recording. Virgin paid for it. I can't understand why I took the group to that TV studio in the first place. I suppose we gave in, didn't we?

Scandinavian Tour

Steve Jones   That was a laugh, it was just that everything closed at ten o'clock. Gorgeous crumpet though, knew everything. Not like English birds, all fat and sweaty—these were dolls, little blonde beauties. They had this gang out there, called the Raggare, this biker gang, a real pain in the ass, they used to beat up all the punters when they came out of the gigs. Idiots.

Paul Cook   We'd done a couple of gigs with Sid, the Screen on the Green, Notre Dame hall. Then we did the Sweden tour, and then it just went to his head and he went mad. That was it, he went off the rails. And very quickly too, I was surprised. He was quite an intelligent bloke, it was just an act he used to put on.

Roadent   I did Sweden. People kept mistaking me for John, so I dyed my hair black and people mistook me for Sid. It was good, a fun tour.

John Tiberi   In terms of playing, the group were really good. Better than America. It had been a long time. It was quite a simple tour, in a van. There was a private airplane at one point. We went up to the very top, a very strange gig. It was summer, so it wasn't that cold, but it was bizarre. They liked the idea of being in a group, playing quite well. It was okay. The gig in that town was in a bar, there was no nightclub. Just a saloon. Sid was away for a very long time from the table, and Paul volunteered to go look for him, and he was gone for a bit, so when I got in there, there was Paul getting this guy from behind, who had Sid held by the padlock, the chain, up the wall, going white in the toilets. He was a big guy. I doubt if he knew who he was holding. It was the only time Sid was threatened, and it had to happen in the northernmost part of Finland.

All the gigs were strange. There was this fanatical teddy-boy element in Stockholm, which was a problem. They broke up the gig, outside, and the police put the group in a van, blue lights flashing, and driven through town to the hotel, then they went away. The hotel had to barricade the doors, because these guys were coming in through the gardens, bashing at plate glass doors, it was crazy. We couldn't go out, but Steve went out. He had a black leather jacket, and he pretended to be one of them. He had to go out and find some chicks. I liked all that, it was like the Beatles in *Help!* There were places where there was no stage. Those photographs Dennis Morris took, with some punk going mad and John six inches from his face with a microphone. It was totally different from the 100 Club. At that point they hadn't played anything bigger than a 300–400-seater cinema. The Swedish gig that was filmed was the biggest gig they had ever done, in a college. After two weeks they were tired but happy.

John had the words for that song, "Holidays," but he didn't actually write it until the sound checks for that tour, it was the only time they put together any of those songs. "Bodies" was put together in the studio, more so than any other song. The studio Sex Pistols song. But as far as I remember they were both written during those sound checks.

Dennis Morris   That was brilliant. That was another situation where we turned up in this hotel, there were at least two rooms short. Boogie and Roadent didn't have rooms. Nor did Jamie. And there were no facilities for Roadent. That was how he got his name, because he always ate what was left. And whatever floor was left, that's where he'd sleep. The first place was this club, the stage was like this high, and there was a rope as a security barrier, and all these Swedish kids who had been into, I don't know, Status Quo or something, and bung them onstage and they just went berserk. I suppose because they were into heavy metal, the whole thing was like heavy metal to them, but being that close it made them go completely berserk. But it was easy for them. The only problem was the usual spillage on the stage, people knocking over equipment. But it was never ever the right setup. Bad mikes, bad PAs. But it was good for them to unwind.

13 JULY 1977   **Daddy's Dance Hall, Copenhagen, Denmark**

14 JULY 1977   **Daddy's Dance Hall, Copenhagen, Denmark**

15 JULY 1977   **Beach Disco, Diskotek Ostra Stranden, Halmstad, Sweden**

16 JULY 1977   **Mogambo Disco, Helsingborg, Sweden**

16 JULY 1977   **Tommy Vance interview with Johnny Rotten is broadcast on Capitol Radio, during which he played some of his favourite records. Included were tracks by Tim Buckley, the Creation, Augustus Pablo, Fred Locks, Culture, Neil Young, Lou Reed, Peter Hammill, Captain Beefheart, John Cale, Ken Boothe, Can, and Peter Tosh.**

Al Clark	The world, certainly the music business, was longing for a way to humanize them. The interview that John did with Tommy Vance, where he played Tim Buckley and Peter Hammill records, was used that way. He has taste after all!

17 JULY 1977 **Discotheque 42, Jonkoping, Sweden**

19 JULY 1977 **Club Zebra, Kristinehamn, Sweden**

20 JULY 1977 **Pinvinen Restaurant, Oslo, Norway**

21 JULY 1977 **Studenter Samfundet, Trodheim, Norway**

23 JULY 1977 **Barbarellas Disco, Vaxjo, Sweden**

24 JULY 1977 **Barbarellas Disco, Vaxjo, Sweden**

27 JULY 1977 **Happy House, Student Karen, Stockholm, Sweden**

28 JULY 1977 **Happy House, Student Karen, Stockholm, Sweden**
This was recorded and filmed. The set list was: "Anarchy In The UK" / "I Wanna Be Me" / "Seventeen" / "New York" / "EMI" / "Submission" / "No Feelings" / "Problems" / "God Save the Queen" / "Pretty Vacant" / "No Fun"

29 JULY 1977 **Orfi, Linkoping, Sweden**

Roadent	I remember being in the hotel in Stockholm with Charles Shaar Murray, running up huge bar bills, taking the piss out of everything. He was an old hippy. The record company insisted that all the papers came over, and John insisted that if they came over there they had to pay for themselves, not to let the record company pay for them. Consequently they had six double-page spreads, three weeks of double-page spreads. Having to pay for themselves, they wanted to get their money's worth.

30 JULY 1977 ***Sounds* Sex Pistols front cover, with article on the Swedish tour by Ross Stapleton**

4 AUGUST 1977 ***NME* Sex Pistols front cover, with article on the Swedish tour by Charles Shaar Murray**

19 AUGUST 1977 **The S.P.O.T.S. tour "S.P.O.T.S." (Sex Pistols On Tour Secretly)**

Barbara Harwood	When the band came back from Sweden and the SPOTS tour came up, Roadent left the Clash and went to roadie for the Pistols, and I went with him. I'd been friendly with the Clash, spent a fair amount of time in Camden Town. I took the band around with Boogie in one of those twelve-seaters, and Roadent took the lorry for the equipment. No longer everything crammed into a small space, and they went one day ahead. It was strange, out of London. Up till then, everything for me had been mostly in London, and suddenly it was off to these corners of Britain. There wasn't much to do. There was just us, instead of us and all our friends with places to go and things to do. There was just us. I was trying to concentrate on the job, while this riot went on in the back, people coming up to pour packets of crisps and peanuts over me. Coca-cola. In the front I drove and Sid or Boogie sat up front next to me, with Paul and John and everybody in the back. We'd arrive at the place, plug in, and away we'd go. It was quite riotous. The audiences were starved of anything, and all hell broke out when the band came on. Roadent and I trying to keep control, keeping an eye on Sid, if he was too out of tune to turn his volume down so that nobody knew he was turned off. Stuff like that. I used to get down behind his speaker and give him encouragement. "Come on Sid, get it together!"

19 AUGUST 1977 **Lafayette Club, Wolverhampton**
Pictures Kevin Cummins, words Charles M. Young

Sophie Richmond	I went up to Wolverhampton. That was the only one, it was great. They played very well, an enthusiastic crowd, lots of money at the end of it then back down the motorway to London. Rock 'n' roll.

Steve Jones	That was real good, there were a lot of fans, queuing up around the block, and they went nuts when we played. It was like how it should have been, a band playing to an audience which dug you. Before all that, we were playing good, but it was all these northerners who didn't know what the fuck we was. There was a lot of trouble. But this was playing to people who wanted to come and see us.
Roadent	The SPOTS tour, that was great fun. Wolverhampton was the first one, and somehow lots of people had figured out it was the Sex Pistols, coachloads from Manchester. Bouncers were standing on the front monitors, holding onto the ceilings to balance themselves, and nobody could see the band, it was chaos, a brilliant atmosphere where everything is threatening and exciting.

24 AUGUST 1977   **Outlook Club, Doncaster—"Tax Exiles"**

25 AUGUST 1977   **Penthouse, Scarborough–"Special Guest"**

26 AUGUST 1977   **Rock Garden, Middlesborough–"Acne Rabble"**

Pauline Murray	We went to see them at the Middlesborough Rock Garden, which is a really small club, renowned for its violence. It wasn't the same, it had gone back down again. I think Sid might have been in the band by then. It was lacking in the original fire, it had a different sort of energy, more violent. They weren't making a message, it was more a barrage. It seemed disconnected somehow. It was still great, but it was odd by that time, like they didn't know where they were going.

31 AUGUST 1977   **Woods Centre, Plymouth–"The Hamsters"**

Barbara Harwood	We went go-karting. I think that was in Plymouth. Sid kept trying to knock me off my kart. When we were in Plymouth I got a sense that the image was in charge of him, when he got quite upset in the hotel, in a real mess, and he wanted me to go away with him for a bit, and for me to help him get himself together. He was asking me about homoeopathy, why I was doing what I was doing, why I was with the band. Why I didn't take him away and sort him out. I was rather flippant about it, thinking that that wasn't what the band needed. The band needed Sid as he was. It was quite a weird conflict, knowing that he needed his image, the whole persona that he had, and he depended on that, and the band depended on it, and here he was suggesting that he wanted to get himself together. It was all so momentary, standing looking over the sea. I didn't take him very seriously, and anyway, I couldn't possibly afford what he was asking me to do, it was more than I could give him. I had kids back in London and everything, I couldn't do that. So he got on with the show.

1 SEPTEMBER 1977   **Winter Gardens, Penzance–"A Mystery Band of International Repute"**
                Filmed by Julien Temple, photographs by Dennis Morris

Jah Wobble	John was already having rucks at the 100 Club, walking off and refusing to come on again and stuff, so you had the antennae out, you could feel monkey business. At the 100 Club, it would send a shiver up your back, and that had gone.
Dennis Morris	Sid broke down in Penzance. He went back to the hotel and he couldn't eat anything. It was drugs, but it wasn't just that. The audience was real close, and expecting a lot. He broke down from that, he was sick all the time, throughout the day. It was at that point that he had his first joint, he never used to smoke before. He threw up straight after it. But it got to him then. It was the worst gig they ever did, as far as I'm concerned. Penzance was a good gig, but it was one number then literally about twenty minutes before the next one, one of those. Wobble was there, that was when everybody realised something was going down, because John was being really friendly towards him. It was the beginning of the end, and the start of something new.

19 SEPTEMBER 1977   **Demo recording of "Belsen Was a Gas" in Denmark Street, produced by John Tiberi**
                This was eventually released on the 35th anniversary 4 x CD release of *Never Mind The Bollocks* box set.

AUTUMN 1977	**Nancy**

Sophie Richmond August or September 1977. Sent Sid off to the dentist, and we'd just got his Maida Vale flat, and the idea was to put Nancy on a plane back to America. It was completely mad and I don't know why I landed myself in it. What it resulted in was me and Nancy standing in the street arguing for three hours, and then I called the office and said, "I can't do this," and Malcolm and Boogie came down, and had no better success than I did. The idea was to take her to Heathrow and I had her in my car actually. We didn't get as far as Heathrow. We just had this endless argument, about Sid and Malcolm and things.

11 OCTOBER 1977   **Russ Meyer walks off the set of the Sex Pistols film, *Who Killed Bambi?*, after one day of shooting. Lack of finance is the main problem.**

Al Clark There are many reasons why Meyer left. There's the story about how he got one of his friends to shoot the deer and the crew walked off in disgust, and they were left stranded in the middle of the countryside. About him and John falling out. And then there's the great story Malcolm came out with, whose veracity I've never been able to settle one way or the other, about Princess Grace being on the board of Twentieth-Century Fox. That was a cracker.

20 OCTOBER 1977   ***Rolling Stone* magazine features the Sex Pistols on the front cover, with a picture of Johnny Rotten captioned, "Rock Is Sick and Living in London." Charles M. Young's story captures the events of August 1977, with the secret tour and Russ Meyer's increasing irritation at his treatment by Johnny Rotten.**

Al Clark John and Malcolm were falling out. John was fed up with being a puppet, and he had enough pride and spirit to feel that if it was going to work, it had to be according to the way he viewed things. Malcolm in turn wasn't going to give all that up. Malcolm still wanted to channel the group emotions towards another great moment. In the early autumn of 1977, the distance increased over *Who Killed Bambi?*, which John wasn't at all keen to do. Malcolm was very keen on it. John made his displeasure very clear to Russ Meyer, who wasn't accustomed to that kind of rudeness. Meyer is a tough, Good Old Boy, but once again, he wasn't used to all this from this little shit.

28 OCTOBER 1977   **Release of the album, *Never Mind The Bollocks Here's the Sex Pistols* (V2086).** Because of the fractious atmosphere between Virgin and Glitterbest and the haste in which the album was released—largely to combat French imports on the Barclay label—the sleeve came in at least two different forms and with different track lists. The record was a quick success, entering the charts for the first of 58 weeks on the 12th of November and rising to number one on November 19th.

14 OCTOBER 1977   **Release of the Sex Pistols' third Virgin single, "Holidays In The Sun" / "Satellite" (VS191). It enters the chart on the 22nd of October and stays for six weeks, reaching number eight.**

John Lydon One of my *tour de forces*, I thought. Even though Steve was accused of ripping off the guitar part from the Jam. That's Paul Weller being silly.

2 NOVEMBER 1977   **Press jaunt to Radio Luxembourg**

24 NOVEMBER 1977   **Trial in Nottingham Magistrates Court of Chris Searle, the manager of Virgin** Records Nottingham, on charges under the 1889 Indecent Advertisements Act. This related to the fact that Virgin shops were heavily promoting the Sex Pistols' album with the "obscene" word "Bollocks." Virgin hired John Mortimer, QC, and experts including Caroline Coon, in their successful defense of the action.

John Tiberi Virgin had a sort of over-educated view of it all. I always cite the "bollocks" case, misconstruing the whole point of it. It must have cost them five grand, and they won the fucking case. With Rotten there. Having Johnny Rotten coming out winning the court case is not the image this group wanted. The press didn't report it that much. The court case wasn't what we wanted. What do you do, win a court case to make the word "bollocks" legal, and retire? The Pistols were not in the press in the way they should have been, because there was nowhere for them to play.

Directors

M.McLAREN
S.FISHER

Registered Office,
23 Great Castle St,
London, W.1.

GLITTERBEST LTD

40 DRYDEN CHAMBERS
119 OXFORD ST
LONDON W.I.

01-734-1137
01-734-1138

NO FUTURE

1)
God save the queen — And the fachist regime
It made you a moron — A potential H bomb

God save the queen — Shes not a human being
There is no future — In Englands dream
    Dont be told what you want
    Dont be told what you need
    No future no future no future for you
God save the queen — God save windowleen
God saves ——— human beings

2)
God save the queen — tourists are money
Our figurehead — Is not what she seems
God save history — Save the mad parade
Lord have mercy — All crimes are paid
    When theres no future how can there be sin?
    We are the flowers in the dustbin
    We are the poison in the machine
    We are the romance behind the screen
    God save the queen — we mean it man
    We love our queen — God saves

Repeat 2'nd verse

End on No future etc....

153

153   Winter 1976/1977. Lyrics to "God Save
       the Queen" written in Johnny Rotten's hand,
       utilized for a publishing contract. Note that
       the song was still called "No Future."

154   **ABOVE:** Original picture sleeve for the New
       Zealand release of the Sex Pistols' "God
       Save the Queen" on Virgin Records. **BELOW:**
       Seditionaries' "God Save the Queen" pro-
       motional T-shirts.

155   Sex Pistols "God Save the Queen" sleeve
       variations. **ABOVE:** West Records (W 8),
       Turkey. **CENTER:** Express Records (EXP
       .0330), Thailand. Various artists EP, includes
       "God Save the Queen." **BELOW:** Virgin
       Records (6079 202), Brazil.

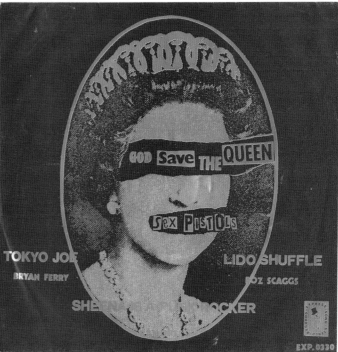

Directors

M.McLAREN
S.FISHER

Registered Office,
23 Great Castle St,
London, W.1.

GLITTERBEST LTD

40 DRYDEN CHAMBERS
119 OXFORD ST
LONDON W.I.

OI-734-II37
OI-734-II38

NO WRONG

I dont mind the things that you say
I dont even mind going out of my way
I try and do things for you
But why should I do it if our love is untrue

Chorus I did you no wrong
Going out of head

Aint seen you off the screen
But those films are in my dreams
And I can't take much more of you
Cos the loghole's no place to remember your face
—   cant you see Im going out of my head
Can't you see Im a little insane
Oh can't you see I fell out of my head
Cant you see Im going loney again

chorus— I did you no wrong
Going out of my head

———

158

VIRGIN information

SEX PISTOLS

Double Crown - straight - 1,000 posters

Plain black and white picture of the Queen's head - not defaced or written on.

3,000 Quads

Four black and white images of Queen's head on coloured Union Jack background. Queen's head will be overwritten with "Sex Pistols" and "God Save The Queen".

3,000 stickers x 2

Will contain the Queen's head with safety pin and photo of the Queen with cup of tea / or boot.

Streamers - 3,000

These are ragged cut-outs of the words "Sex Pistols" and "God Save The Queen".

150 Transfers

Queen's head plus the words "Sex Pistols" and "God Save The Queen".

T-Shirts

Will be the same as the sample already seen - Queen's head and safety pin.

The Double Crown Straight pictures of the Queen will be sited on the backs of 50 London Transport buses (on central routes) for a month, starting on 27 May.

The Quad posters and streamers will be fly-posted on normal sites (and some not-so-normal).

Transfers will be placed on white china mugs and sent to media people. Large distributors will also be consulted as to the possibility of making them available for sale on a large scale to the public.

We have tentatively booked the "Olympia Banner" for two weeks beginning 1 June. The artwork would have read "Sex Pistols - God Save the (Queen's head)." Two weeks before us   Queen is advertising   Queen and two weeks before that again a Queen's Jubilee banner will be up. However as the album title is now in doubt, it might not be a clever thing to do after all, especially as it will cost us £540.

Virgin Record 2 4 Vernon Yard 119 Portobello Road London W.11 01 727 8070

Difference on Bidget

A number of red paint aerosols will be made available to certain
lunatics who will proceed to scrawl "Sex Pistols" over any available surface (this is impossible to cost at the moment, but ardent
fans will no doubt get to work for a can of lager and a bent
safety pin). *(NOT VERY FUNNY)*

The full page Music Press ads. will hopefully consist of the
Queen's head and the words "Sex Pistols" and "God Save The Queen'
in the usual place, but as this particular ad. and indeed others
of the same ilk will probably be banned by the respective
journals, then we have another standby ad. which consists of a
photograph of the Queen's head accompanied by a teacup. Both
the band and myself feel that this is a very strong ad. in its
own right. It would be nice to place four different ads. if
enough acceptable ads could be found.

The 7-second TV commercial could go out any time at approximately
11.30 p.m. when a suitable preceding programme is found, and this
ad. could be held back and placed at the time of release of the
single or album. It could of course be repeated at any time
thought judicious , and would also make a very good Teaser for the
album if repeated at a very cheap rate.

We may also consider the giant Newscaster in Leicester Square for
a day, a week, or more. One week would cost approx. £200, giving
us 770 exposures and will be visible to approx. 980,000 people.

*(ALSO IDEA OF USEING
WALL SPACE & MURAL!
NOT A GOD. ING.*

ALBUM:
① - BLOCK OUT WHOLE OF RECORD
SHOP WINDOWS?
② - WALL PAPER COVER WALLS
OF SHOP

PENDING ON L.P. TITLE!

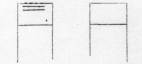

Difference on Bidget

VIRGIN RECORDS LTD.   Catalogue No:

PROMOTION BUDGET ANALYSIS

Title: God Save The Queen   Artiste: Sex Pistols

		BUDGET	ACTUAL
Release Date: 27 May 1977			
Sales - UK & Export only	units		
at average value of £	= £		
Promotion Total as per analysis below	£		
Promotion as a percentage of sales	%		

TYPE OF EXPENDITURE	DESCRIPTION	SPLIT	TOTAL	SPLIT	TOTAL
		£	£	£	£
Press Ads	Back pages & spot colour in				
Production	Melody Maker	650			
Magazine	N.M.E.	540			
	Sounds	500			
	Time Out	300			
			1990		
Radio Ads					
Production					
Station					
TV Ads	7 sec. ad on Thames				
Production		200			
Station		300			
			500		
Posters/Stickers	1000 dble. crwn. straights 20" x 30"	200			
	3000 quads 30" x 40"	700			
	3000 stickers x 2	200			
O.H.O.'s	3000 quads x streamers	400			
	150 transfers	100			
			1600		
Window Displays					
Sundry Promo	200 T-shirts	260			
(T-shirts)	Buses	200			
	Banner?	540?			
	Fly posting	200	1200		
Video					
Tours (Hotels etc)					
Promotional Albums	____ units at average cost of £ ____				
Promotion Total			5290		
Difference on Bidget					

WESSEX SOUND LIMITED

INVOICE

ARTIST ~~SS~~ NO WRONG		Date:
VACANT ✓		Our Ref:
17 ✓	WANNA BE ME?	Your Ref:
N Y ✓		Invoice No:
PROBLEMS ✓		
SATELLITE ✓		VAT Reg. No: 232 3270 04

NO FEELINGS ✓
LIAR ✓
~~E.M.I.~~
ANARCHY ✓
SUBMISSION ?
HOLIDAYS
EMI

Total excl. VAT	
VAT	
Total payable	

164   7 June, 1977. The Sex Pistols' Silver Jubilee boat trip.

165   7 June, 1977. Johnny Rotten on the Sex Pistols' Silver Jubilee boat trip.

166   7 June, 1977. Tracey O'Keefe being arrested at the Silver Jubilee boat trip.

167–170   June 1977. Jon Savage's eyewitness account of the Silver Jubilee boat trip.

Before the police came, it was a great party. Make that a capital G.

Lets take all this sequentially: after an hour of waiting, the "Queen Elizabeth" left Charing Cross Pier at 6.30, and, after a moment's hesitation, decided to head downstream. If you aren't on the List, you aren't On. Nobody jumps......not even Palmolive. Bye bye. Begins very restained - too too 'vous-etes', but come Rotherhithe, some booze and more food, and everyone gets mellow, if such a thing is possible. I mean its a nice evening (albeit a bit chilly) and there's space all around instead of tower-blocks, so why be surprised ? The disparate crowd mixes surprisingly well - the only jarring note in fact is the refusal of the bar to serve doubles.......never know what these notorious punk-rockers might get up to. Downstream aways, we turn as a banner is unfurled along the length of the boat - red on yellow, it proclaims proudly 'Queen Elizabeth - the new single by the Sex Pistols, or something similar. Really low profile. is "God Save the Queen";

Inside, the conversation's covering some pretty recherché terriotry, but, hey, upstairs, in the covered area, the tapes start rolling. Dance. Great selection - moving from arcane dub to the Ramones, thru Paul Revere and the Raiders. More boozing/dancing/yammering - general party patter - but expectation is height-ened. They Have to start playing outside the Houses of Parliament. We repass under Tower Bridge, picking up a police boat on the way - sniff sniff sussy sussy - but it falls behind: meanwhile Jordan's telling me about this group she's managing called the Ants. Upstream it gets chiller - most take refuge in the downstairs bar (big boat this), ostensibly for a film that never happens. There's no pretence now: we're waiting. More turns (Battersea funfair - for the detail-obsessed) and it's home run time.

The Pistols take the 'stage' - at the back of the raised covered area: the conditions are appalling, and it's amazing that any sort of sound comes out. The main one is feedback - this delays their start, and is never fully resolved Any blasé traces are swept away - pulses race/everyone rushes to be front. Pure mania.

2

Rotten gives up on losing the feedback,and the band slams into 'Anarchy',
right on cue with the Houses of Parliament.A great moment.It's like they've
been uncaged - the frustration in not being able to play bursts into total
energy and attack.Rotten's so close all you can see is a snarling mouth and
wild eyes,framed by red spikes.Can't shake that feedback: he complains,won'
sing for the first verse of 'No Feelings'but the others carry on.More frus
to explode.By now the atmosphere is electric/heart thumps too hard/people
pressing,swaying - it's like they have to play to blast them away.They're a
playing for their/our lives - during 'Pretty Vacant' and the next song two
police boats start moving around in earnest.Now all adrenalin is flat out
doitdoitdoitdoitnownownowNOW- suddenly in 'I wanna be Me ' they get inspir
and take off/'No Fun' SCREAMED out as the police boats move in for the ki
is one of THE rock'n roll moments EVER.I mean EVER.(Think about that).What
suddenly we're in the dock n the power's off and Paul Cook's beating the h
out of the drums n there are all those police and WHAT'S HAPPENING and wh
the fuck IS this........

     Now here I have,against my will,to be VERY careful.There's this little
thing called 'contempt of court' which occurs if you make ANY comment abou
a pending case (sub judice) which,catch this,'tends to interfere'with the
course of Justice.The question isn't whether it DOES.So any unfettered acc
will have to wait,I'm afraid,until August/September,when the 'accused' com
for trial.

     Fax.We dock.The power is off.The bar is closed.Suddenly no more party.
Suddenly a lot of police on the quay.Altercations begin.Nobody wants to
                    went us to leave. So does the owner.
leave.The police ~~want us to leave~~.The owner can terminate the contract o
hire at any time.Small print,baby.Richard Branson loses his £500.Richard
Branson doesn't want to leave.Tension.Indecision.People trickle off,slowl
after a half-an-hour.Most stay on.More police.The police move on the boat
People move off.Nothing happens,bar a bit of pushing and shoving either s

Someone gets nicked.Now things start getting crazy.People are 'aided' up the long gangway.Explosion of movement.Fear.Confusion.Flash/people running/Ted restrains/'Get'Im'/crying faces/spin around/black marias/no objectivity/each for himself/quick spurts of movement/hate/'Youre shit'.And there's II people in the marias and we're on the pavement wondering what's been happening.Very quick.

We leave.We go to Bow Street ploice station,via the Zanzibar (whose cutesy-poo decadence is sickening).No message.No bail.No press.No,not an IPC card. 'There are people we'd like to arrest but we don't know who they are'.A direct hint.Buzz off.And don't wait on the pavement.No help.And then the 7 of us REALLY slip into I984: we move to this pub where everybody is enacting this weird ritual which involves the wearing of red/white /blue hats and 'singing' arcane folk-lore.They want us to join in/ we can only make silly jokes out of pain.Zoom zoom / 'I don't wanna grow up: there's too much contradiction'. Chickens come home to roost baby,you'd best believe.

Some jubilee.But look: I mean McLaren's brilliant at the Theatre of Pro-vocation,didN't he set all this up ? To an Exhnt. Provocation,yes,incitement,no.OK,I mean all of us were expecting SOME interference,let's be frank - but not emotional overreaction.Because WHATEVER the rights and wrongs of the individua cases,objectively,yeah,Responsibly,that's what it was.You know - nothing doing in the centre of town and these xo allegedly 'notorious-foul-mouthed-punk-rock -Sex-Pistols'.......Image vs. reality.I'm so confused......

The charges run like this (approximately): Malcolm McLaren /'Using Insulting words likely to provoke a breach of the peace': Vivien Westwood/'Obstructing a policeman':Sophie Richmond and Alex McDowell / 'Assault': Debbie and Tracy /'Obstruction':Ben Kelly and Chris Walsh/'Obstruction': José Esquibel /'Threat ening behaviour':Jamie Reid /'Assault'.All have denied the alleged charges,and have been released on bail/surety until their case will be heard.

No future,eh ? Feelings are bound to run high.But wait.Neither 'side' ~~are~~ is

blameless,but there are a few things left to say:To a certain extent the bar

are down a bit more.That means if you look anything like a Sex Pistol,or a

'punk-rocker',you're likely to get pulled in.Right: No martyrs,No victims,
that means -

No heroes,No stereotypes.No games,on this score,No provocation.Things have

gotten a bit more serious.No escalation................?

Uuuh .Um.Is it too late for me to say that It was a Great party and that the

Pistols were amazing ? Oh,it is,but its a shame,because that's a part of the

evening too......

© Jon Savage June 1977

DAILY Mirror

I'm stayi...
says Do...

BRITAIN'S BIGGEST DAILY SALE   7p   Tuesday, June 21, 1977
★

SLASHED!

Razor attack on Rotten, the Punk Rocker

JOHNNY ROTTEN, king of punk rock, has had his face slashed in a frenzied razor attack by a gang who ambushed him outside a pub.

The pop world fears the slashing is only the start of a savage backlash against punk rock groups such as the Sex Pistols, with whom Rotten is lead singer.

The Sex Pistols are believed to be prime targets because of their anti-Royal record "God save the Queen" — an outrageous disc banned by the BBC — that condemns the Queen as a moron.

The attack on Rotten — whose real name is John Lydon — was the second on the group within days. A Sex Pistols art director was beaten up in the street last week and left with a broken nose and a broken leg.

Marked

Rotten had his face slashed on Saturday night in the car park of the Pegasus pub, near the Wessex Sound Studios in Highbury, London.

Two men with him — recording studios manager Bill Price and record producer Chris Thomas — were both wounded and needed hospital treatment.

Bill Price said last night: "We were probably marked down for attack when Johnny Rotten was recognised in the pub.

"As we left, the gang — about nine men, all in their thirties — pounced, waving razors and knives and aiming for Johnny.

"They cut his face and his arm but didn't manage to do any serious damage.

"Chris also got his face cut by a knife or razor and I got a deep cut in my arm trying to fend off the blows.

"It was obvious Johnny was the target. He's not too popular

By STUART GREIG

because of the record about the Queen.

"We were lucky to get away in one piece.

"The attackers seemed to be out to mark us rather than kill us."

A spokesman for Virgin Records said: "It looks like punk rockers are in for a hard time.

"A lot of people were upset at the record about the Queen and that could be part of the problem.

"Johnny is a target because he is the king of the punk rockers — the figurehead.

"But he is non-violent and we're going to have to take special care to protect him."

A Scotland Yard spokesman said last night: "We are investigating this apparently unprovoked attack."

JOHNNY ROTTEN ... a backlash victim — with more to come?

Tommy Docherty

By STEVE ... and BOB ...

TUG-OF-LOVE ...
Tommy Docherty ... staying with ... United.

And with 3... Brown, wife of ... therapist.

Docherty, the ... glory back to ... said yesterday h... confidence from ... — just 24 hours ... revealed his lov... two Mary.

But her grief — ... Laurie — a clo... colleague of the ... during his fo... reign — turned ... branch from Doc...

As the Doc w... desk at Old Tr... Laurie Brown st...

And he indica... room for the tw... same club.

But Docherty, ... directors' backin... gambled his job ... Mary.

And how he ... feelings for her ... tant than his dev... most exciting soc...

"I was fully ... everything — inclu... said the 49-year-...

"But the dire... stay, and I wan...

Diffi...

Docherty, who ... his wife Agnes ... added: "I knew ... I was fully prep... the consequences ...

He said he an... a great deal o... their romance.

"It wasn't e... added. "We man... affair a closely g... three years."

Asked how, he ... "No comment."

Of Laurie Bro... Doc commented: ... the problems for ... him to come a... would be difficult ...

"It would dep... big enough to ov... lem. It certainly w...

Today, Docher... Lisbon with th... team for an eight...

AMIN SURVIVES ARMED RAID ON HIS CAR

By NICHOLAS DAVIES
Foreign Editor

UGANDAN President Idi Amin was last night recovering from an assassination attempt after his car was fired on by gunmen.

A diplomat in Kampala said last night: "We understand his car was

hit by at least two bullets when two gunmen opened fire in an ambush near Entebbe."

Since the ambush — understood to have occurred early on Saturday — nothing has been heard of Amin.

There has been no mention on Uganda Radio about the assassination attempt.

But Kampala was a nervous, tense city last night.

Heavy concentrations of troops were in Kam-

pala and Entebbe throughout the weekend.

In neighbouring Kenya it is believed the assassination attempt was the work of a group of desperate Ugandans determined at any cost to rid the country of Amin.

172

DAILY Mirror

BRITAIN'S BIGGEST DAILY SALE   7p

Thursday, July 14, 1977

★

TOP OF THE PUNKS!

Pistol Johnny Rotten

The Pistol poster

Did slave gang kill my Fiona?

By MIRROR REPORTER

THE outrageous Sex Pistols shoot back into Britain's homes tonight . . . on BBC TV.

The punk rockers will appear on Top of the Pops, favourite show of millions of teenyboppers.

They will sing their new disc, Pretty Vacant, in a filmed recording

The BBC decision to put punk rockers on TV is certain to enrage thousands of parents and other viewers.

For the group, who include Johnny Rotten and Sid Vicious, have caused two furious storms recently . . .

STORM No. 1 came when the group appeared on Thames TV's Today programme and filled the air with four-letter words.

. STORM No. 2 came when they released an anti-Royalist record God Save the Queen, as Britain was celebrating the Jubilee.

The BBC banned the record, which described the Queen as a "moron."

Even so, it leapt to the top of the charts.

Row as Beeb give 'Pistols' a TV date

3 DEAD IN SHIP DRAMA

A MAJOR alert went out in the Channel last night as a ship carrying explosives caught fire.

Three seamen on the Lebanese vessel Astrid were feared dead.

An RAF helicopter saved two others who leapt overboard.

The Navy survey ship Bulldog and a lifeboat raced to the scene 17 miles off the Kent coast.

All other vessels were warned to keep clear as the 200-ton cargo ship blazed from end to end.

The dead were believed to be in the engine room.

The two survivors were airlifted to Canterbury hospital

From MARGARET HALL in PARIS

A RUTHLESS white-slave gang are thought to have murdered 18-year-old holiday girl Fiona Topham, above.

She vanished nine days ago within hours of arriving in France. Her naked body has been found in a secluded wood near Paris.

The chief of Paris police said last night: "It's quite possible she fell victim to white-slave procurers."

At the weekend Fiona's pa Kaye and Rex Topham, left home near Shoreham, Kent, to the streets of Paris for their m daughter.

They were unsuccessful — an Topham said: "I think she's abducted and taken to some br

Yesterday the couple return Paris to identify Fiona's body, girl had been battered and det think she may have been because she put up a fierce str

Hundreds of girls of all nation vanish in Paris every year an in brothels in Africa and the states.

Many are snatched at the railway station where Fiona a to meet a girl friend.

Her body was hidden under twelve miles aw but detective convinced she killed somewhe and dumped t

To make iden tion difficult, killers took clothes away.

The plot wor some extent the body was on Saturday was Tuesday it was identif

● Girl who ha thing — See Pages.

HEALEY AXES HIS TAX CUT

By TERENCE LANCASTER, Political Editor

CHANCELLOR Denis Healey's offer to cut 2p in the pound off income tax looks as dead as the social contract.

The offer will be withdrawn as one of the first consequences of the decision by the miners and transport workers to end hopes of a firm pay deal.

Ministers will hear details of the Chancellor's NEW proposals

when they meet today to discuss the funeral arrangements for the social contract.

They will be sitting appropriately around a table shaped like a coffin in the Cabinet room.

The 2p offer was made n the spring Budget. It was conditional

on reaching agreement with the unions about a continuing pay policy.

The withdrawal is symbolic of the tough attitude now being shown by Chancellor Healey to his fellow Ministers.

There could still be some in-

come tax relief — but it won't be the full 2p.

Members of the T.U.C. Economic Committee met yesterday following their talks the previous night with Chancellor Healey.

Afterwards Frank Chappell, the moderate leader of the electricians, said there was no chance" of a Phase Three deal.

Turn to Page Two

Dea r Malcolm ~~MacLaren~~

This time last year I spent a considerable number of blood
hours fighting people at Granada to get a band I had seen at the
Lesser Free Trade Hall on a TV show. A pile of fucking energy used up b
it wasn't wasted as you may remember from the nicest piece of action
on your video from SIG.

This time, this year, I've spent as much energy tr ing
to get the same band on TV only this time, it has been a complete waste
and what's more its been just a little bit more degrading, and a lot
more like dealing with the Rolling Stones or any fur other fucked up
rich man's band who treat media lackeys like me with the same ammount
of contempt, and revel in their position of impreganable power, due
to that strange position of being much-wanted.

I totally sympathise with your fears of being swallowed up
by the six billion dollar industry, of becoming exactly the kind of
commodity music you set yourselves up to destroy; but don't hold me
responsible for that piece of substandard crap on Top of the Tops, or
for those disgusting "I've got my finger up Sid's ass" pieces by
Shaar Murray and Dadomo. I have no interest in expressing to the world
the important news that 'I've had breakfast with the pistols and we got
on just great'. I am interested in a movement in music which has shat
on the appalling monopoly of corporation music, the dead , lifeless
overproduced stuff that rock had become, the eght eight track cassette
fodder for your Porsche etc.............yo u led this movement, you
were the first gust of the new air, but to tell us that doing a So it Fo
(which incidentally we have already said would be totally in your hands;
Julian to direct the film and all of us to put the show together; Sid
can present etc etc etc....whatever gets the message across, messages li
the 'Does it threaten???????' page in your mag) would compromise you

seems to lose sight of the two most important arguments; the people an
the commodity.

First off, more important tha n you, safety pins or Steves
rapidly improving guitar playing are the kids, all those youngsters
with new reasons, new thoughts and new excitements. You were the
first band to show them the potential in stepping outside the dried
skin of the music world. Your greatest contribution has been almsot
as missionaries; but don't tell me the fucking mission is over. The
only new wave album to really make it has been Rattus whatever by the
load of technically proficient crapheads who make people like Mike
Appleton(BBC) and Bart Mills(Cosmopolitan) feel really safe. The Strang
still stuwk in that asinine hierarchy of technique are the only ones to
get really up there....the kids who are buying their stuff and the ohes
who are buying the yes albums....they deserve the excitement and
hope that posessors of that £2-00 anarchy single have already found.
Don't be a fucking elitist, get your invaluable message overnto more
kids.........get them to form more bands.......I know you're planning
a tour for this purpose, but why not use television for the same
thing.....because I think your way is 7/8 correct I'm offering my
metaphorical anus to be USED........we want to give you a show, so you,
and we can get over to the people, the kids, all the possibilities...
........and all we get in the end after three weeks of being fucked
around is the simple instruction to fuck off.

Number two and this'll be the last bit......commodity theory.
I don't know where exactly you're coming from, whether the Bakunin
T shirts were a aftuous joke or whether we really are talking about
the 'Poverty of everyday Life' and the avoidance of spectacular
existence and the divorced sense of reality etc etc.........but if this
is what we are talking about, the fear that the Pistols will also
become part of that world, just another alienated experience;"only 3-95
mate, and a lovely inside sleeve picture..." then your Rod Stewart
style retreat into the shadows, punctured ohly but by the occasional

brown-tongued NME exclusive and exorbitantly priced import singles,
turns you into exactly the kind of mythologised distanced product
that you wished to avoid. We want you to play...yes folks, play music,
to something like three million kids for half an hour, and the poor
bastards won't have to sit at the other end of Wembley stadium.

Whatever went wrong with music in the past, in 58-62 or 70-76,
although it can bee seen as the prevailing culture buying itself a
piece of the revolution, and draining the blood out of it by so doing,
it is also the history of the artists proximity to his audience; Keats
had this thing about the artist being a fairly irrelevant tool just
like this typwriter , and he compared it to an Aeolian harp... a greek
stringed instrument, that was played by the action of the wind blowing
over it......for wind read mass consciousness, tge audience, the Zeitgei
or whatever,...........all I'm trying to say is the audience is
the important factor and in telling me to take a running jump you
are saying exactly the same thing to all those kids in Aberdeen,
Wigan and Slough who aren't going to get to see you but who desrve to.

Those are my arguments, you knew them anyway, but
it helps exorcise a little of the anger I feel at having been
quite considrably fucked arpund.

Tony Wilson

PS If you're going to be so damned purist about going
on So It Goes, at least do me the favour of being equally purist in
other fields and avoid all the other crap, so I don't have to read
Shaar Murray snivelleings etc......and get the fucking LP out...and
make it cheap.   Nice talking to you.

SPACE TRAVEL

an official guide
for san francisco
commuters

SeX PisTOls

pretty vacant

NO FUN

OUT THIS SATURDAY ON VIRGIN RECORDS   VS184

178   Original picture sleeve for the Sex Pistols' "Pretty Vacant" on Virgin Records.

179   **ABOVE:** June 1977. Sex Pistols in *Melody Maker*, photographed by Barry Plummer.
       BELOW: 1 July, 1977. Screen grab from the Sex Pistols' *Top of the Pops* performance of "Pretty Vacant."

180   Promotional poster for the Sex Pistols' "Pretty Vacant."

181   Early 1977. Jamie Reid's sketch of "Nowhere Bus" for an unpublished second issue of *Anarchy in the UK*.

SEX PISTOLS
SKANDINAVIEN-TURNÉ

```
ONSDAG 13 JULI  -  KÖPENHAMN (DADDY'S DANCE HALL)
TORSDAG 14      -     "              "
FREDAG 15       -  HALMSTAD (DISKOTEK STRANDEN)
LÖRDAG 16       -  HELSINGBORG (MOGAMBO)
SÖNDAG 17       -  JÖNKÖPING (DISKOTEK 42)
TISDAG 19       -  KRISTINEHAMN (CLUB ZEBRA)
ONSDAG 20       -  OSLO (PINGVIN CLUB)
TORSDAG 21      -  TRONDHEIM (STUDENTSAMFUNDET)
LÖRDAG 23       -  VÄXJÖ (BARBARELLA)
SÖNDAG 24       -     "          "
ONSDAG 27       -  STOCKHOLM (GLÄDJEHUSET)
TORSDAG 28      -     "            "
FREDAG 29       -  LINKÖPING (DISKOTEK ORFI)
```

183   March 1977. The Sex Pistols at the Berlin Wall.

184–186   July, 1977. Pages from Swedish teeny-bopper magazine *Poster*, featuring photographs of the Sex Pistols touring in Sweden.

187   July 1977. Swedish announcement of the Sex Pistols' tour of Scandinavia.

188–189   Bootlegs

The demand for Sex Pistols output in 1977 led to numerous bootleg LPs being issued before the Sex Pistols had an official full-length album released. *The Good Time Music of the Sex Pistols*, also released as *No Fun* and featuring a recording from the Manchester Lesser Free Trade Hall concert, appeared in record shops in August 1977, almost three months prior to the release of *Never Mind the Bollocks*. The notorious bootleg LP *Spunk*, also released as *No Future*, featured demo recordings and was released just a couple of weeks before *Never Mind the Bollocks*. Around the same time, *Anarchy in Sweden*, packaged in a red ink–stamped sleeve and held together with an actual safety pin, also showed up in record shops.

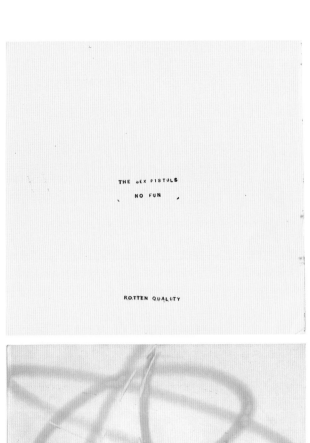

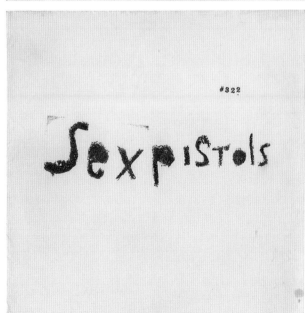

188   **ABOVE LEFT & RIGHT:** Front and back of *No Fun, AKA The Good Time Music of the Sex Pistols: Live at the Manchester Lesser Free Trade Hall. June 4, 1976.* **CENTER LEFT & RIGHT:** Alternate sleeve and label of *The Good Time Music of the Sex Pistols*, featuring the vocalist of the Manchester punk-prank band The Worst. **BELOW LEFT & RIGHT:** Autumn 1977. Early edition of *Spunk* under the title, *No Future UK?*, with silkscreened sleeve.

189   **ABOVE LEFT:** Sex Pistols *No Fun*. Original edition of *The Good Time Music of the Sex Pistols*. **ABOVE RIGHT:** Early version of *Spunk* (some claim the first edition). **CENTER LEFT:** A version of *Spunk* with a spray-painted sleeve. **CENTER RIGHT:** Early edition of *Spunk*. **BELOW LEFT:** Early edition of *Spunk*. **BELOW RIGHT:** Sex Pistols, *Anarchy in Sweden*.

ROCK GARDEN

208 NEWPORT RD. M'BRO. 241995/6

BRITONS PREMIERE
MYSTERY GROUP

ACNE REBBLE

26 AUG. 8-1

BEST SOUNDS IN 'ROCK MUSIC'

190   August 1977. Flyer for anonymous Sex Pistols gig in Middlesborough.

191   September 1977. Flyer for the Sex Pistols gig at the Garden, Penzance. Note their billing as the "Mystery Night" notice in top left corner.

GARDEN

PENZANCE
ROCK PROGRAMME SEPT./OCT. '77

THURSDAY 1st SEPTEMBER

??? Mystery ??? Night ??

guaranteed appearance of top
international British group

Adm. £1.00

TUESDAY 6th SEPTEMBER

Jam Session

with many
local musicians

ADM. FREE

THURSDAY 8th SEPTEMBER

the Adverts

supported the Damned on their recent visit
went down a storm!

Adm. £1.00

TUESDAY 13th SEPTEMBER

beaver

ADM. FREE

THURSDAY 15th SEPTEMBER

STRIFE

Adm. 80p.

TUESDAY 20th SEPTEMBER

WELCOME BACK
Bert Jansch

WITH HIS BAND:
DANNY THOMPSON
& MARTIN JENKINS

Adm. £1.25

THURSDAY 22nd SEPTEMBER
'NEW WAVE' SPECIAL

the Boom Town Rats

Adm. 80p.

TUESDAY 27th SEPTEMBER

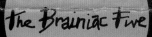
The Brainiac Five

ADM. FREE

THURSDAY 29th SEPTEMBER
"NIGHT OF THE MONTH"

Dave Edmunds Rockpile

Adm. £1.25

THURSDAY 6th OCTOBER

MEAL TICKET AND "contraband"

Adm. £1.00

THURSDAY 13th OCTOBER
FOR CONNOISEURS!

Quantum Jump

Adm. £1.00

TUESDAY 14th OCTOBER
ROCK N' ROLL SPECIAL

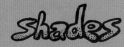
Shades

ADM. FREE

TUESDAY 18th OCTOBER

The Daga Band

ADM. FREE

THURSDAY 20th OCTOBER
Welcome back

Spiff Spingham & the Big Rocks.

ADM. FREE

TUES 25th OCTOBER

The Brainiac Five

ADM. FREE

THURSDAY 27th OCTOBER
ONE OF THE MOST
ENTERTAINING GROUPS TO APPEAR THIS YEAR

BURLESQUE

Adm. £1.00

COMING: THURS 10th NOVEMBER

VAN DER GRAAF GENERATOR

BELGIUM
YEAR ROUND HOLIDAYS 1977

NEVER A DULL MOMENT WITH BELGIAN TRAVEL SERVICE

192   Original graphic source for Jamie Reid's "Holidays in the Sun" record sleeve.

193   **ABOVE:** Original Sex Pistols "Holidays in the Sun" withdrawn picture sleeve.
           BELOW: Autumn 1977. Promotional postcard by Jamie Reid for "Holidays in the Sun" campaign.

194   Jamie Reid's Suburban Press–era *Nice Collage*, used for the reverse of the "Holidays in the Sun"
           picture sleeve.

195   25 October, 1977. Cease-and-desist letter from Belgium Travel Services regarding images
           appearing on the "Holiday in the Sun" picture sleeve.

R. T. P. WILSON   G. E. HUDSON
A. C. T. COCHRANE   P. R. H. DIXON
A. G. F. YOUNG   C. L. SIMON *
N. A. BONHAM-CARTER   D. W. ANDREWS
R. R. VALLINGS   H. LIPWORTH *
B. J. PARKER †   G. R. GREENHOUS
A. J. GIBBS   A. C. HAND
M. J. ELKS

ADMITTED N.S.W. †   ADMITTED S. AFRICA *

CONSULTANTS:
SIR EDMUND SARGANT   S. F. T. L. ROBINSON
S. L. LLOYD   R. C. HUBBARD
E. H. FRANK

<u>BY HAND</u>

RADCLIFFES & CO

SOLICITORS

10 LITTLE COLLEGE STREET · WESTMINSTER SW1P 3SJ

Telegrams: Dracliffe London SW1 - Trexag London SW1

Telephone: 01-222 7040

Telex: 919302

LDE Box No.113

J. Reid Esq.,
Glitterbest Limited,
90/98 Shaftesbury Avenue,
London, W1

Your ref

Our ref V/CS

25th October 1977

Dear Sir,

Belgian Travel Service Limited -v- Virgin Records Limited and Branson

We act for Belgian Travel Service Limited and on behalf of our clients we have obtained an **Injunction** against Virgin Records Limited and Richard Branson, a Director of that Company in connection with the sleeves for the Sex Pistols record Holidays in the Sun. We enclose a copy of the Injunction Order.

We understand from Virgin Records Limited that the sleeve was designed by you on your own behalf or on behalf of Glitterbest Limited. In the circumstances, unless we receive from you the original artwork together with any record sleeves in your possession, power or control and an undertaking in the form of paragraph 2 of the Order, our clients will reluctantly have no alternative but to take proceedings against you inter alia for the appropriate Injunction.

We look forward to hearing from you as soon as possible.

We are, dear Sir,
Yours faithfully,

Radcliffes & Co.

COPY FOR JAMES REID.
(Also to Malcolm McLaren).

195

VIRGIN STUDIOS

10 SOUTH WHARF ROAD, LONDON W2 1PA   724 0500

2-4 VERNON YARD, 119 PORTOBELLO ROAD, LONDON W11 2DX   727 8070

DATE:	ARTIST:		TITLE:				PRODUCER:			
11th Oct 1977	Sex Pistols						Chris Thomas / Bill Price			

CAT. NO:	~~XXXXXX~~	ENGINEER:	COPIED BY:	SPEED	~~XXXX~~	EQ:	24TR	4TR
V2086	COPY	Bill Price	Christopher Blake	~~XX~~ 15 ~~XX~~	~~XX~~	NAB	16TR	2TR

MATRIX NO:	REEL	OF	CLIENT:	¼" / 2" / ½" / 1"	~~XXXX~~ STEREO	8TR	FULL
V2086A	1	2	Glitterbest				

TITLES	TIME	REMARKS
TONES		
Tones at head of reel of 1kHz-12kHz-3kHz-150Hz-45Hz at reference level of 200nWb/m		TAPE WOUND TAILS OUT ~~X5XXX~~
SIDE ONE/~~XXX~~		
Holidays in the sun		
Liar		
No feelings		
God save the Queen		
Problems		

VIRGIN STUDIOS

10 SOUTH WHARF ROAD, LONDON W2 1PA   724 0500

2-4 VERNON YARD, 119 PORTOBELLO ROAD, LONDON W11 2DX   727 8070

DATE: 11th Oct 1977	ARTIST: Sex Pistols		TITLE:			PRODUCER: Chris Thomas / Bill Price		
CAT. NO: V2086	XX6X5X / COPY	ENGINEER: Bill Price	COPIED BY: Christopher Blake	SPEED: XX 15 XX	XXXX XXX	EQ: NAB	24TR	4TR
							16TR	2TR
MATRIX NO: V2083B	REEL 2	OF 2	CLIENT: Glitterbest	¼" 2" ½" XXX		STEREO	8TR	FULL

TITLES	TIME	REMARKS
TONES		
As per side one		
		TAPE WOUND TAILS OUT HEADS XXXX
SIDE ONE/TWO		
Seventeen		
Anarchy in the UK		
Bodies		
Pretty Vacant		
New York		
EMI		

196-197   11 October, 1977. Virgin Studios master tape assembly of the *Never Mind the Bollocks* album.

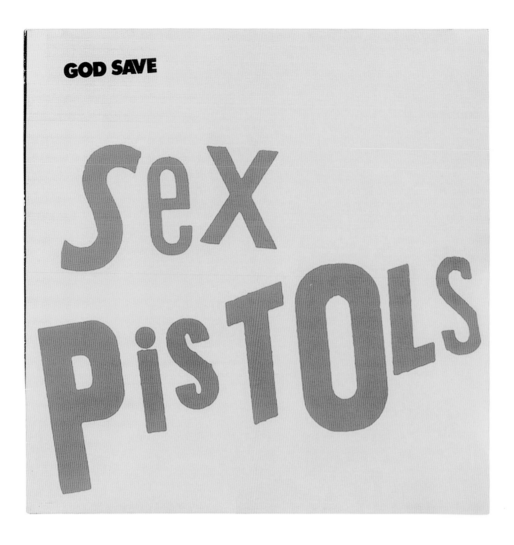

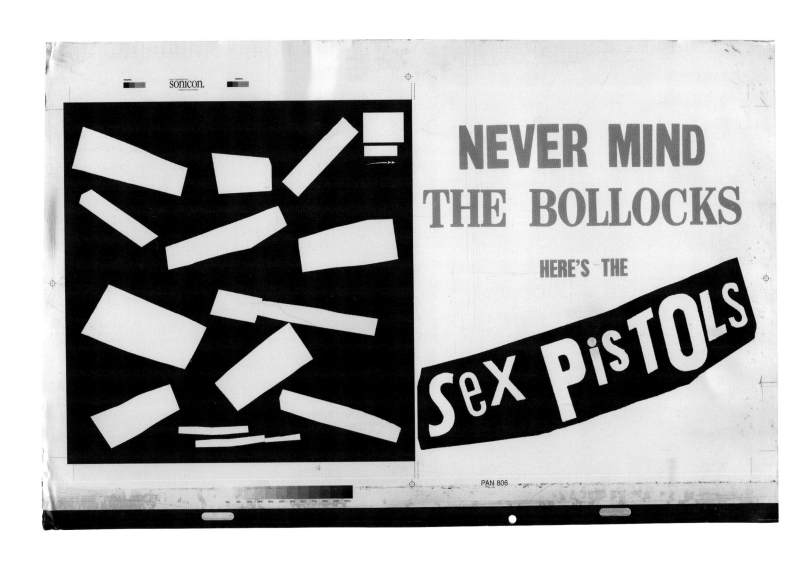

POLICE NOTICE

Her Majesty's Police Force are contemplating prosecution of the person or persons responsible for this Sex Pistols advertising material under the Vagrancy Act 1824 and/or the Indecent Advertisements Act 1889.

The Vagrancy Act states that

"Rogues and vagabonds can be put in the house of correction and have their cutlasses and bludgeons forfeited to the King's majesty."

Also liable to prosecution are any persons

"pretending to tell fortunes, exposing their persons, exposing wounds or deformities to gather alms and every person wilfully exposing to view in any street, road, highway or public place any obscene print, picture or other indecent exhibition."

The Indecent Advertisements Act states that

"whoever exhibits to public view in the window of any shop any picture or printed or written matter which is of an indecent or obscene matter..."

shall be liable to prosecution.

Pending further investigation of this matter, the police have masked or removed the advertising material in question.

The police would like to reassure any members of the public who feel their personal freedom is restricted by these actions that we know best.

Control Department CP/F1320 B

1977 "BOLLOCKS" INDECENCY TRIAL

Prosecution brought against Nottingham Virgin Records store

PROCEEDINGS: David Ritchie prosecuting, John Mortimer Q.C. defending.

Mr. Ritchie said the display measured 9 ft. by 6 ft. with sleeves fitted around the posters with the word "bollocks" displayed prominently. The display consisted of three large posters and eleven sleeves. The word "bollocks" was in letters four inches high, and the whole display was featured prominently in the front window of the shop. Sgt. Stone spoke to Seale again and asked him if he was responsible for the display and Seale said he was. Sgt. Stone informed Seale it "appeared to be a deliberate breach of the law" and Seale was placed under arrest.

Mortimer then said that he wished to call Professor James Kingsley to give evidence as to the meaning of the word bollocks. Mr. Ritchie objected to the witness being called. However, the chairman said, "Let's get it over with," and Kingsley was called.

Kingsley told the court he was the Reverend James Kingsley, Professor of English Studies at Nottingham University. He said he was a former Anglican priest and also a fellow of the Royal Academy. Under questioning from Mortimer he then went into discussing the derivation of the word "bollocks." He said it was used in records from the year 1000 and in Anglo Saxon times it meant a small ball. The terms was also used to describe an orchid. He said that in the 1961 publication of Eric Partridge's *Dictionary of Slang*, he had not taken into account the use of the word "bollocks" in the Middle Ages. He said it appears in Medieval bibles and veterinary books. In the bible it was used to describe small things of an appropriate shape. He said the word also appears in place names without stirring any sensual desire in the local communities. Mortimer said that this would be similar to a city being called Maidenhead, which didn't seem to cause the locals in that vicinity any problems. Mr. Kingsley said that Partridge in his books wrote that "bollocks" remained in colloquial use down through the centuries and was also used to denote a clergyman in the last century. "The word has been used as a nickname for clergymen. Clergymen are known to talk a good deal of rubbish and so the word later developed the meaning of nonsense," he said. "They became known for talking a great deal of bollocks, just as "old balls" or "baloney" also come to mean "testicles," so it has twin uses in the dictionary.

Mr. Ritchie asked him if he was just an expert on the word "bollocks" to which Kingsley replied that he was an expert on the English language who felt he could speak with authority on the derivation of a word such as "bollocks." Mr. Ritchie asked Kingsley if the words "fuck," "cunt," and "shit" also appeared in the *Dictionary of Slang* from which he had quoted. Kingsley replied, "If the word "fuck" does not appear in the dictionary it should."

Mr. Mortimer in summing up the case for the defense said:

"What sort of country are we living in if a politician comes to Nottingham speaks here to a group of people in the city center and during his speech a heckler replies 'bollocks.' Are we to expect this person to be incarcerated, or do we live in a country where we are proud of our Anglo-Saxon language? Do we wish our language to be virile and strong or watered down and weak?"

Upon returning to the courtroom some twenty minutes later the chairman of the bench made this finding:

"Much as my colleagues and I wholeheartedly deplore the vulgar exploitation of the worst instincts of human nature for the purchases of commercial profit by both you and your country, we must reluctantly find you not guilty on each of the four charges."

Directors

M.McLAREN
S.FISHER

Registered Office,
23 Great Castle St,
London, W.1.

GLITTERBEST LTD

40 DRYDEN CHAMBERS
119 OXFORD ST
LONDON W.I.

OI-734-II37
OI-734-II38

PROBLEMS

Too many problems, so why am I here
Dont need to he me cos your all too clear
And I can see theres something wrong with you
But what do you expect me to do
At least I gotta know what I want to be
So dont come to me if you need pity
Are you lonely and you got no-one
Got your body in suspension

Problem — you got a problem — and the problem is you

Eat your heart out on a plastic tray
If you dont do what you want then you'll fade away
You wont find me working nine to five
Its too much fun just being alive
Using my feet for my human machine
I aint dedicated to a t.v. screen
Got your mind castrated
Got your brains dehydrated

Problems — you got your problems — the problem is you — so what you gonna do

I a death trip but I aint automatic
You wont find me just staying static
So dont you give me any order
Cos to people like me there is no order
Bet you thought you had it all worked out
Bet you thought you knew what we were about
Bet you thought you solved all your problems
But you are the problem

Problem — you got a problem — the problem is you so what you gonna do

(This wonderful work of art is followed by an ad-lib verse then ended)

208

Problems

new
MUSICAL
EXPRESS

Editorial Department

King's Reach Tower, Stamford Street, London SE1 9LS
Telegrams: Verditure SE1. Telex: 915748 MAGDIV LDN
Switchboard: 01-261 5000
Personal Telephone Number:

Too many problems so why am I here
I dont need ble me because yer all too clear
And I can see theres something wrong with you
But what do you expect me ta do
At least I gotta know what I want ta be
Dont come to me if ya need pity
Are you lonely and you got no-one
Cot yer body a suspension
        Problem

Eat yer head out on a plastic tray
If you dont do what you want then you'll fade away
You wont find me a working 9 to 5
To much fun being alive
Using my feet for my human machine
You wont find me living for the screen
Are you lonely all needs catered
Cot yer brains de hydrated
        PRoblem
I a death trip but I aint automatic
You wont find a just staying static
Dont you give me any order
Cos for people like me there is no order
Bet you thought you had it all worked out
Bet you thought you knew what we were about
Bet you thought you solved all my problems
But you are the problem

ipc magazines

Registered Office: IPC Magazines Ltd., King's Reach Tower, Stamford Street, London SE1 9LS
Registered Number: 53626 England. A subsidiary of Reed International Ltd.

LIAR

Liar
    Tell me why Tell me why, why do you have to lie
    Should have realized should have told the truth
    Should have realized, you know what I'll do!

I know
        Why you never look me in the face
        Broke a confidence just to please your ego
        But you should have realized
        Cos I know what I know!

INTERIM
        I know where you go, everybody you know
        I know everything that you do or say
        So when you tell lies I'll always be in your way
        Im nobodys fool I lie no more cos I know

Liar
        I think your funny, your funny ha! ha!
        And I dont need it, dont need your blah! blah!
        ~~Cos I know~~ You should have realized I know what
                                                              you are

YOUR ONLY 29 GOT A LOT TO LEARN
BUT WHEN YOUR BUISSENESS DIES
YOU WILL NOT RETURN

WE MAKE NOISE COS ITS OUR CHOICE

ITS WHAT WE WANT TO DO
WE DONT CARE ABOUT LONG HAIR
WE DONT WEAR FLAIRS
AND SEE MY FACE NOT A TRACE, NO REALITY
I DONT WORK I JUST SPEED
THATS ALL I NEED
LAZY SOD

208–209   Autumn 1977. Lyrics for the Sex Pistols' "Problems" in Johnny Rotten's hand.

210   Autumn 1977. Lyrics for the Sex Pistols' "Liar" in Johnny Rotten's hand.

211   Autumn 1977. Lyrics for the Sex Pistols' "17" in Johnny Rotten's hand.

212   28 October, 1977. Postcard from Bob Gruen to *Punk* magazine, sent on the day of the release of *Never Mind the Bollocks*.

213   29 October, 1977. Internal Warner Brothers Records memo regarding the Sex Pistols' birthdates.

INTER-OFFICE MEMO

WARNER BROS. RECORDS INC.

TO: The department FROM: Merlis

SUBJECT: Sex Pistols birthdates

DATE: 10/28/77 COPIES TO: Liz, Les, Gary, Marion, Donna, Stacy, Pam, Heidi, Veron ica, Melenie, Suze, Nancy, Kathy

Following are the birthdates of the Sex Pistols.

Keep them on file somewhere (Sex Pistols clipping or bio file would be approiate, don't you thing) as people are starting to ask us these strange questions.

Johnny Rotten: Jan. 31, 1956

Steve Jones: Sept. 3, 1955

Paul Cook: July 20, 1956

Sid Viscious: May 10, 1957

I hope none of you try to figure out what signs these geezers were born under because, take it from me, they wuz all born under a bad sign.

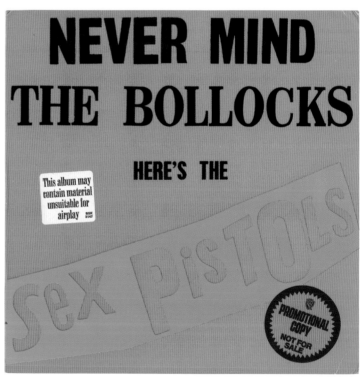

US Sex Pistols release **ABOVE:** Warner Bros. Records (USA) in-house art department flat for *Never Mind the Bollocks* album cover artwork. It includes a color key bar and handwritten amendments for the production run. **BELOW:** *Never Mind The Bollocks, Here's The Sex Pistols*. Warner Bros. Records (BSK 3147) USA. Original first issue promotional copy record with language warning sticker attached for unsuspecting DJs. Note that the black tone used in the color scheme has been corrected in comparison to the proof artwork above.

LEFT, FROM TOP: International versions of *Never Mind the Bollocks*: Columbia House mail order edition, (BSK 3147), USA; Virgin Records (2933 710), Greece; Nippon-Columbia (YX-7199-AX), Japan; record label unknown (511), South Korea. **ABOVE RIGHT:** Warner Bros. Records (USA). Original bromide for advertising material with artwork, including a slogan from the lyrics. **BELOW RIGHT:** Warner Bros. Records (USA). Color proof copy for advertising material with artwork, including a slogan from the lyrics.

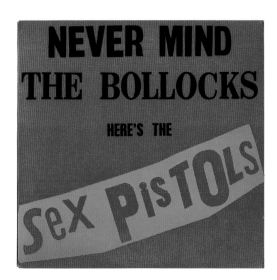

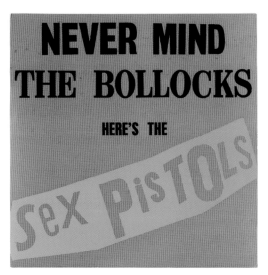

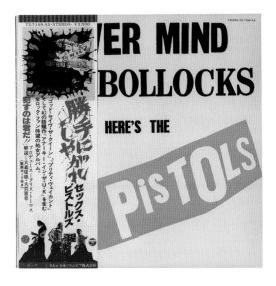

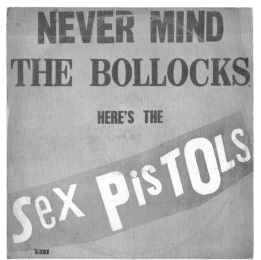

EMI Limited
135 Blyth Road, Hayes,
Middlesex UB3 1BP,
England.

Telephone 01-573 3888 Ext: 2919
Telex No. 22417
Telegrams Emitron, Telex, London
Cables Emitron, London

The Managing Director,
Virgin Records Limited,
2-4 Vernon Yard,
119 Portobello Road,
LONDON W.11

2nd November, 1977

68119/   014731

Dear Sir,

Our attention has been drawn to a record issued recently for
sale by your Company by the 'Sex Pistols' under reference number V2086.
You have used the letters "EMI" on the reverse side of the outer sleeve
in which the record is contained and on the label for Side Two of that
record.

As you are aware, EMI Limited is the proprietor in the United
Kingdom of Trade Marks which consist of the letters "EMI" and Marks of
which those letters form a substantial part. In particular, we
would wish to refer to the following registration numbers:-
B644561, 809580, B809581 and pending application number B1039376.
These Trade Mark registrations cover the use of the letters "EMI"
on or in connection with, 'inter alia', records and tapes. Your use
of "EMI" on the cover and label of the above-mentioned record appears
to constitute an infringement of our rights in these Trade Marks under
the Trade Marks Act, 1938.

Having hereby notified you of the ownership of the "EMI"
Trade Marks, we wish to reserve our rights to take whatever action
we may consider to be necessary for the further protection of our
Trade Marks, whether in respect of the above-mentioned record or
any other record which may be issued by you.

Yours faithfully,

D.C.C. Pick
Group Trade Marks Executive

DCCP/TRS

216   **ABOVE:** Front cover for *Never Mind The Bollocks, Here's The Sex Pistols*. Warner Bros. Records (BSK 3147) USA. Inadvertent 3-D effect added to Jamie Reid's iconic cover design by out-of-register printing. **BELOW:** Back cover for *Never Mind the Bollocks, Here's The Sex Pistols*. Warner Bros. Records (BSK 3147) USA.

217   2 November, 1977. EMI confronting Virgin Records about the usage of "EMI" on *Never Mind the Bollocks*.

218   November 1977. Telegram from Nick Mobbs, the Sex Pistols' A&R man from EMI records, congratulating Malcolm McLaren and the Sex Pistols on reaching number 1.

219   8 November, 1977. Letter from Richard Branson to Sophie Richmond at Glitterbest regarding legal costs of the Silver Jubilee boat trip.

Virgin Records Limited 2-4 Vernon Yard Portobello Road London W11

Sophie,
Glitterbest Ltd,
90-98 Shaftesbury Avenue,
London W1.   8th November, 1977

Dear Sophie,

As I mentioned to you on the telephone, nobody has ever
asked us here if Virgin would pay for the legal costs
relating to the Jubilee Boat Trip. We helped one person
out on his fine because he was bust.

I suggest that we should go 50/50 between Glitterbest and
Virgin on anybody that can't afford their own costs.

Best Wishes,

Richard Branson
Virgin Records Ltd

Directors: RICHARD BRANSON NIKOLAS POWELL SIMON DRAPER KEN BERRY
Registered Office: 2-4 Vernon Yard Portobello Road London W11 Registered No. 1070953(England) Telephone: 01 727 8070 Telex: 22542

ANARKi&KAOS

APRIL -78 NR 4

THROBBING GRISTLE

BLONDIE

FRANK ZAPPA

KEVIN COYNE

IAN DURY

PATTI SMITH GROUP

REGGAE

FANZINES

30 SIDOR SEX PISTOLS 5:-

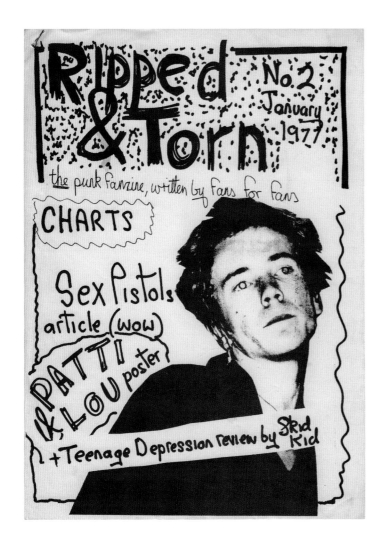

Ripped & Torn

No. 2 January 1977

the punk fanzine, written by fans for fans

CHARTS

Sex Pistols article (wow)

PATTI & LOU poster

+ Teenage Depression review by Skid Kid

March No. 8

$1.00

PUNK

Sex Pistols

BONDAGE

NO. 1 TERMINAL '76

JUST ANOTHER COUNTRY

SEX PISTOLS

The JAM

EATER

SEX PISTOLS

ON STAGE !!

at last !

LONDONS OUTRAGE !

On stage the pistols are the most aggressive, nastiest band ever

SEX PISTOLS

Punk rock violence is sinister

BY JOHN BLAKE

What the Nazis did, Arendt said, was something new: they altered the limits of human action. In doing so, the Nazis provided humanity with more than a burden—the need to comprehend their actions—they also provided a legacy: "It is in the very nature of things human that every act that has once made its appearance and has been recorded in the history of mankind stays with mankind as a potentiality long after its actuality has become a thing of the past. ... Once a specific crime has appeared for the first time, its reappearance is more likely than its initial emergence could ever have been..."

STER SQUARE ++ ADMISSION £1.00 ++

これがわたしたちの文化だ、こんなに音もなく滑りながら
稔りのない海の平野を進んでゆく、どこか行く手に
懐疑派の東洋か、戦争か、新しい花か、新しい衣裳か。
--- 誰もわからない、
一番の恥さらしは誰なのか、誰が金持になるか、
誰が死ぬかを。

SeX PiSTOLs

words： *W.H.Auden   Kim Chi Ha*
edit. by *BOREDOM 1978 1.*
150 yen   PHONE 0422 54 6663,

Special thanks to Sophie of the Sex Pistols' H.Q.

220-224   Punk-era fanzines covering the Sex Pistols.

225-226   10 November, 1977. Legal document regarding trademark application in the US and UK for Sex Pistols.

LADAS PARRY, VON GEHR, GOLDSMITH & DESCHAMPS

HIGH HOLBORN HOUSE
52-54 HIGH HOLBORN
LONDON, WCIV 6RR

TELEPHONE: 01-242 5566
CABLES: LAWLAN LONDON, W.C.I.
TELEX: 264255 LAWLAN G

IAIN C. BAILLIE
NEW YORK BAR
LOUIS STEVENSON
ILLINOIS BAR
IAN SHERIDAN
NEW YORK BAR
————
NEW YORK OFFICE:
IO COLUMBUS CIRCLE
NEW YORK N.Y. IOOI9
————
LEONARD J. ROBBINS
S. DELVALLE GOLDSMITH
OF COUNSEL

SIDNEY DESCHAMPS
MARCEL DESCHAMPS
W. MALCOLM PARRY
H. GEOFFREY LYNFIELD
GABRIEL M. FRAYNE
PAUL B. MOROFSKY
PAUL B. WEST
STEPHEN A. GOLDSMITH
LESTER HORWITZ
HERBERT L. BOETTCHER
IRVING M. BRAVERMAN
LAWRENCE E. ABELMAN
IAN J. KAUFMAN
ELLIOTT BOWDEN
ROBERT BLACK
FREDERICK REICHWALD
JOSEPH H. HANDELMAN
NORMAN D. KANTOR
ALLAN S. PILSON
JAMES N. PALIK
(MEMBERS N.Y. BAR)

PARIS OFFICE:
7 RUE DE LA PAIX
PARIS 2, FRANCE

WILLIAM J. REZAC
(MEMBER N.Y. BAR)
————

CHICAGO OFFICE:
IO4 SOUTH MICHIGAN AVENUE
CHICAGO ILL. 60603

CHARLES J. FOXGROVER, JR
JOHN J. CHRYSTAL
THOMAS E. PETERSON
THOMAS J. HOFFMAN
RICHARD J. STREIT
(MEMBERS ILL. BAR)
————

LOS ANGELES OFFICE:
3600 WILSHIRE BLVD.
LOS ANGELES CAL. 90010

GEORGE VON GEHR
RICHARD W. KEEFE
W. NORMAN ROTH
(MEMBERS CAL. & ILL. BARS)

L 8475/T77-1287/1286   10th November, 1977

Glitterbest Limited.,
90-98 Shaftesbury Avenue,
London,
W.1

For the Attention of Miss Sophie Richmond

Dear Miss Richmond

Re: Trade Mark Applications in the United Kingdom
      and the United States for "Sex Pistols"

This will confirm our recent telephone conversation in which we advised that we had been asked by Steven Fisher to file Trade Mark Applications in the United Kingdom and the United States for "Sex Pistols".

The British applications have been filed and the details are as follows:-

Trade Mark: Sex Pistols
Application No: 1085921
Goods: Paper and paper articles all included in Class 16,
                 paper iron on transfers, printed matter, comic books,
                 picture books, colouring books, painting books,
                 drawing books, posters, photographs, artists materials
                 (other than colours or varnish), instructional and
                 teaching material (other than apparatus) and ordinary
                 playing cards - Class 16.

Cont/..............2

Trade Mark: Sex Pistols
Application No: 1085922
Goods: Articles of sports clothing, suits for men, blouses
and dresses, overall, jackets, skirts, shirts, T shirts,
articles of underclothing, sleeping garments, swimwear
and tights all being articles of clothing, shoes, boots
sandals,canvas shoes,socks (for wearing), stockings,
ties, caps, and belts all for wear, scarves, playsuits,
costumes and sweat shirts - Class 25.

Both of the British applications were filed on November 1st, 1977, but we do not expect the Patent office to act on the applications for approximately 6 months. We will keep you fully advised of all developments.

As for the applications in the United States, it is necessary to make some nominal use of the Trade mark in commerce in the United States before Trade Mark applications can be filed. We are making the necessary arrangements and we expect to be able to file the applications in the United States in approximately 2 weeks time. The coverage of the applications will be the same as for the United Kingdom.

Our two debit notes for the filing fees for the two British applications are enclosed together with copies of the official filing receipts and copies of the application forms as filed.

Sincerely yours

....

L. STEVENSON

LS/DC

GLITTERBEST LTD.

90/98 SHAFTESBURY AVENUE
LONDON W.1.

01-734 1137
01-734 1138
Telex No: 298361

Registered Office:
25/27 OXFORD STREET
LONDON W.1.

Directors:
M. McLAREN
S. FISHER

2.12.77

Richard Branson,

Virgin Records,

Vernon Yard,

Portobello Road, W11

Dear Richard Branson,

I am very concerned with your insidious methods of laying the blame
of a massive export of albums to the U.S. on me, via Robert Lee, to
Warner Brothers. In Italy; in Hollan; in Scandinavia - we have
received reports that the album pressed by Virgin was in their shops
before it was released even here.

Your attempts to stall delivery to your European licensees in order,
it appears, to make quick profit from pilfering and pirating exports
into these countries, has damaged our chances of success here, and to
hide behind Barclay Records does not, and will not, wash with me.

I have made attempts to reconcile the problem with Barclay and have
continued to do so, and will win. But, if this problem as well as
other problems, regarding illegal merchandising, with your company
come to my notice again,

I will seek legal advice to strengthen my position in no small
manner

Waiting on your- but not for too long!

Malcolm McLaren.

5

227   2 December, 1977. Letter from Malcolm McLaren to Richard Branson.

228–229   September 1977. Johnny Rotten and Sid Vicious circa the Sex Pistols' anonymous secret tour.

Virgin Records Limited 2-4 Vernon Yard Portobello Road London W11

Malcolm McLaren,
Glitterbest,
90-98 Shaftesbury Aven,
London W1.   5th December, 1977

Dear Malcolm,

I know it's not your policy but it would be nice if, just
once, you gave some credit to people who have worked
as hard as we have this year. We have talked and dreamt
Sex Pistols for months. We do not expect at the end of
it all to receive the kind of letter you wrote today.
I do not think we deserve it either.

We all intended simultaneous release of the Pistols'
album worldwide on 10th November. As you know, at the
very last minute you wanted "Submission" added to the album,
which obliged all our licencees to hold everything up for
the new tape. All was well until we learnt that Barclay
were shipping records WITHOUT "Submission" and that you,
furthermore, had not insisted that they include it.
Consequently we rushed our release date forward to combat
imports from Barclay and messed up our licencees in the
process. We have had a very close relationship with all
our licencees for four years. We are certainly not stupid
enough to "pilfer and pirate" from them on purpose.

As far as U.S.A. is concerned all Robert told Warners was
that it was Barclay who was shipping large quantities and
not us. Naturally, he mentioned the "Submission" problem,
but merely because (a) Warners blamed us and (b) they thought
Barclay was one of our licencees.

I also cannot understand your sudden concern over merchandising
items. You have been aware and encouraged Virgin's involvement
in this activity and have even been one of our biggest customers.

                                   Cont'd..

Directors: RICHARD BRANSON NIKOLAS POWELL SIMON DRAPER KEN BERRY
Registered Office: 2-4 Vernon Yard Portobello Road London W11 Registered No. 1070953(England) Telephone: 01 727 8070 Telex: 22542

2

<u>Cont'd</u>

If you want us to stop we will after we have disposed of our
existing stocks. As you know we do this solely as a promotional
purpose - it has actually cost us in excess of £15,000 - and
if in future you want to conduct merchandising on a different
basis why don't we discuss this. In the meantime, Robert and
Stephen are sorting the position out regards rights etc. (We'd
be happy to sell all our stocks at cost to you or whatever).

Yours ,

<u>Richard Branson</u>
<u>Virgin Records Ltd</u>

c.c. R. Lee

AVAILABLE FOR THE FIRST TIME,
THE ORIGINAL, AUTHENTIC

SEX PISTOLS POSTERS

Ⓐ 'PRETTY VACANT' 27"x 39" 1 colour £1.00

Ⓑ 'GOD SAVE THE QUEEN' 27"x39" 3 colours £1.50

Ⓒ 'BOLLOCKS' 27"x39" Full colour £1.75

Ⓓ 'BOLLOCKS' 60"x38" DAYGLO 3 colours £2.50

Ⓖ 'HOLIDAYS' 27" x 39" 2 colours £1.50

Ⓔ 'PRETTY VACANT' 1 colour £1.00 27"x 39"

Ⓕ 'ANARCHY' 27"x39" 3 colour £2.00

FREE 'GOD SAVE THE QUEEN' STREAMER WITH POSTERS!

Original designs by Jamie for the Sex Pistols.
© Glitterbest Ltd. 1977

See overleaf for Pistols Special promotions!

232

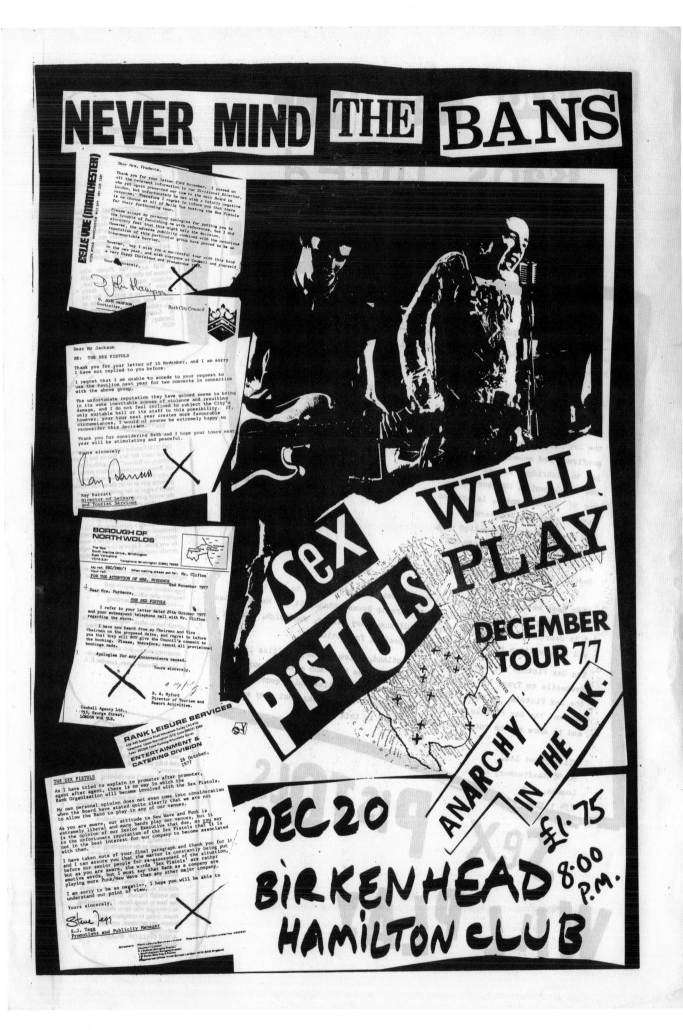

IF you WANT THE
Bans lifted
It's UP to you!

December 3, 1977 SOUND

...ST 4ND.

Sign in stranger

AFTER LISTENING to the Radio 1 interview of Johnny Rotten and Sid Vicious, and hearing Johnny's remarks about how apathetic punks are, ie not doing much about getting the authorities to let them play an official gig, I have decided to launch a campaign.

WILL any *True Punks* who wanna be able to hear the Pistols without aggro from the law, please try to get as many signatures on a petition for the same, and send them to me at this address: **Megan G Hughes, 1 St Georges Road, Kingshill, Dursley, Gloucestershire GL11 4DN.**

PRESS STATEMENT DEC 12

SEX PISTOLS BAN LIFTED

Sex Pistols will play. Sex Pistols national tour starts 16 December, London, Brunel University.

After 12 months of complete rejection by every local authority in England, Scotland and Wales and by the major independent owners of ballrooms, Mecca, Rank, Trust Houses Forte, certain towns have given their permission for the Sex Pistols to play under their own name. The following gigs have been confirmed and announced:-

Dec 16 Uxbridge, Brunel University

Dec 17 Coventry, Mr Georges

Dec 18 Wolverhampton, Lafayettes

Dec 19 Keighley, Nickers

Dec 20 Birkenhead, Hamilton Club

Dec 22 Rochdale, Champness Hall

Dec 23 Newport, Village

Dec 24 Cromer, Links Pavilion

Kids have been organising petitions to their local councils to let the band play, among them, Molly Gilligan, 19 Taranto House, Shandy St E1, Megan Hughes 1 St Georges Rd, Kingshill, Dursley, Gloucs, Anne Gallop, Woodleigh, Reading who have written to the music press appealing for action.

The Sex Pistols are still banned in Scotland, Wales and major cities like Newcastle on Tyne. All help will be given to the kids who actively support the Sex Pistols. We will fight to expose the authorities which continue to prevent the Sex Pistols and other young people from saying what they mean and to show up the censorship which exists in this country.

Glitterbest Ltd,
90-98 Shaftesbury Ave,
London, W.1.
734 1137/8

NEW MUSICAL EXPRESS

November 26th, 1977

DO YOU realise that it is now almost a year since the Sex Pistols last played publicly in Britain? The authorities are doing everything in their power to stamp them out. Are we really such pathetic gits as to let them win? How much longer is the greatest group in the world going to be oppressed and opposed by every petty little mind in existence while we go on living our boring comfortable little lives?

I'm starting a petition to the GLC (because they're the most influential council) and it must be big or it won't be any good. I appeal to every single person reading this to gather as many signatures as possible everywhere you go and send them to me. And all you hypocritical music papers and fanzines who whine about 'freedom' — bloody well do something constructive!

You may think I'm just a soppy crank but so what. Anyway what else can we do so short of taking a machine gun and mowing down the vile Brook-Partridge and all his contemptible toadish minions?
MOLLY GILLIGAN, 19 Taranto House, Shandy Street, London E.1.

LISTENING TO Johnny Rotten and Sid Vicious on Radio One, one remark really stuck. The interviewer said: "Do you want to go to America" and John answered: "Yes, out of curiosity".

By this time I was thinking 'Turncoats, sell outs'. Then Johnny said something very valid, he said: "What have we got from this country anyway? We can't play, we can't even go out, and I haven't seen many complaints to the town halls or councils about it either."

It's true, what have we done about it? Nothing. I know I haven't, that is why I want to do something now. I don't blame them if they do go to America, what have they got here except rising record sales and more money. We would be really angry if they did go, wouldn't we. Are you content to lose the best rock band in the world? I'm not. British, so let's do our best to keep them. I'm appealing to everyone who cares about rock music today to complain, write letters, get petitions, anyway just do something!
ANNE GALLOP, Woodley, Reading, Berks.

Sex PISTOLS
WILL PLAY

George Cruikshank

They are Dickensian-like urchins who
with ragged clothes and pock marked
faces roam the streets of foggy
gas-lit London. Pillaging .....
Pill

Setting FIRE to Buildings. Beating-up
old people with gold chains.
Fucking the rich up the arse.
Causing havoc wherever they go. Some of
these ragamuffin gangs jump on tables
amidst the charred

236

debris and with burning torches play rock 'n roll, to the screaming delight of the frenzied pissing pogoing mob. SHOUTING AND SPITTING 'anarchy' one of these gangs call themselves the SEX PISTOLS. This true and dirty tale has BEEN CONTINUING THROUGHOUT 200 years of teenage anarchy and so in 1978 there still remains the SEX PISTOLS. Their active Extremism is all that they come about because that's what WHAT COUNTS to JUMP RIGHT OUT of the 20th CENTURY AS FAST YOU 21st CENTURY possibly can in order to CREATE an environment that you can TRUTHFULLY RUN WILD IN Oliver Twist.

THE LONDON PUNKS

ALL ABOUT PUNKS PART-①

パンクからエキサイティングなヤング魂を学ぼう。

キミたちよ ヘイワにどっぷり浸っていてはダメ。いま ロンドンをベースにして派生したシャープな若者感覚〈PUNK精神〉で武装しよう

取材：岩崎三貴也
撮影：辻 帛
構成：守永隆伸／海野一雄

238–241　Autumn 1977. Japanese *All About Punks* magazine article. A translation of the accompanying interview appears on page 320.

DESTROY

SEX PISTOLS

N・Yパンク
なんてゴミよ

ポール・クック

FIGHTING!

Is Fucking Way?

IT'S ONLY NOW !!

Do Something Defferent!

"100 CLUB" Oxford St

"ROCK GARDEN" Convent garden, No.3の人気店

ナゼかパンクスには黒人が多い

一見デビット・ボーイ風のメークだが チェーンサドパンクスだ

パンク・ダンスは
ファイトが要素

興奮のあまり楽器を壊すのは日常茶飯事

サングラスはすべて '60年製

LONDON & PUNKS

SEX PISTOLS

And We don't care

'VORTEX', Wardown St.,

HOPE & ANCHOR

...igh & Thurs...
...HAPMAN & BAN
...CHAPMAN & BAN
...Keef Hart...
...Cleaves plus
...Ian

No Future

SEX PISTOLS

ホモ! ましてもな
奴よりマシさ

241

"NO FUTURE FOR YOU!!!"

So says Johnny Rotten and it's not all lies--.
Punk Rock exposes the joke of man trying to save himself from the curse:

"The soul that sins will surely die."
So says God and he can't lie

no future for you...

not in music, in social friends, in plans and good deeds, and not in the rebellion that Punk Rock peddles...

BUT

There is a Life and a Future Forever: Jesus came to make a way back to

A FUTURE FOR YOU:

There is a Johnny Rotten inside each of us and he doesn't need to be liberated--
he needs to be crucified.

Our sin nature must die at the cross of Jesus Christ that we can be born again in the resurected Christ

TURN FROM YOUR PUNK WAYS AND BE BAPTIZED INTO THE DEATH AND LIFE OF JESUS...

242 12 January, 1978. Anti-Sex Pistols handout during the Sex Pistols US tour, Tulsa, Oklahoma.

243 **LEFT:** Randy's Rodeo matchbook.
    RIGHT: 8 January, 1978. Flyer for the Sex Pistols at Randy's Rodeo.

244-248 The Sex Pistols' 1978 US tour. *Punk* magazine photographer Roberta Bayley's photo
265-279 documentation of the tour is breathtaking. The selection here is a small excerpt from
    this body of work.

Dutch Tour

Roadent

The last real tour I did with them was Holland. Everyone taking turns staying up all night with Sid to try and keep him away from smack. There was some crazy idea of Malcolm's that we had to get the band out working to keep Sid away from smack dealers, so he sent us off to Holland.

5 DECEMBER 1977 **Eksit Club, Rotterdam, Holland**

6 DECEMBER 1977 **Maastricht, Holland**

7 DECEMBER 1977 **Pozjet Club, Tilburg, Holland**

8 DECEMBER 1977 **Stokuishal, Arnhem, Holland**

9 DECEMBER 1977 **De Effenaar, Eindhoven, Holland**

10 DECEMBER 1977 **Huize Maas, Groningen, Holland**

11 DECEMBER 1977 **Maf Centrum, Maasbree, Holland**

14 DECEMBER 1977 **Eksit Club, Rotterdam, Holland**

Never Mind the Bans Tour

16 DECEMBER 1977 **Brunel University, Uxbridge**

John Lydon

I remember Brunel University being awful, it was hideous, a fiasco. We were in that big hall, which was jam-packed, nobody really knew why anybody was there, least of all us. I was very confused by the sheer popularity of it, and I thought, "This is horrible, it shouldn't be like this." I'd seen us as a small clubby band at that time, we were way ahead of ourselves. We didn't know how to cut it onstage, how to get past the first twenty rows.

The good gigs were when we were taking the piss out of ourselves, our situation. That didn't happen at Brunel. We were all terrified, there were too many people, we didn't know how to deal with it. And there was a real nasty mood in that audience, all trying to out-punk each other, and the fun had gone. Sid was out of his tree, thinking he was God, because by that time Nancy was telling him he was "the only star in this band." The fact that Sid made no recorded contribution to any record didn't occur to him to be important.

Dennis Morris

Brunel was the disaster. That was the one Virgin used as their showcase. Branson himself was there, Simon Draper, just about everybody. The PA was about 1K including the monitors, and the hall holds about two thousand people. When they arrived there was big friction between John and Sid. At that point John was on his own. You'll see from the pictures that by then the Public Image thing had started to creep in, the white jacket, the tie. The Ferry thing, with the riding boots and the leathers. But he was on his own. And then everybody else from London turned up and it was, "God, everyone's here to see us!" Branson going, "Hi Guys!" They walked onstage and there was nothing, John couldn't hear himself, no one could hear him. It was utter disaster, and that was when they realised that the merchandising was going on. After the soundcheck we left the hall to get some Kentucky, and there were these guys with everything: Pistols badges, T-shirts, everything. John and everybody walked up and just turned the whole thing over, you know? Who's getting the money? When they came back the whole thing just erupted, a lot of violence from the audience. Toward the band.

17 DECEMBER 1977 **Mr. George's, Coventry**

Roadent	At Mr. George's in Coventry, I remember all these drunken Coventrians coming up saying, "Why are they on so early?" and getting real stroppy and violent about it. I remember packing a microphone stand by my side and thinking, "I'm going to have to use this any moment now." That was the night that Sid smashed the room up.
Dennis Morris	It was decline for Sid in some ways. He was getting really out of it. He missed Nancy, he wanted to bring her on tour, and John said absolutely no way. She came to the Brunel gig, because John conceded. Sid missed her, he was a very lonely character and he fell for the trap that McLaren may have instigated, he fell for it. He fell for the whole rock 'n' roll trip. After people screaming at you, wanting to get at you, and you're dumped in this square room, with just about enough of everything to keep you going. That's the other thing, if you had a bit of this to smoke, or a bit of speed, it's just enough to get you on the edge, and he always fell for it, so he used to wreck his room. Then in the morning McLaren would just turn up with this wad of notes, and he knew the cost of the hotel rooms, and the guy would look at the wad and go, "Yeah, alright." It was over, and McLaren would leave it up to him about whether to ring up the papers and say, "They wrecked my hotel!" One thing he always avoided was public police prosecution. It's better to pay the guy. Once the guy got paid, anything else was perks.

19 DECEMBER 1977	**Nikkers Club, Keighley**
21 DECEMBER 1977	**Lafayette Club, Wolverhampton**
23 DECEMBER 1977	**Stowaway Club, Newport**
24 DECEMBER 1977	**Links Pavilion, Cromer**
25 DECEMBER 1977	**Ivanhoes, Huddersfield (Afternoon show for kids)**
25 DECEMBER 1977	**Ivanhoes, Huddersfield (Evening show)**
	USA Tour 1978
28 DECEMBER 1977	**Leona Theatre, Homestead, Pennsylvania—CANCELED**
5 JANUARY 1978	**Great South East Music Hall, Atlanta, Georgia**

John Tiberi	Warners took over the minute we got there. Nice customs clearance, I must admit. We did the immigration thing like normal people, then this little ferret bloke Mel Monk comes along, and all the luggage comes straight through on a trolley. Warner Brothers started to talk. Then in the lobby, NBC tour manager coming back to the States, on this bus. This is the bus to the car park! TV, the lot.
	The tour was straight into Atlanta, first gig, because we were late. That first night Sid disappeared, went AWOL to get a feel for America, man, fans! Sid found these fans, straight out of Ziggy Stardust. Glitter, makeup. I think they came back, actually. That night he went missing in Atlanta he just showed up again in the morning. There was a later occasion when he couldn't get what he wanted... maybe that was the night he turned up with a massive gash in his arm, because he couldn't get a spike. The alcohol wasn't working. It was cold turkey. These kids were good at dressing up, but they couldn't get him anything.
	Sid had a spike relationship, which is quite a separate thing. People have been known to get off shooting up water. He had these massive Quaaludes, horse tablets, but they weren't hitting the spot he wanted. You could say, "Why weren't you looking after him, Boogie?" But there you go. I ripped the phone out of the wall. Whatever had been happening in the days preceding this, had been happening whilst I was arranging visas, he and Nancy had been at it for four days solid. Sid went home and had his private life, and it wasn't a case of me looking after him, shaking his willy and putting it away afterwards. It did develop that way later, in Paris, and I have to be reminded of that. That wasn't the way any of us wanted things to be. I was doing it to make a film to get us all off the hook, I suppose. Minding the sick drug addict.

6 JANUARY 1978	**Taliesyn Ballroom, Memphis, Tennessee**

Joe Stevens	The *NME* called me and said, the Pistols are touring, how would you like to go on it? They gave me $167 to do an eleven-day tour, and all the flights. I missed the first one. This sounds like my deposition for the Rotten case. I missed the first gig, which was Atlanta. A bit of trivia: if the Pistols had fulfilled all their engagements in America, their first gig would have been in Philadelphia. That didn't happen. Jimmy Carter's administration were having trouble deciding whether they should be given visas. They were given a two-week visa to do eleven dates. That is rare. Even today, dodgy bands from England don't get treated like that. Luckily they were aligned with Warner Brothers, and Warners, being all gangsters, pulled some strings. I'm still trying to track some of it down, through people who cover the White House. Whether it actually happened in the Oval Office, Jimmy Carter confronted with making a decision whether to let the Sex Pistols into America, I don't know. But I heard that happened.

I met them in Memphis, found the hotel. The gig that night involved Sid getting a lot of trouble with his security. He was brought over to detox, and to do gigs, and we saw the man, Sid Vicious, walking around, cold turkey, in the lobby. The rest of us are having a nice gin and tonic, and sandwiches... they weren't speaking to each other. Cook and Jones hung out together, they'd go bowling. Rotten would have nothing to do with McLaren. Sophie showed up for that gig. The first thing she said to me, she described them as "this fucking poxy band," in conversation just before they went onstage. I began rooming with McLaren. They all had twin rooms, and his other bed was going unused.

John Hölmstrom	I showed up an hour or two after they were supposed to go on, and a riot had just happened, they're not letting anyone in. I happened to run into Gary Kenton, the Warners publicity person, and he very nicely let me in. I was totally confused, standing there with a suitcase, looking at broken glass and police sirens and people wandering all over the place, very angry. He lets me in and I'm listening to Alice Cooper, *Killer*, the first side, and I go to someone, "Great record," and they go, "Yeah," but they've been playing it over and over for three hours. Everybody's pounding on the floor, there'd been a riot because they'd sold too many tickets and had to turn people away, it was pandemonium. The Pistols went on, and they weren't very exciting.

What I did next was go to the British press, the *Sun*, the *Mirror*, the *Evening Standard*, and I said, "How would you like a daily briefing, from the inside?" Because McLaren didn't want the British press to know where the gig was. He told Warners, "Don't give them anything." That was the idea, to wind them up. They're used to this, we've been doing it in England, it's like a circus. They'll find the gig, they'll buy their own tickets. No comp tickets for the press. I was an exception, because I was in the inner circle. So I'd give press briefings in the lobbies of the hotels. This is what happened last night: Sid almost fell out of the window. Rotten is spitting up this big green stuff, McLaren's got a bad cold, Sophie's threatening to go back to London, blah blah. McLaren was on the phone to the lawyers for six hours last night, keeping me awake, "Anything else you want to know?" They'd say, "Yeah, where's the fucking gig tonight, you cunt?" And I'd whisper, "It's in a bowling alley, wherever... " The gigs were not announced to the press. The kids would find them, and sell it out.

8 JANUARY 1978   **Randy's Rodeo, San Antonio, Texas**

Paul Cook	That American tour was so heavy with paranoia, the whole tour. Malcolm wasn't helping, he was really paranoid, saying that people were following us around, and we did have to be careful. Sometimes there were policemen with guns standing at the side of the stage while we were playing, two on each side. I got the feeling someone was going to get killed at any time, it was really heavy. And there was that stupid film crew following us around. There's so many loonies in America just waiting to latch onto something. Thousands of people came out of these little towns to see us. Tons of stuff thrown at us onstage, mainly cans, but dead rats, pigs' ears, stuff like that. Really sick. It was hard to play with all this stuff going on around you. Which is why some of it sounds so ropey. But I've seen some clips of that American tour, and it looks so exciting... so much tension.
Roberta Bayley	I got on the plane the next day and went to Texas. I'd seen the Ramones the night before and been to a party and got on the plane. I got there and everything was weird and secretive. John [Hölmstrom] was going, "We've got to find the Pistols, they're hiding." I think they were trying to keep the Pistols away from the press, they were traveling on this bus, so John and I spent the whole time trying to find what hotel they were in, it was really strange. We went to the gig,

the soundcheck. That was the Rodeo, the most insane show, all these rednecks throwing bottles for the whole show, and that's when Sid hit the guy over the head with his bass, and there was all this shit going on. You definitely felt there was going to be a riot or something. There were very few people there who cheered for them, it was definitely Texans who had come down to check out what this shit is, these macho guys... and there were all these weird people selling safety pins, nobody knew what punk was. It was in Texas and it was totally strange. I thought they were amazing, but I wasn't getting up close, even to shoot pictures. I thought, "This is too frightening."

Rory Johnston   San Antonio was fantastic, its still the best rock 'n' roll gig I've ever been at in my life. Complete mayhem. They were throwing everything they could get their hands on: hot dogs, popcorn, beer cans. Rotten was getting smacked on the head, Sid didn't know what was going on, basically. The night before, or the night before that, he'd carved "give me a fix" on his chest in a moment of frenzy. "All you fucking cowboys are a bunch of fucking faggots!"—Rotten from the stage. They were fighting in the audience, Indian guys and Mexicans fighting with the cowboys. This bottle of Jack Daniels comes flying over the PA column, and there's a little sheriff standing there all done up in his guns and everything, and the bottle smacks him on the head, and he staggered back. I saw him go for his guns, I thought, "Fuck, he's going to start shooting somebody." I was the first person he was going to see, I thought he'd probably shoot me. I ran up to the board, and the crowd was so wild. I said to Boogie, "I think we're going to get fucking done in here." It was radical. It was such an incredible shame they didn't film that gig. I've still got the clippings from the next day: "The Battle of the Alamo II," or something.

John Hölmstrom   I think the San Antonio gig was one of the best I ever saw, if not the best rock 'n' roll show. It was insane, there were bottles flying everywhere. They were responding to the audience. That was the one with the famous incident, where Sid hit the guy, and the lights went off, I thought there was going to be a riot. The Pistols rose to the occasion, they were amazing. It's captured a bit on the DOA thing. But I wish they could have shown more of that, no matter how bad the filming was. They were amazing.

It was a very hostile type of thing, but if you wanted what punk rock was supposed to be, this was the ultimate show. They got the audience into it, too. The incident with the guitar happened very early on. There was a great headline: "Pistols Win the San Antonio Shoot-out." It was like that. The audience seemed ready to kill the Sex Pistols as soon as they came out. There were rednecks in the audience, but it was a mixture. Who are these punks from England? Let's go down and show them what Texas is about. Malcolm had mentioned this as the place he wanted, he was hoping there would be this kind of incident. They were throwing full beer cans at the Pistols. I saw Sid take a full beer can right in the mouth, and he took it and dared them to throw more, and they realised they were for real. Then they started throwing things for fun. Johnny got a pie in the face. After the show you couldn't see the stage for the beer cans piled on it. I've never seen such a mess, and the Pistols loved it, they came out and talked to the press for the first time. I think the only time they came they talked to people. They were under rein for the first two shows. Under a lot of scrutiny, and if there were any riots they weren't at Atlanta. The Sex Pistols didn't throw up or kill anybody, and by the time they reached San Antonio, a lot of people dropped off the tour and they were themselves.

Joe Stevens   One of them was the second best rock 'n' roll show I'd ever seen in my life. San Antonio. It had everything. It had violence, great music, the band was storming, even with Sid screwing up. Rotten was on top form, his voice had cleared out. Annie Leibowitz, who was doing a cover story for Rolling Stone, Charles Young was doing the whole tour. She had everything stolen from her bag at that gig, including all the shots from the night before, lenses... I thought I was being fondled by some girl behind me. Turned out it wasn't a girl at all, it was a little guy, stealing my lenses. I couldn't move, you know? I'm sure you've seen the photographs. Beer cans flying. At the end of the gig, the beer cans on the stage were about three feet deep. Unbelievable gig. That was the one where Sid clunked a kid over the head with a guitar, then went after him again. The security guys finally grabbed him.

9 JANUARY 1978   Kingfish Club, Baton Rouge, Louisiana

10 JANUARY 1978   Longhorn Ballroom, Dallas, Texas

John Hölmstrom	The next show was great too, at Dallas. That was where Sid got hit on the nose, and was bleeding. They were hanging out talking to people before the show in Dallas too, things had loosened up.
Rory Johnston	Malcolm was on the tour, traveling with the band until either San Antonio or Dallas. I think Dallas was the last trip he made on the bus. Then he decided he had to fly from there, and I went with him from Dallas to Tulsa. Then when we got to Tulsa, Jones and Cook said, "Fuck it, we don't want to travel on the bus anymore." Sid was really fucked up, difficult. I think Malcolm realised about midway that it was out of control. I didn't know enough about what had preceded it. He'd given up on the band, and decided to put it in the best light, based on what the Pistols were all about, tried to create a situation that left the idea of the band intact, so that the structure was left, but the building collapsed.
Paul Cook	John and Sid were obviously the most striking, they got the most attention and they needed more looking after, I suppose. Me and Steve could always go off and mingle. But Sid was driving everyone mad, so me and Steve started flying to the gigs, because otherwise it was driving in the bus for ten hours at a time in the snow, ridiculous. By the time we reached San Francisco, we'd had enough of it all, and that's when the split occurred.
Sophie Richmond	Sid was quite out of it, but they did play well and it was packed with lots of interested people, it was quite wild, and Dallas was a place that appealed to me anyway. The nicest bit that I remember was the bus journey between Baton Rouge and Dallas, and it was snowing, driving across America, great articulated lorries turned over by the side of the road, stopping to buy little souvenirs, little key-rings with guns and so forth. Sid was ill, John was pissed off, and Steve and Paul were relatively quiet, their usual selves.
John Hölmstrom	The Pistols were all pissed at Malcolm, because he was flying everywhere, but he wanted the Pistols to stay on the bus so they could see the country, or something. He had some wacky idea. Then somehow Steve and Paul got on the planes, but I heard Sid and Johnny wanted to be in the bus, they liked their traveling party, they were getting along great with the bodyguards. Sid I think needed somebody to watch him all the time. Noel Monk was the bodyguard. He was creepy, such a fascist. They were spending a lot of time with those guys, I think they thought they were new friends. But once they broke up, they couldn't even talk to those guys. I think they found they weren't such great friends. They were horrible to us, I think Noel Monk had Roberta practically beat up in San Francisco.

12 January 1978   **Cains Ballroom, Tulsa, Oklahoma**

13 January 1978   **Travel to San Francisco. KSAN interview with Paul Cook and Steve Jones.**

14 January 1978   **Winterland Ballroom, San Francisco, California**

John Lydon	It was very bad. Sid was misbehaving appallingly, no one was talking to anyone. Steve and Paul and Malcolm flew everywhere, and ignored us, and all the time Malcolm was behind this, plotting and scheming and breaking things up. He couldn't control me, Malcolm, and that really upset him. I wasn't talking to them, they weren't talking to me. I was just as bad as them, don't get me wrong. I have my faults too, my faults are really quite intense. There's huge catalogue of complaints about me, this I know. But there just didn't seem to be any way of connecting it all, ever more. I meant it—no fun. Ever get the feeling you've been cheated? Well I meant that from here, because I felt cheated. I knew it couldn't go on.
Steve Jones	I had a cold, Sid wasn't playing a note and he wasn't even plugged in half the time. Me and Paul just wanted to play. I kept cutting out, strings breaking left right and center. And all these people going about thinking it was great, what's going on. It was such a relief being on that plane to Rio. Go and see Biggsy.
Paul Cook	It was all right. It was alien to us, because we'd never played in such a big place. By the time we got there, we'd originally been booked to play a 500-capacity place, but because of all the publicity it was the Winterland, six thousand people. By far the biggest venue we'd ever played. But we got away with it, people loved it.

Roberta Bayley	That was the night they tried to keep me out of the concert for being a CIA agent. Paul had given me my tickets and then they said the band doesn't want you to see the show. They met us at the door, threw us out of the soundcheck. Once again, we couldn't work out what was going on, something to do with Tom Versade but we couldn't figure what it was. Then it was like a regular rock concert, it's just a big city and a big venue. In a way it was exciting, because it was the Sex Pistols, but there wasn't any challenge, there was no danger, everybody was there because they wanted to see them. So it was different to the other shows, where it was fifty-fifty.
Rory Johnston	The atmosphere was really dark. Malcolm was trying to get this other band on the bill, and Bill Graham didn't want to add another act to the show, and I was trying to deal with that. We got the Avengers on, but we wanted Pere Ubu to do the first half of the tour. We hooked up with a zydeco band for New Orleans. Sid was turned off completely on the night. It was just Steve and Paul really. We switched Sid off completely, as soon as he started going to pieces.
Sophie Richmond	They played brilliantly, it was very powerful and a huge place, everybody reacted very well, though obviously the problems with Sid drove everyone to despair. It did seem funny to me, at the time, that they should come to the heart of hippy land and be defeated, in a sense.
V. Vale	For all of us, we had all read a lot about the Sex Pistols in the British press, we had a whole set of expectations, a whole scenario. We knew he would try to make fun of San Francisco, that he would spit on them metaphorically if not literally. We knew that he doesn't come to praise but to (attempt to) destroy. And you had the Winterland as setting for this little psycho-drama, which is this huge cavernous hall, the very opposite of the intimacy of punk that we had experienced. We talking January 1978, after only one year of punk in San Francisco, which was very personal, very intimate—and of course we got what we expected, which was a totally alienated concert, someone screaming something in an English accent, which is hard, by the way, for Americans to understand. You had the very thing which the Sex Pistols supposedly set out to critique, you had a spectacle, and I don't know if there is a way you can defeat a set of expectations by being a band playing on a stage about ten feet above the audience, with bouncers, burly jock-like characters hired to stop people getting onto the stage. That was unheard of at the Mabuhay, anyone could go onstage any time they wanted. You wouldn't do it, really, but you didn't have any 200lb security guard standing there to keep you off. There was oppressive, police state kind of atmosphere, and we'd already heard all the songs and deciphered all the lyrics, and read his interviews, and it was exactly what I thought it would be. It was a zombie performance, people who were already dead, re-animated for a while, going through their motions. They were media-saturated, they'd run out of message to deliver. But there were people who were so dense, these fifteen-watt lightbulb people, somebody was buying those T-shirts, with Sex Pistols slogans from eleven years ago. There was a terrible PA set up. It was inadequate. The sound people were probably third string Bill Graham technicians who were in contempt of the musicians. I saw them, with ponytails down to their waists, and you could tell they had total contempt, they thought it was all noise. Their ears couldn't differentiate the basic components of rock guitar band music, plus vocal. To me it was a generic experience.
Legs McNeil	I was there at Winterland, their last show. It was the worst rock 'n' roll show I've ever seen. The sound was terrible, the place was too big, nobody was having any fun on that tour, everyone was completely miserable, I just didn't want to be around them. I went backstage and watched them. Sid was sitting there going, "Who's going to fuck me tonight?" I was really jealous that they were paying attention to Sid, but of course they were rock stars. Really beautiful teenage girls, black leathers, prime fucking condition, and Sid didn't look like he even knew how to undress them! "Who's going to fuck me tonight?" And this girl's saying, "Don't I even get a kiss first?" Then there was Paul and Steve, going, you know, "Who's got the can opener?" Looking like they could have been working a gas station and been happy all their lives. And Annie Leibowitz there to take a picture, with her assistant, wearing a black leather jacket. *Rolling Stone* does a punk story! It was so pathetic. She wanted a picture of the whole band and nobody would get up. That was real funny. They never seemed to drop it. The Ramones would do that for the press, then they would drop it and have a good time, but the Sex Pistols didn't seem to know who to trust. All Americans were all Americans, there was no distinction. They finally got John in the bathroom. "Is my hair all right?" Being an obnoxious asshole. You

felt like asking them if they wanted to split for a beer, but the Sex Pistols would just stay... they never dropped the pose. Can you imagine if you hung out with Jerry Lewis and he acted that goofy all the time? You'd say, "Fuck you, Jerry." Or whoever. The Three Stooges. I didn't wanna be around them, that's all I knew. They weren't having fun, I just wanted out of there. The only funny guy was Malcolm. I told him he should go try and get Nixon re-elected. He said, "Who are you?" But they were so obnoxious, so British. It was like, Arthur Tree Turtle becomes a punk, you know? It seemed like they were into class and stuff, and punk wasn't about the class system, they were being totally arrogant without humor. They just weren't fun.

John Tiberi   This was the biggest gig they'd ever done, and Mr. Warner Brothers turned up, Bob Regehr. He's in the hotel, talking about the gig with Malcolm, rock 'n' roll rapport, and I'm not really involved, but essentially the issue of where Rotten is, is not part of anything. Nobody's paying any attention. My next clear memory is of going out of this place... that's the beginning of it. It's come from John, directly. John said, "I don't want to stay with the rest of them." This is what I'm told by Noel. As far as I remember, he gave me the address. I'm getting mixed signals, they don't really want me to know, this is a management matter, or something. I don't think Malcolm was letting on if he had noticed. Regehr was just swanning the whole thing.

Joe Stevens   They had to do eleven gigs in two weeks in the States. The next gig booked was in Stockholm. It would have given them about five days to rest up after flying back from San Francisco. Then a Scandinavian tour, I think. McLaren gets this brainstorm: why don't we go to Rio and see Ronnie Biggs? I was the only one in the touring party who had ever been to Rio, so that qualified me for a ticket. So when they went to Bob Regehr, they got eight first-class round-trip tickets. I still have my ticket, San Francisco to Rio, Rio to New York. One of the riders in Rotten's contract was that Warners had to get them into the country to do their shows, and get them out to their chosen destination, wherever in the world that is. Their tickets said Rio, Stockholm, London, and they were back where they'd started out, end of contractual obligations. So I'm on the phone, cooking up McLaren's business. Meanwhile, Rotten is not staying at the hotel, nor is Sid. They wouldn't let Sid in, anyway, So they didn't even try, Warners said they'd put him in another hotel, they were staying in San Jose.

Rotten wasn't told anything about Rio. He rings McLaren's room and he gets me. McLaren is snoring. He had an idea he was being kept in the dark, about everything, and I broke the news to him. I said, "The plan is, you do Winterland, then the next day we all take a six or seven AM flight to Rio, stop off at Mexico City, and do some gigs down there, hang out with Ronnie Biggs, the Great Train Robber." He said, "What? They expect me to sit in a first class compartment with Sid Vicious, to go and fuck around with this guy who beat someone almost to death with a club? I'm not going." He says, "I like sushi and I'm not staying in a nice Japanese hotel like the rest of you cunts. Is Sidney there?" He didn't know where Sid was, there were three hotels. We were in the Miyako, Rotten was in a flea-bag, and Sid was in another one. Actually, I think they let Sid go to Haight Ashbury and watched over him with those girls.

So I said to John, "Why don't I talk to McLaren, I think it's a tragedy, I don't think this has to happen. Maybe rather then getting you guys all pissed off, we should cancel this Rio business. But I'm not the manager here, it's not my business." So I tell McLaren that Rotten wants nothing to do with Rio, nothing to do with Ronnie Biggs. He doesn't think there'll be enough time to do everything and get back to London. McLaren says, "Well, fuck that cunt." They do the gig, it's a disaster. There's a party backstage afterwards, Rotten picks up a girl, brings her back to San Jose, to the motel. We've got another day before Rio.

Rotten calls again from San Jose, gets me again. I tell him I have tickets for him and me, a seven AM flight, and that Warner Brothers security were going to come and get him, and pick up Sid, and we'd all meet at San Francisco airport. It seemed like it was going to happen because Rotten's complaining wasn't having any effect on everyone's plans.

15 JANUARY 1978

Joe Stevens   The next morning, me and Steve and Sophie and Paul get into a taxi for the airport. We never saw Rotten, McLaren, Boogie, or Sid. We saw the flight take off, and we drove back. I've got pictures of them, sleeping in the back. At that point we knew something nasty was about to happen. Lydon had taken a taxi from the San Jose hotel. Initially he'd refused to leave his hotel room, wouldn't go to the airport. When he found out where we were staying, he gets into a taxi and shows up on his own at the Miyako. This is the emergence of Johnny Rotten as a man. He's about to be fired from the band, and he's doing things on his own. He's years away from getting his own cheque book, but this is the first time I'd seen him actually take charge. He's in a foreign country, taking taxis, on his own, dealing in the currency.

John Lydon   The American tour, it was awful. None of us were talking, I had to keep Sid away from drugs, so I had to stay with him on the coach. Steve and Paul were being flown around with Malcolm, booking themselves into better hotels. We had major rows because I was writing different songs, I wrote Religion during the American tour, and Malcolm said, "Oh, no, that's bad for the image, can't do things like that." I wanted to get them away from three chord rock 'n' roll into something a bit more spicy. They wanted to do what Malcolm wanted them to do.

Steve Jones   John wanted to carry on. He was saying, "Let's get rid of McLaren." I was sick of the band, I was saying, "I'm gonna piss off with McLaren, I'm going to Brazil and do something with Biggsy," just to get away from that scene, I was sick and tired of it. My mind was made up, and Paul just followed. The American tour was what really done it, if anything. We weren't talking to one another, there was a lot of needling going on between the band. It was horrible. It used to be a laugh.

Paul Cook   Me and Steve were at the Japanese hotel with Malcolm and John was out of town somewhere. Malcolm had a word with John. Malcolm looked really ill at the end of that tour, it was just getting too much. We just said, "I don't know how much longer we can carry on like this."

Rory Johnston   Sid ran away, we couldn't catch him. We'd checked into the hotel in San Francisco under my name, because the hotel had told Warner Brothers the Sex Pistols couldn't stay there. Rotten was stuck out in a motel somewhere, really pissed off. The next day nobody could find Sid, we finally found him at this girl Lamarr's place, right on the corner of Haight Ashbury, he overdosed the next day. Boogie and I found him just as he'd shot up, he was starting to turn blue. I thought, "So this is how it's going to end, Sid's going to die right here on Haight Ashbury." We tried to walk him around, I went off to find Malcolm, to get a doctor from Bill Graham, I got Boogie to talk to Noel Monk. The doctors arrived and injected him, he started to revive... Sid showed up on the night of the gig with a load of kids, trying to get money out of Malcolm. I think he smacked him actually, right in a hotel room full of people. Rotten went off to the motel... I think he came back to the hotel the day after the gig, or the day after that, the day after the OD. Malcolm was now insisting they go to Brazil. Warners wanted them to go back and do these other dates, I wanted them to do that too, but Malcolm wasn't having it, he said Warners were sucking the life out of the band.

Joe Stevens   So, he shows up. McLaren is still crashed out upstairs. McLaren used to spend about two hours a day awake. If there was a gig or something, then he'd go right back to bed again. Which was very weird. Rotten walks into the restaurant, and there's Steve and Cook and me. We're having Japanese food and drinking lots of beers. We'd gone up to Steve's room, smoking joints. What could we do? He didn't show up. We were sure it wasn't going to be Rotten's fault, it was going to be Sid's fault. They could find Sid dead or something. We hadn't heard yet.

The three have a talk. Steve's saying John was stupid, that they should have gone to Rio. Cook was sort of agreeing. So I say, why don't we go up and see McLaren, catch the magic two hours before he goes back to sleep again. And we went upstairs, and that was the break-up. They sensed that the manager wanted nothing to do with it. Cook and Jones were very pro-McLaren, but they saw there was no way to get McLaren going on this anymore, he wanted nothing to do with the band, and Steve just said, "Well, that's it, I'm pissing off." And that was that.

John said, "You're a miserable stupid cunt, you've been stitching me up ever since you met me. With the police, with people beating me up, robbing me, calling my house in the middle of the night, annoying me, telling lies about me to the press. And now you want me to sit on a plane with Sid Vicious for hours, you stupid cunt. To talk to some idiot who coshed somebody on a train."

McLaren said, "You're turning into another fucking Rod Stewart, we don't need you, go and find some cocaine." It was bitter. And there's me walking around saying, "I'll book the guys into Madison Square Garden, two dollars a head, two nights." I know the rental is seventy thousand dollars, I can get it from the mob. They're looking at me—because at that point they didn't really know what Madison Square Garden was. And I could have done it.

John Tiberi   John came over to the hotel, in a room, and Malcolm went in and came out again, and that was about it. Steve and Paul were in another room and Sid OD'd. I had to drive back to the hotel. One of the kids he'd found, same tactic, phoned me up, because they knew what hotel it was, because they were groupies. They said, "You better come and find us." An easy address: the corner of Haight Ashbury! Talk about irony. It was a squat, and he was going blue on a mattress on the floor. I picked him up and walked him around, and he was very lifeless. Those fucking kids... it wasn't their fault, and they were pissed off. They were brats, they didn't live there, it was just a shooting gallery for rich kids. They got this alternative doctor type person, a very powerful kind of guy, and we drove him up to Marin County to this doctor's place, and gave him acupuncture. This was in the morning, when I got back to the hotel Rotten had arrived back. Sid was asleep. I had to go back there and Sid was waking up, looking like he'd never even been in the Sex Pistols. Suddenly the whole weight of the thing has hit him. "Oh right, yeah, I got to get out of here." I think Steve came up there with me.

17 JANUARY 1978   Sex Pistols split up

Paul Cook   The problem was, we were due to tour in Sweden straight after, and nobody fancied it after America. We should have just canceled it, rested for a few months. There was no way that was going to happen, so we split up instead. Malcolm was trying to set up this thing in Rio, and we were into it. I was anyway, but John wasn't, and Sid OD'd somewhere in San Francisco. Some girl turned up crying her eyes out, and me and Steve rushed over there, Sid was laid out on the floor, the doctors had just got there, girl punks crying all round him. I thought, "Oh God." Then he was in hospital... There was no way we could have gone on tour anyway, with Sid like that. We went to see John and he turned up with Joe Stevens, and we just said, "We can't handle this anymore, we're going to Rio, are you coming?" And he had a talk with Malcolm and he didn't want to go, for some reason. So we went down there, and had a great time.

John Tiberi   The next day we all went out separate ways. Steve and Paul flew to Los Angeles. I went with Sophie to Los Angeles to wait for my connecting flight, for my ticket, with Sid. I think John went to New York. We went to a doctor who prescribed some methadone pills, then we got the plane to New York. A red-eye, probably, and Sid flaked out, he must have had something else too, he just didn't wake up. We were in first class, too. We took him in an ambulance to a hospital and they plugged him in, and he'll be okay. It was a drug induced coma, which was a pretty big deal, I suppose. It wasn't an OD. Then it snowed, everything was snowed in, even the roads.

Rory Johnston   Steve and Paul went straight off down to Brazil, they came to LA, stayed a few days and then off they went for a holiday and to meet with Ronnie Biggs. Malcolm had never been to Brazil, he didn't know what the fuck he was going to go on down there. It was underway because Malcolm saw Biggs as this Robin Hood character. There was another plan to go to Finland. But it got out of control, he let Rotten get so alienated for that critical moment. He didn't have to do that, even though Rotten may have hated his guts, he would have come around. He just felt abandoned by the whole thing, and Malcolm should never have let that happen. He had no emotional follow-through, he gets things rolling, and then pulls back.

Malcolm set it up for Jones and Cook to tell Rotten he was fired. It shouldn't have happened like that. Even if Sid was incapable of carrying on, Rotten and Cook and Jones should have kept it going. But at that time all Malcolm was interested in was the film, and Brazil, and Ronnie Biggs, the next buzz, which wasn't a very feasible proposition when you think about it. It was going to be a novelty at best. But Rotten didn't want to go to Brazil, because it wasn't real, it wasn't what he was meant to be doing. It wasn't an essential ingredient in the Sex Pistols saga that Ronnie Biggs get involved in it. It was a nice idea maybe, but it wasn't that important in itself.

Roadent	While they were away, there was a call at the rehearsal studios from the *Sun*: "Is it true you've been banned from Finland?" I phoned up the Finnish Ambassador's office, which is listed in the phone book, thinking I'd get some flunkey, and I got the Finnish Ambassador on the phone. I said, "What's this about us being persona non grata in Finland?" Apparently it was true. They were supposed to go straight to Finland from America, but that didn't happen, and then I heard the band had split up. Me and Jamie went out and got blind drunk, and we made up this press statement which apparently the *Guardian* printed, which we later withdrew on Malcolm's orders, he was worried it was libelous or something.

We went down to the 100 Club and all these people were crying. We bought three bottles of blue label vodka between three of us, me and Jamie and Sue [Steward], and went and celebrated, there was a lot of tension. I was given orders, keep it quiet. Jamie would remember better than me. It was in the *Guardian* though, I think they were the only people who printed it. Typically Nicolas de Jongh or whoever it was. The crew of the PA and the lighting company had got onto the plane to fly to Stockholm, all the equipment was over there and then I was told to cancel the tour, to get what money we could back, and the crew were paged off the plane. They were well pissed off because they had to give their duty frees in.

18 JANUARY 1978

John Lydon	They left me with no plane ticket, no money, and no way of getting home. I called up Warners and they said, "Oh no, we know it's not you, Malcolm told us you've gone back to England." Great.
Joe Stevens	The Sex Pistols had broken up, we're back in my apartment, a big blizzard is covering New York, and Forcade lived round the corner, gets my number. The *New York Post* printed this article, picked up from the *Sentinel / Sun*: "The Sex Pistols broke up in San Francisco the other night, Sid Vicious OD'd and he's in a hospital in Queens, Malcolm McLaren doesn't want to speak to the press, Warner Brothers in New York wants nothing to do with the whole case. Johnny Rotten is staying in the apartment of his friend Joe Stevens in New York." So, all of a sudden my apartment becomes real popular with the press. I was doing press briefings on the steps.

Rotten was staying at my house, Forcade is round the corner, he calls me. I'm screening calls for the guy, he's just lost the best job he ever had. He's still a young man, he's never been to New York, he's freezing. My apartment's heat's been cut off. We don't have any money because this lab is suing me. They didn't leave him with any money. Forcade says, "I can take care of that right away, I can come around with a shoe box full of greenbacks, all he has to do is sign a release for whatever we want to use in the movie." His part of whatever licensing for his appearance. I said, "I don't know, I'll have to talk to him about it. What kind of money are we talking about?"

He said, "Well, this is what I want." He stated what he wanted, and said, "That is worth fifteen thousand dollars, I'll bring it over." So I tell John, and John says, "No fucking way. I don't need that money now, I'll need it at another point." He was so smart. I wasn't pushing him on, but switch it around, I would have gone for it. The movie came out anyway.

Anyway, we got in the car, and on the radio we hear, "From Jamaica Queens Hospital, we have an interview with Sid Vicious!" We go up to Spanish Harlem, I have this punk girlfriend, the bass player from the Erasers, pick her up and we're driving around with Rotten in the back, smoking drugs and drinking beer, listening to Sid doing interviews from the hospital. Amazing. They had yet to play New York.

He was snowed in, they couldn't get flights out, so, five days. I said, "John, you're a Warner Brothers recording artist. Do you mind if I call my connections at Warner Brothers, they could put us onto bigger people, and then they can send some idiot down with some money. You can pay me back what you owe me, I can cook, we'll have some money for pot." So I did it, and they stonewalled him, they wouldn't have anything to do with Rotten, at all. They didn't know which one they wanted. Which punk, which little dirt-bag. You know who it was who was in charge of stonewalling us? Liz Rosenberg. I see her name in print every fucking day now.

| **20 JANUARY 1978** | **Roberta Bayley calls Sid in Jamaica Hospital, Queens and records the call** |

Al Clark — The diminuendo for me happened later when they broke up in America. After that, despite the numerous records that were released under their name, it did have a very ritualized quality. It was mostly to do with Sid's habit, and peripheral aspects. It was always Sid and Nancy at the Inverness Court Hotel, it was always to do with Sid, really.

EARLY FEBRUARY 1978 — **Steve Jones and Paul Cook Rio recording sessions for two tracks with Ronnie Biggs, "No One Is Innocent" and "Belsen Was A Gas." Filming is also done with Biggs and actor Henry Rowland playing "Martin Bormann."**

Al Clark — The one Glitterbest contradiction that I found a bit tricky, for all Malcolm's barrow boy persuasiveness, was the one that used swastikas so much, and the Nazi references. They would always say they were trying to demystify it, and bring it out into the open and all that kind of stuff. Essentially it had rather a nasty aftertaste, and having that guy dress up as Martin Bormann, and Sid with his Nazi T-shirt, I know that he walked through the Jewish quarter of Paris with it on, a Situationist act. I wonder how many times Sid just did acts of stroppiness, and then Malcolm thought he was being Situationist... but no, I didn't like the Biggs single.

LATE MARCH 1978 — **Recording sessions in Paris for Sid Vicious's "My Way" single**

John Tiberi — After the split, I'm the only guy who can look after Sid, and that aspect comes into Paris. Malcolm hasn't got any money to make this film, Warners aren't signing any more cheques. Sid was all we had left of the Pistols at that point, and I didn't want to go. I got on with them all. I didn't get on with Julien. I like the guy, but I don't like the way he thinks he has to work. I didn't go. They phoned me up and asked me to come, and Malcolm is very difficult to say no to... they've got meetings, and they don't know what to do. The first meeting is in the bar at the hotel, talking about the footage they've already got, which is fuck all. It was a dodgy time, he'd run out of steam. We were talking about "Belsen Was A Gas," as a single. They weren't too keen on that, Fabrice and the other guy. We've got a nice catalogue! Johnny Halliday... and that was how "My Way" came up. Malcolm liked it because it got the French going. Who's going to tell Sid? Sid isn't so sure, but we worked it around him. The development of the scene was worked out between Julien and myself, and Sid and Malcolm. But when it came to the actual shooting of it, Sid worked it out himself. We did a rehearsal, and it was great, and we said, "Okay, can you just... " and he did it again, exactly the same. He knew exactly. He had great intuition about cameras. He understood perfectly.

29 APRIL 1978 — **John Lydon sends a letter to Glitterbest demanding a statement of accounts: this is beginning of a long and tortuous court case that would not be resolved until 1986.**

John Lydon — Not only did they leave me stranded in America, but when I came back they wouldn't talk to me at all. That was the situation and the only way around it was the courts. As soon as I got back. I got no joy out of them at all. All of them, the whole staff wouldn't talk to me, it was ridiculous, really petty. A sort of, "You're not in our gang anymore," that kind of attitude. Because I didn't go to Rio, apparently. I wasn't even asked to go to Rio. The band didn't know that, they were told something completely different. They were told that I'd refused to go. Very sad.

Everything was with held from me, all monies, everything. It was a ridiculous situation. I was literally stranded. Enter Brian Carr.

27 MAY 1978 — ***NME* front cover, interview by Neil Spencer with John Lydon's new group, Public Image Ltd.**

30 JUNE 1978 — **Release of the Sex Pistols fourth Virgin single, "No One Is Innocent (A Punk Prayer by Ronald Biggs)"/ "My Way" (VS220). It stays in the charts for ten weeks, reaching number 7.**

Al Clark — I didn't like the Biggs single. I liked "My Way" a lot, but that was the side that I played. Now there was an icon that needed demolishing—possibly the most narcissistic song of all time, closely followed by "I Write The Songs"—I write the songs, I am the songs!—so I suppose the play element took over, from then on it was pure play, what could we do next to get up people's noses, now there isn't a group?

I remember ringing up Biggs once. I called him up to ask him if he would do a few interviews on the phone to promote the single, and he said, "Well, I don't want to do anything until I'm paid some money," and I said, "Well, what money? What are you owed?" He said, "I did this deal with Malcolm and he hasn't paid me yet." I said, "Oh I see, well, we can't pay you, legally or even technically, because we're a company and we can't send money to a man called Ronald Biggs in Brazil." And he said, "Well, do you think I'm due some then?" I said, "I expect you are, you're entitled to some royalties unless you've signed everything over to Malcolm." He asked me, "Where did the record get to? I understand that if you get into the top five you get a house and a car." That was such a gloriously late-fifties pop star's mother and father talking. I said, "No you don't, you just get some money." And he said, "Look, why don't you bring the money over to Rio in a suitcase, and when you get here you'll have the best time of your life." This sounded promising. Anyway the whole thing was in the hands of the Receiver by then, and so Ron just got whatever Malcolm gave him on the spot, and nothing more.

MAY–JULY 1978	**Reworking of Goodman demos for *The Great Rock 'n' Roll Swindle* soundtrack: "No Lip," (I'm Not Your) Stepping Stone," "Substitute," "Road Runner/Johnny B Goode," "Whatcha Gonna Do About It."**
AUGUST 1978	**Filming *The Great Rock 'n' Roll Swindle***
28–30 SEPTEMBER 1978	**Sid Vicious plays Max's with a pick up band including Jerry Nolan, Arthur Kane, and Steve Dior. These shows form the basis of the *Sid Sings* album, released December 1979.**
12 OCTOBER 1978	**Sid Vicious arrested for Nancy Spungeon's murder at the Chelsea Hotel, New York. On the next day he is granted bail. Malcolm McLaren flies to New York.**

Joe Stevens   I went there. Nancy was still in the bag. They were talking to Sid in another room. They took him to a downtown police station, I never did find out. As soon as I had the chance, I called McLaren in London, who was prepared to fly out that very moment. He alerted Ma Vicious, she showed up about twenty-four hours after he did.

The legal people who handled Sex Pistols business in America, Prior Braun Cashman and Sons, they were entertainment lawyers, they didn't know shit about criminal law. They had the case, and they sent some guy down to the courts, and McLaren and I show up in court for the bail hearing. This entertainment lawyer got Sid out on fifty thousand dollars' bail, after he's been accused of killing an American citizen. I couldn't believe that an entertainment lawyer swung that. Something fishy happened there, but I wasn't keeping track of it all. I think there was a bribe. I don't think McLaren really knew what was going on. I think maybe the lawyers had some friends in the criminal division of the courts, and they decided to pull a string. A kid called Sid Vicious, looking like that, from the Sex Pistols, just got out on bail? What is going on? No-one ever tracked it down.

Anne Beverley   Malcolm could never be a friend of mine, I didn't like the guy, but I could never put him down the way other people have, because I think he was as much carried along as everyone else. He couldn't handle it. One ought to feel sorry for him, rather than castigate him. He's bananas, really. Sid knew he was selfish and careless, and he loved him for it.

16 OCTOBER 1978   **Anne Beverley arrives in New York and visits Sid Vicious in Riker's Island prison.**

Anne Beverley   He was very down. Perhaps I was the most unfortunate person for him to be with, because I'm really good at advice in a way that people can act on, for somebody who's in deep trouble, to someone who doesn't matter that much to me. I can communicate if I'm not involved. If I love someone, I can't talk, I can hold them, stroke their hair, but I can't talk, because I'm so frightened of saying the wrong thing, I don't know why.

It was an absolute nightmare. I was rushing round, because when people make a statement it has to be signed by a notary, and I was gathering statements. People were very good to me. I found New York rather depressing, but that could have been the state I was in. I could hear people screaming at night, and thinking, "Somebody's being murdered," practically every night. But I met nothing but kindness, from all and sundry.

It took hours to visit anybody. Visiting day would come around and you'd get out there at ten o'clock in the morning and sometimes you were lucky if you got to see your visitor by three in the afternoon. I think he was all right. I was very worried, because being called Sid Vicious, somebody's going to want to have a go. But there again, they used to let him sit in the corridor under a light, and read a book, because he couldn't sleep at night. Things like that. He made me laugh once, he said the governor wanted his autograph, for his daughter.

17 OCTOBER 1978   **Sid Vicious granted bail.**

22 OCTOBER 1978   **Sid Vicious attempts suicide and is hospitalized at Bellevue.**

Joe Stevens   They put him with his mom, he's got to get his passport, got to go for urine tests, when you go for methadone. So, he's got to watch what he takes. He's staying in this flea bag hotel, Seville Hotel, uptown, like a welfare hotel. So he's there, McLaren is crashed out on my couch. Sid hates staying with his mom. I'd taken pictures of him standing with his mom, and he looks real uncomfortable.

I get a call in the middle of the night, Ma Vicious. "Joe, is Malcolm there? You got to wake him up. You've got to get over here right away, Sid's done something to himself." So I wake up McLaren, we go flying uptown, we get to the hotel room and there's Ma Vicious, doing circles. There's Sid on one of the twin beds, in the corner, near the window, and he's opened up one of his arms, but he's done it the wrong way. He's done it with a throw away razor, just stomped on it with his shoe.

He had the same problem Nancy had, they were haemophiliacs. If you're a junkie, your kidneys and liver don't heal, so you bleed to death. Nancy bled to death out of negligence. She hadn't been murdered, the incision was only half an inch. That's a little-known fact. The prosecution was going to have a hard time convicting him of first-degree murder, when it was revealed that the wound was a half-inch incision below the navel. If you want to kill somebody, you'll have to cut them up. This was not a real murder.

So there he was on the bed, and I'd been out the day before on an assignment, with my micro cassette recorder and camera, doing something. It was still in the bag, and I took it out of the trunk of the car. I didn't take any pictures of Sid at that time, he was close to death, mom doing the spins. Malcolm goes over to the bed and says, what have you done this for? We were going to get you out of jail, you stupid cunt. We're both thinking he's on his death bed.

Sid is saying to Malcolm, "You've got to get me something to finish me off. Get me some Quaaludes." So Malcolm says to Sid, "I'll get you some Quaaludes, don't worry." And what he's really doing is going up to the payphone and calling an ambulance—Ma Vicious hadn't done that yet. He calls Bellevue Hospital, quite close to where the Seville was, leaving me on the second bed, my bag between my legs, and I lean over and say, "Why the fuck you wanna do that? McLaren is busting his chops, the record company is coming up with all the money to get you out of jail"—because I thought I was talking to the soon-to-be late Sid Vicious.

He just said, "I want to be with my Nancy, I want to be left alone. I don't want to talk to any more New York City policemen. I don't want to be with my mum," he says. "I'd rather be in the hospital ward on Riker's Island than be with my mum. I hate that cunt."

9 DECEMBER 1978   **Sid Vicious assaults Todd Smith, brother of Patti, at Hurrah's, and is taken back to Riker's Island the next day for breaking the terms of his bail.**

25 DECEMBER 1978   **Public Image Ltd. play their first UK date at the Rainbow Theatre, London.**

Sid Vicious is released from Riker's Island. A celebratory party is held at the flat of his girlfriend, Michele Robinson. Sometime during the night he dies of a heroin overdose.

Paul Cook   Just before [Sid] died, me and Steve were going to fly out to New York to do an album with him, to raise some money for his court case. Some standards, and write some new songs. Sid was actually quite a good singer, a performer.

Joe Stevens   I think he was in there over the Christmas holidays, they cleaned him up beautifully: vitamins, sleep, he no longer has scabs on his arms, he puts on a bit of weight. I hadn't visited him on this one, he's bottling people. I hear that he's being released on bail the next day, and I introduced him to a girl called Michelle Robinson, and he walks into Max's and it's, "Hey Joe, buy me an Amaretto and cream," a favorite junky drink. So I went for that, and he starts hitting on this girl that I'm with. I warned her, he might give you a fuck, but he might kill you. I knew he'd probably go right to her house when he got bail. He did.

I didn't know what Ma Vicious was preparing; I wasn't part of that crowd, didn't want to be. She knew he was getting out, she got his favourite meal together, spaghetti bolognese, and she figures he's going to want to score, so she calls up the dealer, a British guy living in New York, I'd rather not say who. So Nolan and all these guys are there, and they're eating spaghetti bolognese, about five or six people walking around the room, Sidney's looking great, and the smack arrives, and the dealer says there's a problem with the smack, its one hundred percent. Five weeks before it was unheard of, no-one is selling 100% smack, but something happened to the smack scene during that time, and it was 100% pure. Sid says, get outta here, but the dealer says, please, just take a little bit, and Sid takes a little bit, but just before he adds water to it, he adds a little bit more. He turns blue, lost respiration, what they describe as bouncing against walls, having trouble breathing—but survives, doesn't die.

The party disperses, Ma Vicious on the couch, Sid and Michelle in her bed in the back room. In the middle of the night he gets up, apparently goes to Ma's Purse, grabs the smack, shoots up a load, goes back to bed and dies. She wakes up, she's got to get him to a methadone clinic at 9 o'clock—he has an appointment, you can't go cruising into a meth clinic at any time. She tries to wake him, and he's stone dead. They call the police. At this point, I'm leaving my house down town. Walking past a café like this and they have FM radio on, and I hear, "Sid Vicious found dead in girlfriend's Greenwich Village apartment. Stay tuned for more details," so I go down there. I assume that since they're announcing on the radio, they've already removed the body. I should know better, but when I arrived they'd already taken him out, there's a cop outside. I go up the steps and he says, "Get outta here," but Michelle sees me and she gets me in. I didn't take any photographs but I taped some stuff. I thought he would be gone. Ma Vicious is freaking out, Michelle was taking time out from freaking out, then getting back into it again. I said to Michelle, "You know, Hendrix died, and all those people and the story starts to change after a while, so why don't we set the facts down now, and who knows, the truth might just stick." So we go into the bathroom and she tells me the story about the party and everything, and I go back into the living room and I tell the same thing to Ma Vicious, "Be straight with me, I won't fuck you. Keep it straight." She says, "Let's go in the back room where it's quiet." In the back room there's a little table lamp, the bed all rumpled, and I still think Mr. V. is gone, and she tells me how she got her son his final smack. "I thought he was going to buy some anyway, I thought I'd make it easy for him." At this point I don't have much room on the bed so I push something away, and it's Sid's foot, they just put a sheet over him. And there she is, telling me how she bought the smack. That was in the *Express*. Nobody seemed to mind, as long as they got the stories down.

Anne Beverley   We got back to Michelle Robinson's flat in Greenwich Village. I'd invited about eight people. I was going to do a spaghetti bolognese in celebration of Simon getting out. But Michelle's dishes were dirty, and I wasn't gonna wash up and cook the meal, so after a couple of hours I went out and bought the ingredients, did the washing up, cooked the meal. Simon had had a fix early in the day, supplied by this guy called Martin, which had so little in it that it didn't do anything. Then later on, this Martin said he could get some stuff, and I said to Simon, "Look, you've already had some today, I know it didn't do anything for you but you're only out on bail, and if they decide to take a blood test and you come up positive, you could be inside again." He was a well known person. Everybody would recognize him. If I had said no, he would have just walked out, gone and got it himself. So if he did that, he was going to get nicked, because he was Sid. So I had to go along with it.

What are you going to do, put a collar and a lead on somebody, lock them in a room? You can't. So the guy left. I cooked the meal, the guy came back, we all had the meal. Whoever was going to do it went out into the bedroom, and about a quarter of an hour later, they all walked back in, and Simon had a rose pink aura around his whole body. I said, "Jesus, son, that must have been a good hit, or whatever." He was elated, quietly so. Elated on the inside, coming out, creating the aura. I've never seen anything like it before. Five minutes later he went back into the bedroom and someone said, Simon's collapsed. I went in, he was sliding down the bed, what should I do? Should I take him to the hospital, which was just up the road, and say, I think he's OD'd, he's had a fix, can you do anything for him? Next day, he's back in Riker's Island? Do I sit it out and hope he comes around? What do I do?

We put him on his side. Hope he slept it off, which he did. He came round. "Oh fuck, I was so worried about you." He didn't want to go for a walk, and he had to report to the nick in the morning, so I said, "If you don't want to go for a walk, I think we should just go to bed." So they went to bed. I slept on the couch in the sitting room.

That night, after they'd taken it, I said, I'll have the rest of it, thank you very much, I don't want you taking anymore, and I put it in my back pocket, and the next day when the police came in, I saw them turning the place over, I watched them doing it, and it didn't penetrate at all. It wasn't until hours later when I was in the police station, when they said, "Do you think he took some more?" And I said, "No, he couldn't have. They took it for analysis, and it was 93% pure. You never get that on the street. It had come before adulteration. In other words, Martin knew someone who had got it first. The head of the chain.

It would have come out that it was a suicide pact, and she died and he didn't, which made him guilty of manslaughter, and sorry, here's five years, you'll be out in three. Three years in a hard nick in the States? Forget it. He couldn't have done that, because he was not a hard man, he was too sweet and soft. He would never have survived. I'm glad he died, in view of what happened. Nothing can hurt him anymore. And where could he have gone, from where he was at? He couldn't have backed down and done something different, like John Lydon has. There was no way he could have reverted, and been a—a pop singer. He was in a corner. The rug was pulled out from under his feet, and he would never have survived in an English jail, let alone an American one.

7 FEBRUARY 1979
The hearing begins in the Chancery Court re J. Lydon and others versus Glitterbest and Matrixbest.

Joe Stevens   Originally it was Glitterbest against Lydon, which involved Ma Vicious, Cook, Jones, Steven Fisher the crooked lawyer from Glitterbest, and McLaren, against little Johnny. At the very end, Cook and Jones and Ma Vicious had moved over to Rotten's side.

John Lydon   He hadn't produced any accounts whatsoever, and I hadn't received any money. He was claiming that he owned the name and that I didn't deserve any money because I apparently broke contract, which wasn't true, so it went to court to prove exactly that. His initial case against me was absurd in the extreme, it was just character slander, it was nonsense, pure fantasy. He called all kinds of weird and peculiar people to say all kinds of weird and peculiar things. Most unfair.

Paul Cook   I didn't study what was going on, but then we took a neutral position, which was where we were, between John and Malcolm. In retrospect, we should have sided with John right from the beginning, but we were still involved with Malcolm on the film. We weren't interested in court cases, we didn't get into it for all that. It wasn't in our make-up, to sort business problems out. John hated Malcolm he really wanted to take him on. John thought he was being ripped off, and there was this clash all the time.

Steve Jones   I don't remember anything about it. I remember going down to Chancery Lane a couple of times to see these cunts in wigs, but I don't remember anything about it, I was too into dope at that time. I remember I was on Malcolm's side for about half an hour. The last thing I wanted to think about was all that bollocks.

13 FEBRUARY 1979   **Cook and Jones switch sides and lawyers and join Lydon in his suit against McLaren**

Joe Stevens   If you read up the first trial, Steven Fisher, in drawing up the papers to extract Matlock from the band, charged Matlock for the legal papers. They billed Matlock's royalties for the papers to get him out of the group, and the judge, who had done lots of entertainment cases before, looked up and said, "I understand that is highly illegal." The barrister working with Fisher looked up to the judge as if to say, "Jesus, we can't hold this case." They hadn't briefed him properly. McLaren acted irresponsibly in putting Mr. Johnny Rotten out of business. Signed them up at an early age, that he should have been acting as a guardian and was acting as a scoundrel, he was impatient and petulant, and he had no time for what he had started. That's what I said in my piece, and I stick to that.

14 FEBRUARY 1979   **The verdict is delivered: control in Glitterbest / Matrixbest is taken away from McLaren and put in the hands of the receivers Spicer and Pegler.**

19 FEBRUARY 1979   **Release of Virgin single VS 240 "Something Else," an Eddie Cochran cover sung by Sid Vicious. It reaches #3 in the charts, and sells 320,000—becoming the best-selling Sex Pistols single.**

27 FEBRUARY 1979   **Virgin rush releases the album *The Great Rock 'n' Roll Swindle*, which eventually reaches #7 in the charts and stays there for over half a year.**

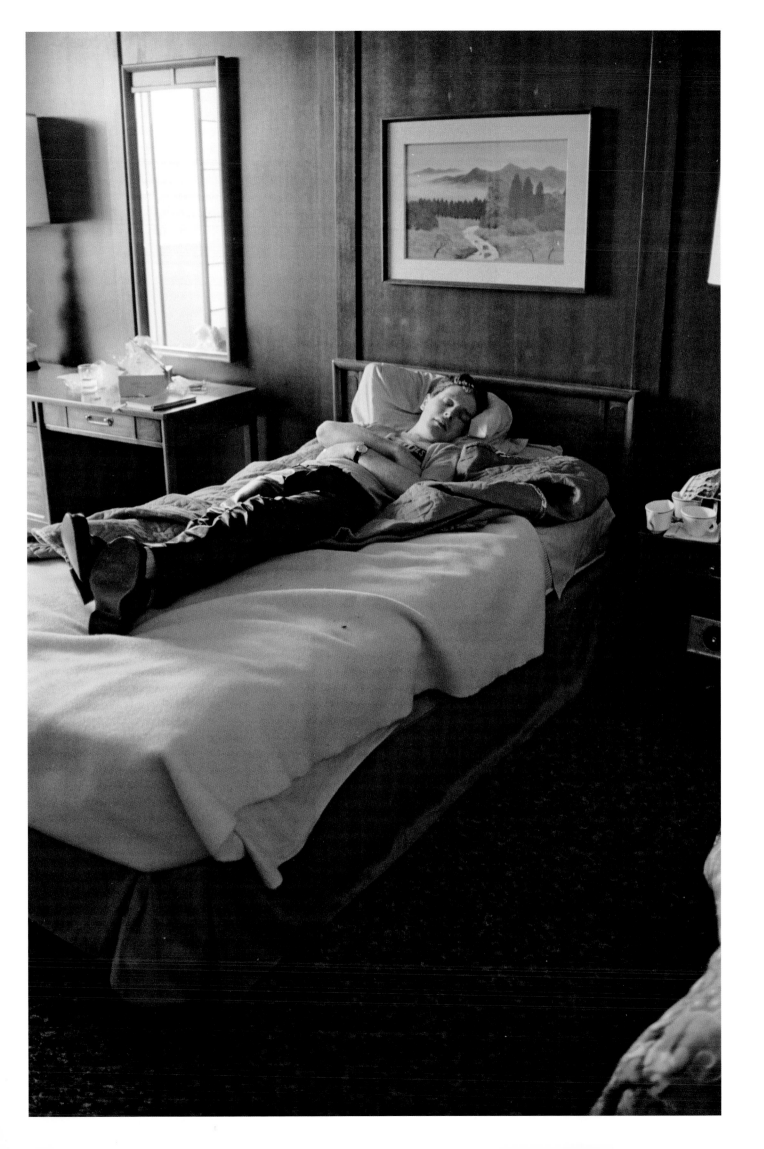

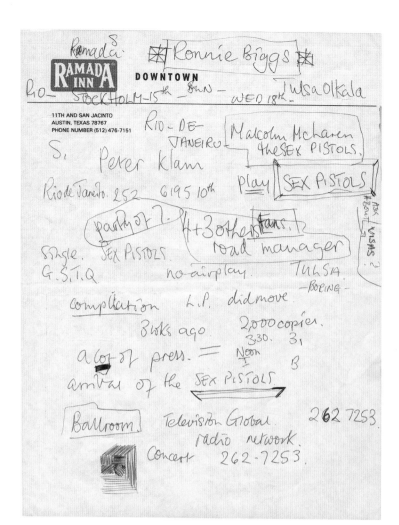

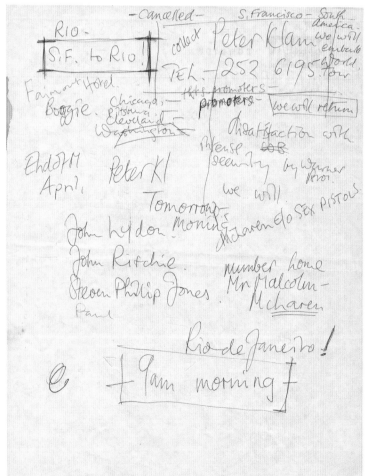

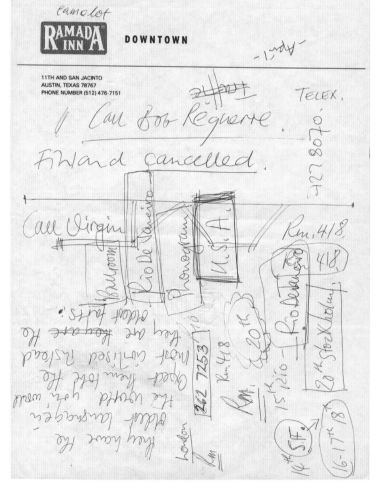

280-281   Malcolm McLaren's notes regarding the
breakup of the band circa the US tour.

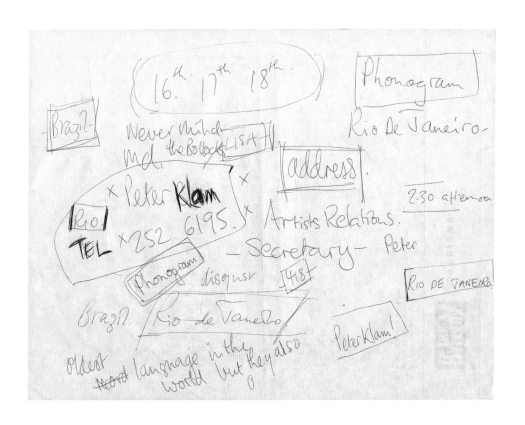

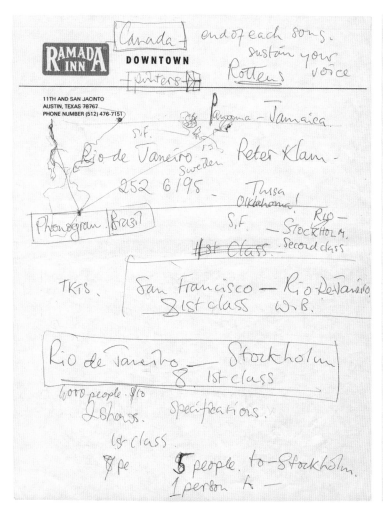

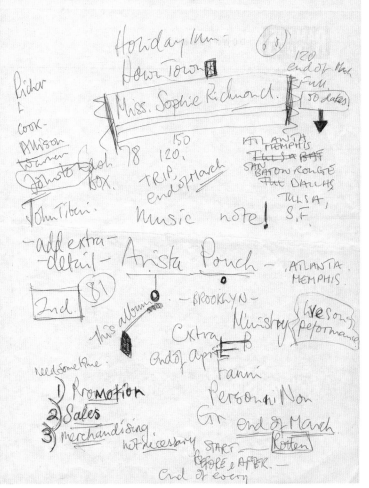

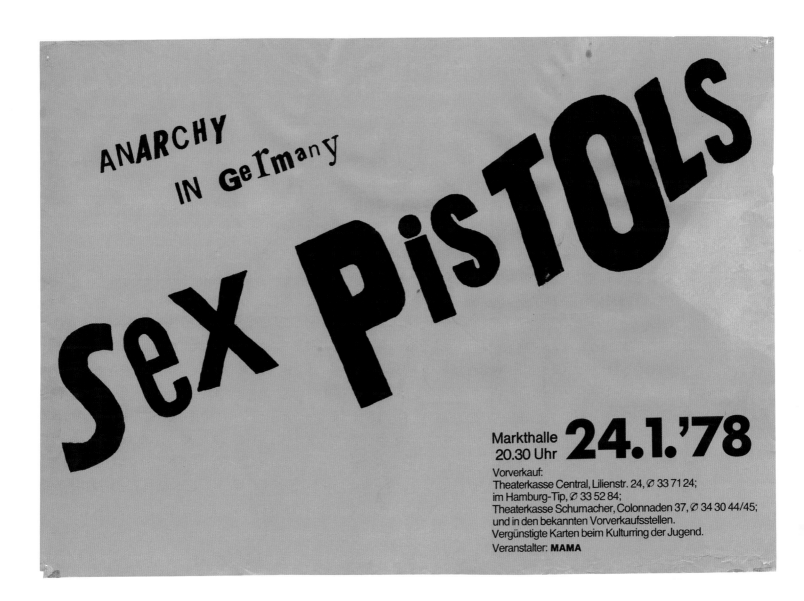

282–283   Posters for shows canceled following the breakup of the band.

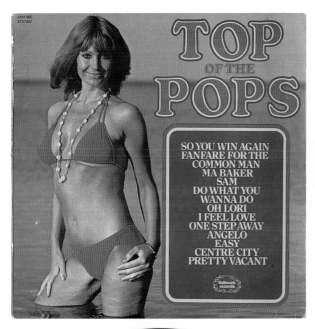

SHM 990
STEREO

TOP OF THE POPS

SO YOU WIN AGAIN
FANFARE FOR THE
COMMON MAN
MA BAKER
SAM
DO WHAT YOU
WANNA DO
OH LORI
I FEEL LOVE
ONE STEP AWAY
ANGELO
EASY
CENTRE CITY
PRETTY VACANT

Hallmark
records

WARNER BROS. RECORDING STUDIOS

45 rpm-stereo   6/23/78
(3:03)

The Sex Pistols

"God Save The Pistols
(Cosh The Driver)"

Warner Bros. Recording Studios • 11114 Cumpston Street • No. Hollywood, Calif. 91601 • 213-846-9090

Creole

Made in
England
Jonjo M. Co. Ltd.
45 RPM
SIDE 1
P 1977
King of
England, B.V.

4 Bank Buildings
High Street
Harlesden
London NW10
England
01-965 9223

CR 139
CR 139A
3.00
Intro: 0.15

GOD SAVE THE SEX PISTOLS
(Arr. King)
ELIZABETH
Produced by J.K.

MANIC RECORDS

Marketed by
Plastic Fantastic Records

A
SIDE
45 RPM
P & © 1979
IMBI/FUNGUS
STEREO

PFUL 1105
PFUL 1105 A
Produced by
Keith Hudson
Mixed by
Tapper Zukie
at Chalk
Farm Studios

PISTOL BOY
(Hudson/Dunn)
MILITANT BARRY

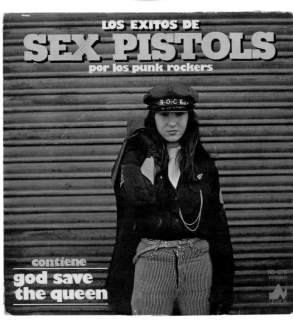

LOS EXITOS DE
SEX PISTOLS
por los punk rockers

contiene
god save
the queen

ND-1276
ESTEREO

LOS EXITOS DE SEX PISTOLS

CARA A   CARA B
HOLIDAYS IN THE SUN   SEVENTEEN
BODIES   ANARCHY IN THE UK
NO FEELINGS   SUBMISSION
LIAR   PRETTY VACANT
GOD SAVE THE QUEEN   NEW YORK
PROBLEMS   E.M.I.

LOS PUNK ROCKERS

284–285   Sex Pistols exploitation records.

284   **ABOVE LEFT:** Pickwick supermarket album with cover version of "Pretty Vacant." **ABOVE RIGHT:** Warner Brothers acetate of "God Save the Pistols." **CENTER LEFT:** Novelty response record of Jonathan King imitating Queen Elizabeth responding to "God Save the Queen." **CENTER RIGHT:** Dub/toast 12" commenting on the Sex Pistols. **BELOW LEFT & RIGHT:** *Los Exitos De Sex Pistols Por Los Punk Rockers*, Spanish supermarket all-cover cash-in version of *Never Mind the Bollocks*, circa 1978.

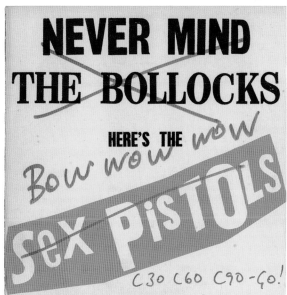

ABOVE: Unused Jamie Reid artwork for *Flogging A Dead Horse*, Virgin Records Sex Pistols cash-in album circa 1979. **CENTER LEFT:** Sex Pistols soundman and demo producer Dave Goodman-produced fake Sex Pistols 12". **CENTER RIGHT:** *Cash Pussies*, 1978. Dave Goodman issued, Fred and Judy Vermorel-produced Situationist commentary on punk, featuring Sid Vicious reading from their book *Sex Pistols*, set to a generic punk-rock backing. **BELOW LEFT & RIGHT:** Bow Wow Wow 12" distributed in *Never Mind the Bollocks* sleeve detourned by Malcolm McLaren, circa 1980.

Incest, torture, murder, sexual assault, bestiality, drug addiction, hepatitis, bad breath, obscenity, lynching, mob violence, piss-soaked furniture, all these things are bad enough. But cruelty to animals is the final straw.

'Ugh!' said Lisa. 'It's horrible. I refuse to have anything to do with this record. That poor little goat! It's got to come off!'
'Come off what?' I asked.
'It's got to come off the cover,' said Lisa
'Do you eat meat?' I asked because I had recently seen Lisa, a girl with a hearty appetite, make very short work of a big steak. There was no risk of getting the wrong answer.
'No, look...' Julie had joined in,'..it's really horrible.'
'They shot it with a crossbow, you know, right through the neck!'
'Horrible!'
'In any case,' I added, 'it's not a goat.'
They all looked at me.
'It's a baby deer. A bambi. They slaughtered Bambi with a crossbow bolt straight through the neck.'

Sue was dreaming. Mick Jagger came straight past her house in a Rolls Royce, driving - or was he being driven - down the narrow lane leading into the heart of the forest. The car stopped - yes! he was being driven because the chauffeur stayed at the wheel - and Jagger got out. He was carrying a crossbow. He wanted to kill something. He seemed to be able to move very quietly. None of the animals could tell he was there. Everyone knew what a good shot he was with the crossbow. Suddenly he stopped. He raised the crossbow and fired immediately. He grinned and ran forwards. Now Sue seemed to be in the Rolls itself. It was moving very quickly through the forest. But the windscreen was red and the bonnet was furry. Perhaps the car was turning into an animal. She didn't like it.
'Get rid of it!' Jagger seemed to say this to the chauffeur. The car stopped and the red faded from the windscreen. The chauffeur was wiping it off. Then the bonnet was metal once more. Relief!

Sue was in a strange, tiny cottage, but one she knew to be her own.She was wearing an odd, almost Tyrolean blose and a prettily embroidered skirt. A largish woman was baking bread. She too was strange, although Sue knew too that this was her mother. For some reason she had been feeling relieved. But now things were beginning to change. She ran out into the garden.

There, by the gate, lay a tiny deer with a huge gash in its throat. Sue screamed. Then, still screaming, she ran back into the house.
'Mummy! Mummy! Someone's killed Bambi! '

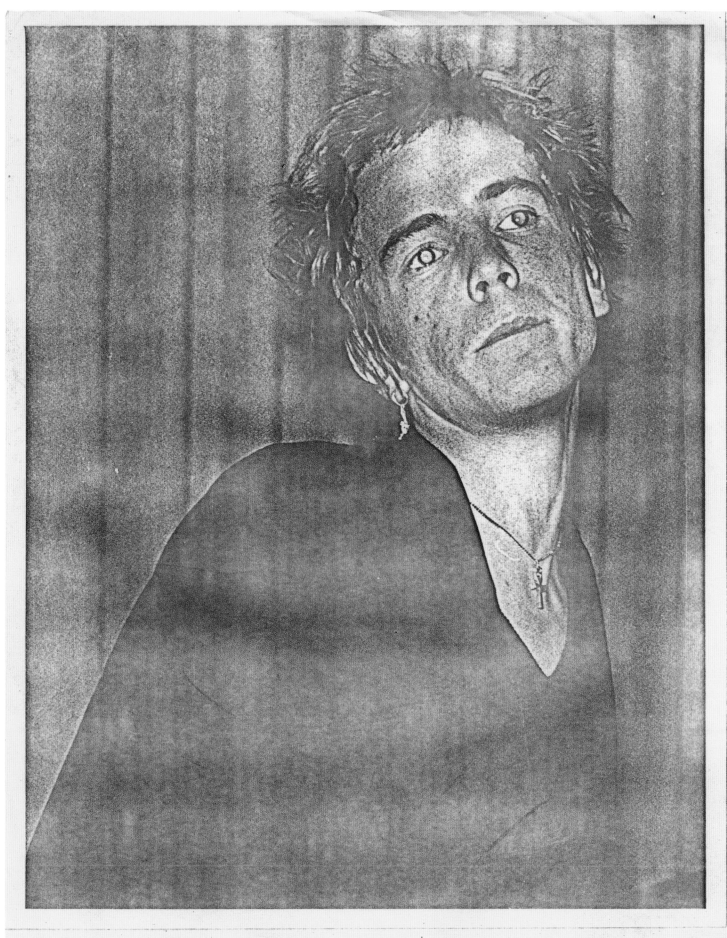

WE ARE ALL
IMBECILES, CROOKS, GIMMICKS
EXILES AND EMBEZZLERS

r. d. March 16, '78

THE SWINDLE

THE SEX PISTOLS ARE AN UNDOUBTED SUCCESS BASED ON AN IDEA CALLED PUNK ROCK, WHICH SETS OUT TO TRAIL BLAZE A PATH OF ANARCHY AND RUIN WITHIN A CULTURE THAT CHOOSES TO DESTROY US BY MAKING OUR DECISIONS FOR US.

PUNK ROCKS CAUSE IS TO CREATE AS MUCH FUSS, HAVOC, EXCITMENT AS POSSIBLE, CRIME PAYS US.

PUNK'S SLOGANS ARE — CASH FROM CHAOS —
— BELIVE IN THE RUINS — NEVER TRUST A HIPPIE —
—ANARCHY IS THE KEY, DO IT YOURSELF IS THE MELODY—
—IN OTHER WORDS, ROT 'N ROLL.

THE MEDIA WAS OUR HELPER AND LOVER AND THAT IN EFFECT WAS THE SEX PISTOLS SUCCESS.
AS TODAY TO CONTROL THE MEDIA IS TO HAVE THE POWER OF GOVERNMENT, GOD, OR BOTH.

IT IS ALL THAT MATTERS TO EXPLAIN OUR GREAT
ROCK 'N ROLL SWINDLE. A TRUE SWINDLE OF IDEAS
THAT GIVES YOU BACK YOUR RIGHT TO DECIDE
FOR YOURSELF.

THE EMBEZZLER

WHO KILLED Bambi

BAMBI IS THE ONE YOU LOVE AND SEX PISTOLS
LOVE ANARCHY!

BAMBI IS UNTAMED INNOCENCE AND AS SUCH
IS ALWAYS A THREAT TO THE POWERS THAT BE—
WHO SEEK TO CONTROL AND CURB INDIVIDUAL
POTENTIAL AND POSSIBILITY.

BAMBI IS IN THE HEART OF EVERY PUNK
ROCKER AND WILL ALWAYS RISE AND STRIKE
AGAIN AND AGAIN AND AGAIN!

Fatty Jones

Chocolate Box

ANARK

PiSS
Lemonade

Vicious BURGER

ANARKEE-ORA

VICIOUS-BURGER

SeX PiSTOLS

POP CORN

popcorn

GOB

Sid Vicious

ACTION MAN

£12·50

E-ORA

ROTTEN bAR

THE GREAT
ROCK 'N' ROLL
SWINDLE
SeX
PisTOLS

Week ending September 1 1956   EVERY THURSDAY

Picturegoer

4d

THE NATIONAL FILM AND ENTERTAINMENT WEEKLY

THE GREAT POP SWINDLE

—by Lonnie Donegan

FILMLAND'S BIGGEST BATTLE YET

you never saw such luxury by DIANA DORS

NILDA TERRACE
—she's rocking on to your screens

18

ROCK'N ROLL— it's a swindle
by LONNIE DONEGAN

STORIES of big swindles hit the headlines daily—and one of the biggest is happening right now on Tin Pan Alley's own doorstep. You won't find it publicised as such. But I'll name it: rock 'n roll.

Yes, I know rock 'n roll is red-hot pop music news. But it's also Big Business for the music moguls. That's why I say the rock 'n roll fans are being taken for a ride.

And who *are* the fans of rock 'n roll? I'll tell you. Youngsters whose musical taste is undeveloped, or those who frankly come into the "tin-ear" category.

Harsh words? Anyone with an atom of musical appreciation would endorse them to the hilt. But just let me go on record as saying that rock 'n roll has no musical value, no variety in sound, nondescript lyrics and a rhythmical beat about as subtle as that of a pile-driver.

Moreover, the majority of the rock 'n roll exponents can't even sing in tune. Yet this is the "music" that is sweeping both the United States and Britain.

Sure, as I've said, a section of the public likes it. But it's only the youngsters who have to be " in the swim." You know, when marbles are the craze—they all play marbles. And rock 'n roll just about comes into the marbles category.

During my tour of the States, I happened to appear on two rock 'n roll shows. The average age of the audience was probably lower than fifteen. Kids of ten and twelve stayed in those shows right through from 1 p.m. to 1 a.m. They brought their own sandwiches and popcorn.

Who can blame them if they started getting restless after the first two performances? With any similar gathering of youngsters, high spirits are soon let loose.

Girls started screaming—just for kicks, mostly—and the popcorn and peanuts began to fly. Those stories of slashed seats, mass hysteria, sobbing fans and initials carved on arms with penknives? Mostly dreamed up by newspaper men short of a story.

It's Still A Menace

But rock 'n roll is a menace in one sense. Musically, I mean. The mums and dads of today's fans had *their* crazes. But at least they listened to men like Benny Goodman, Harry James, Duke Ellington. Good musicians, all of them.

But what sort of musical appreciation is a generation brought up on rock 'n roll going to develop? A pretty debunched one, I can tell you.

There's one ray of hope, though. Rock 'n roll is a gimmick—fostered by the big pop music interests. Like all gimmicks, it is sure to die the death. Let's hope that will happen soon.

Well, I've let off steam. Just let me have one final blast. Nothing makes me madder than to be bracketed with those rock 'n roll boys.

I'm a folk singer. Happily, the public has accepted me as such. And I intend to stay that way. No rock 'n roll gimmicks for me!

Don't tie me with rock 'n roll—I'm a folk singer, says Lonnie Donegan

...and these men are

Frank Sinatra

KILLING IT OFF
by STANLEY NAYLOR

Vic Damone

Tony Martin

IN Britain, the booming rock 'n roll craze is about to take its biggest knock—from music publishers in Tin Pan Alley, now preparing to issue their top song titles for the autumn.

These will be released early this month and despite the increasing popularity of Elvis Presley—advance guard of the U.S. rock 'n roll assault—r report that most music publishers are STILL backing top melody songs.

Tin Pan Alley will urge British singing stars to record songs—mainly ballads—that have a more sustained appeal. They will point out to disc-jockeys the dangers of inciting teenage riots, as in the United States, if they give too much play to rock 'n roll.

Make no mistake, Tin Pan Alley HATES rock 'n roll and is preparing to kill off the craze. Can this counter-attack halt the craze in Britain?

One man who says it can is Les Perrin, spokesman for the American-owned Southern Music Co., one of the biggest and most important publishing organizations in the world.

"There are positive reasons why I say good melodies will be taking over from rock 'n roll soon," he told me.

"There are even indications that rock 'n roll is losing its grip on the American market. At this time the biggest challenge to vocalists like Presley is coming from singers of melodies.

"In America, as in this country, Sinatra's LP 'Songs For Swingin' Lovers' is a top-selling disc; the LP from the show 'My Fair Lady' is also strong.

"I can name many others that threaten rock 'n roll: Tony Martin's 'Walk Hand In Hand,' Vic Damone's 'On The Street,' the 'Moonglow Theme' from 'Picnic.' And this, remember, is only the start of the autumn season."

Song man Perrin uses two basic reasons for rock 'n roll's coming doom in Britain. First: "There is no top vocalist here who is establishing the rock 'n roll personality. British teenagers get it all second-hand from the States. It came become awfully dull, not to see and hear your idols in person."

Second: "The British market for rock 'n roll is really too small to make it an important musical factor. In America, the Negro population is so big that a vocalist could easily sell more than a million rock 'n roll discs to them."

The Southern Music Co.—its past hits include "In Old Lisbon" and "Under The Bridges Of Paris"—is backing a ballad called "Gina," already a big Continental hit, for the hit parade.

Another publisher, David Platz, of the Essex ("Band Of Gold") Music Co., told me: "Publishers just can't afford to let it take hold. Our profits, ultimately, come from the sale of sheet music. Rock 'n roll is too small a market.

"One recent rock 'n roll hit has sold 200,000 records in far—but only 2,450 copies of sheet music. Tin Pan Alley, with these figures, MUST discourage rock 'n roll."

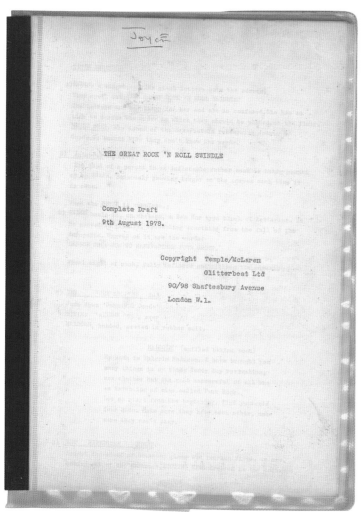

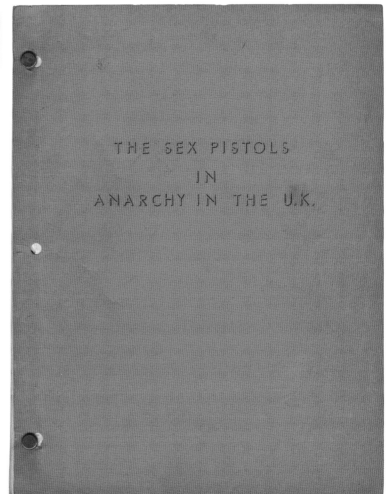

2 weeks time.

2 weeks time / B.B.C. 10th anniversary !
Party   E.M.I   worlds biggest
                         birthday Cake.

2)   Play outside [B.B.1]
                Portland /
        Swish place !

        {So it Goes} | Film Deal . ↕
                      | Serious deal —

              | B.B.1.

OKay!
Anthony Balch .
Columbia Pictures —

I hate Rotten.— The lousy shit!

Rotten is a shit—
cunt — I hate him.

                    PAUL
              ~~Rotten used to be my~~
              ~~pal!~~   4) ?

         ~~Paul~~ is so upset he's lost control. He lashes
         at the desk again, ~~and then starts to cry---~~
         tears roll down his face while he gasps for
         air and is at the verge of blowing up once more.
         He wants to kill the trend-setter of all time---
         and at the same time, he's giving up.

         After all this explosion, Boggs still finds the
         strength to come back: Freaked-out rockers
         are not new to him.

                    BOGGS
                 (ala Zero Mostel)
              Listen, kid----I know where you're
              coming from! I'm from the streets
              myself! I fought my way to the
              top, and you can too! You're my kind
              of guy! You're the real thing,
              Paul! Fuck Rotten!

         Paul turns his back, trying to regain control.
         Boggs carefully reading Paul's emotional state,
         looks out the window (and here again there's
         the faint suggestion of Zero Mostel in "The
         Producers"). He looks down at the crowds milling
         in the streets.

         (Including POV of crowd starting the con)

                    BOGGS
              Look at those poor souls down
              there! They're starving---
              out of work! It's a Depression!
              Let's give them something, Paul!
              A cause---that's what they need!
              Give them a chance to blow off
              some steam!

         Paul turns toward the window uncertainly. Boggs
         expands.

                    BOGGS
                 (the big con)
              I can hear your band playing, on
              every radio and television station
              in the land! On every juke box---
              The Sex Pistols, number one! You'll
              be bigger than the Beatles! Bigger
              than the Army! Bigger than the
              Queen!

                                        CUT TO:

Understand this you bloody
idiot. I don't want to ←———
be in a band with ~~Rotten~~
I've had enough! That
sod spoils everything. ✓

~~Look~~ at last night.
he ~~fucked~~ messed everything up.
And you ——— —— you asshole
——— trying to tell us what to do!
~~Its over~~ —

You can't make a ✗
record with that bastard ✓
~~Under~~ Think of that. You thick dick!

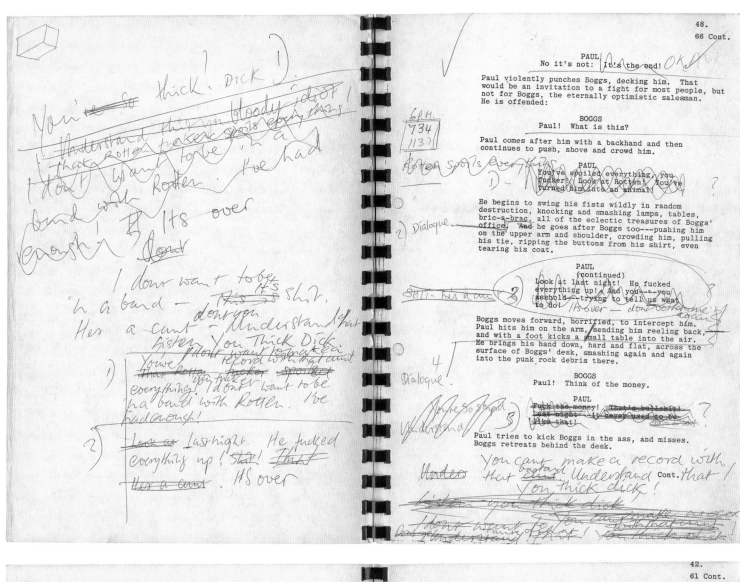

PAUL
No it's not. It's the end! OK!

Paul violently punches Boggs, decking him. That would be an invitation to a fight for most people, but not for Boggs, the eternally optimistic salesman. He is offended:

BOGGS
Paul! What is this?

Paul comes after him with a backhand and then continues to push, shove and crowd him.

PAUL
You've spoiled everything, you fucker! Look at Rotten! You've turned him into an animal!

He begins to swing his fists wildly in random destruction, knocking and smashing lamps, tables, bric-a-brac, all of the eclectic treasures of Boggs' office. And he goes after Boggs too---pushing him on the upper arm and shoulder, crowding him, pulling his tie, ripping the buttons from his shirt, even tearing his coat.

PAUL
(continued)
Look at last night! He fucked everything up! And you---you asshole--trying to tell us what to do!

Boggs moves forward, horrified, to intercept him. Paul hits him on the arm, sending him reeling back, and with a foot kicks a small table into the air. He brings his hand down, hard and flat, across the surface of Boggs' desk, smashing again and again into the punk rock debris there.

BOGGS
Paul! Think of the money.

PAUL
Fuck the money! That's bullshit! Last night--it never used to be like that!

Paul tries to kick Boggs in the ass, and misses. Boggs retreats behind the desk.

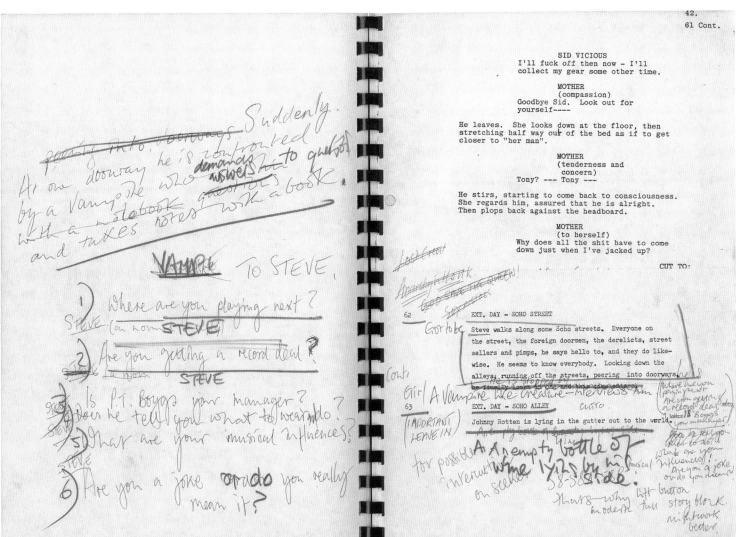

SID VICIOUS
I'll fuck off then now - I'll collect my gear some other time.

MOTHER
(compassion)
Goodbye Sid. Look out for yourself----

He leaves. She looks down at the floor, then stretching half way out of the bed as if to get closer to "her man".

MOTHER
(tenderness and concern)
Tony? --- Tony ---

He stirs, starting to come back to consciousness. She regards him, assured that he is alright. Then plops back against the headboard.

MOTHER
(to herself)
Why does all the shit have to come down just when I've jacked up?

CUT TO:

62   EXT. DAY - SOHO STREET

Steve walks along some Soho streets. Everyone on the street, the foreign doormen, the derelicts, street sellers and pimps, he says hello to, and they do likewise. He seems to know everybody. Looking down the alleys, running off the streets, peering into doorways,

63   EXT. DAY - SOHO ALLEY

Johnny Rotten is lying in the gutter out to the world.

NEVER TRUST A HIPPIE

THE GREAT ROCK 'N' ROLL SWINDLE

CASH FROM CHAOS

BELIEVE IN THE RUINS

THE ONLY NOTES THAT MATTER ARE THE ONES THAT COME IN WADS

They Swindled Their Way To The Top

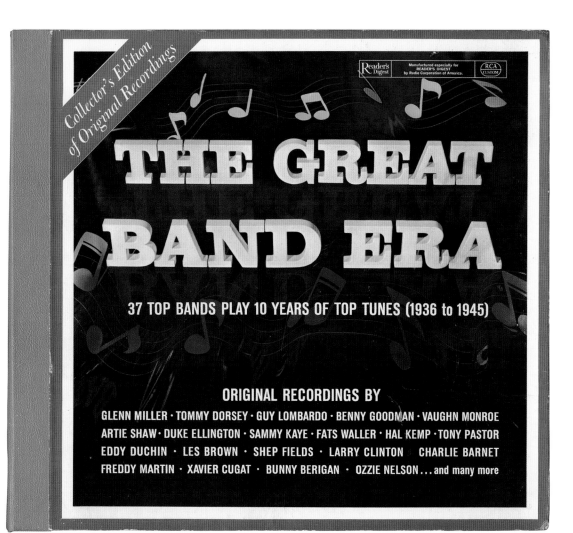

The SEX PISTOLS are an undoubted success based on an idea called Punk Rock which sets out to trail blaze a path of anarchy and ruin within a culture that chooses to destroy us (by making ~~so~~ our decisions for us.

~~Punk Rock's~~ ~~Cause~~ Cause ~~was~~ is to create as much fuss, havoc, ~~crime and~~ excitement as possible. CRIME pays us.

~~Punk's~~ slogans are — Cash from chaos — Beleive in the Ruins. — Never trust a hippie — Anarchy is the key — 'do it yourself' is the melody.

In other words Rot 'n' Roll.

The media was our helper and lover and that in effect was the SEX PISTOLS success. As today to control the media is to have the power of goverment, god or both.

It is all that matters to explain our Great Rock'n' Roll Swindle. A true swindle of ideas that gives you back your right to decide things for youself.

Malcolm Mchaveny ~~Oliver Twist~~. ~~Malcolm Mchaven~~ ~~FAGIN~~ ~~as he was~~.

CRIME PAYS US
WEARGALL CROOKS EMBEZZLERS.
IMBECILES, GIMMICKS
+ EXILES

① NIGEL & CECILIA.

② QUEEN WITH SAFTEY PIN. (NO FUTURE - LYRICS)

③ NO FEELINGS
YOUNG GIRL WRAPPED IN CREPE BANDAGES & PINS AGAINST PHOTO BACKGROUND, OF URBAN REPRESSION

④ DON'T TALK TO US ABOUT OBSCENITY

⑤ LEE'S FIST & PIN PHOTO,

⑥ SUBN - SIBERIA PISTOLS CARTOON.

⑦ OFFICIAL E.M.I. PRESS STATEMENT. AT CR GENERAL MEETING (IT WILL FREAK THEM OUT - I.E. HOW WE GOT A COPY) (OFFICIAL) OF IT,

⑧ ANYTHING THAT HAMMERS HOME POINTS COMING OUT OF INTERVIEWS.

⑨ PUNK IS DEAD
(WITH FIST PHOTO ✓)

⑩ HOW TO IMPROVE YOUR MIND. — LEAVE HOME.

⑪ E.M.I. PAGE (REALLY STIMULD) OWNERSHIP OF I.T.N. THAMES T.V. ETC.

⑫ CARTOON! (DONE AS CARTOON) A POSSIBILITY. COUPLE (IN LOVE). ~~NIGHT ON THE~~ DAY SHOPPING IN LONDON, + NIGHT ON THE TOWN — EVERYTHING CONSUMED OR DONE OWNED BY E.M.I. THEATRES, RESTAURANTS, RECORDS MAG WEAR ETC.
✳ DONE IN STYLE OF TEENAGE GIRLS COMIC.

⑬ LETTERS - PAGE. REQUESTS FOR MAG ETC. (SOPHIE TO SORT OUT THE MORE INTERESTING ONES)

302   1979. *The Great Rock 'n' Roll Swindle* promotional banners.

303   **ABOVE:** *The Great Rock 'n' Roll Swindle* album sleeve visual source material.
BELOW: *The Great Rock 'n' Roll Swindle* album cover art.

304   **ABOVE:** 1979. Jamie Reid and Malcolm McLaren's *The Great Rock 'n' Roll Swindle* working notes.
BELOW: January 1977. Jamie Reid's working notes for the unpublished second issue of *Anarchy in the UK* zine. Note themes that would be revisited years later for *The Great Rock 'n' Roll Swindle* film.

305   1979. Malcolm McLaren's working notes for *The Great Rock 'n' Roll Swindle* film.

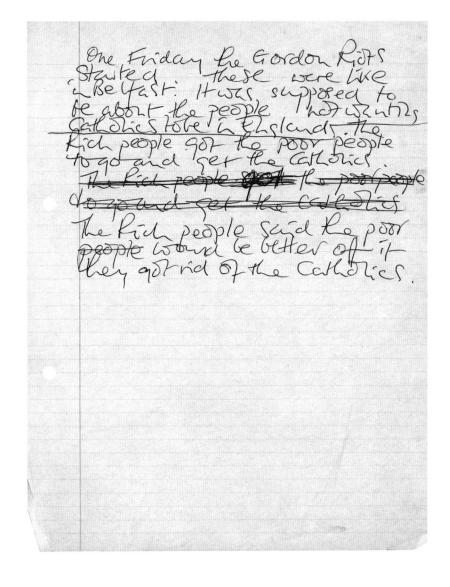

Turn and utilise violence from frustration and boredom make it positive
and directional to destroy, the environment, packaged culture, make it more
interesting Take on that medium which exists and its mechanics and give it
a new life - revitalising - kids become rock 'n roll - band becomes rock 'n roll/
the Intention has grabbed their imagination Fired to make their own culture -
music used as a launching pad for attitudes   annoy as many people as possible.
Band coming together through this mood.

Mention of rehearsals. (Denmark St?)

Malcolm and Viv for source material.

Michael's photos.

September M.M. The Tastemakers.

Interview Linda.

Forum. SEX.

..... (repeat?) you can always change them
    later (is inherent in this section)
SLASH Interview Part 1.

Dutch Film & shop
Peter Clifton 1973 London Rock & Roll Show
Tapes from John Varnham

Kings Road gig W. Wally arranged by
Bernard & Viv.   Café in Kings Rd. pissed
about & fucked up. (w. Cindy Cale rehearse / Brighton
in mini. Glenn fucked Cindy Cale.) Hotel.

73 American Fashion Show. Chelsea Hotel - N.Y.
weirdos. Michael J. Pollard Alice Cooper. Dolls.
Story of Ringo
"Grease" clothes. "Mahler" (Ken Russell.) Bike tyre T-shirt
                                            cross. mini-skirt
                                            swastikas.
                                            Viking woman.

ALL THE POINTS ARISING FROM; POINTS OF POLITICS PHILOSHPHY, PUT INTO MAIN STORY THEME.

① A FAST MOVING, SXTÆRLATING STORY IS NOT GOOD ENOUGH. THE STORY IS A SERVICE OF SELLING THE MORE COMPLEX IDEAS THAT ~~MOTIVATED~~ THAT WERE BEHIND AND MOTIVATED THE EXISTENCE OF THE SEX PISTOLS.

② THE BOOK AT THIS POINT IN TIME IS AN IDEAL VEHICLE FOR COMING OUT INTO THE OPEN AND STATING THESE 'POLITICAL' INTENTIONS.

———

③ HOW THIS IS DONE I.E. IN THE STORY LINE, AS GRAPHICS, AS A CONCLUSION IS A DESICION TO BE MADE AT THE END OF THE FIRST IRDTAL, ROUGH DRAFT. <u>THEY MUST BE THERE</u>

E.G. SWINDLE FOR ITS OWN SAKE IS UNE THING I.E. TRAIN ROBBERS, PIRATING RECORDS

WHAT MAKES THIS STORY MORE EXITING IS THE CONCEPT OF SWINDLING, GETTING MONEY FOR ~~YOUR~~ OWN IDEAS OF SUBVERTING. GET SUBSIDISED BY THE ENEMY YOU ARE ATTACKING SWINDLING TO SUBVERT.

URING, SHOCK, OUTRAGE ETC.

THE PISTOLS WHERE A DEVICE FOR DOING THIS.

———

MAKING AS MUCH MONEY AS POSSIBLE. (ref. UNIONS — MINERS. FORDS ETC) IS <u>REVOLUTY MARX.</u>

MAKING MONEY FOR SUBVERTING IS EVEN BETTER.

(This is not a hard & fast rules but one which applies socially, economically, politically. AT this point in time (expand).

P.T.O.

MANIFESTO - STATEMENT OF COMMENT & INTENT

IF. GRAPHICALLY. ① USE WITH PHOTOS DRAWINGS
CARTOONS ETC OUT OF CONTEXT. ie NOT
PISTOLS BUT PHOTOS OF OTHER PEOPLE, OTHER SITUATIONS
eg. AWAY WITH THE MURDER OF THE BODY!
    ② DEFACE: GRAPHICS. OVER THE TOP. TO STOP THEIR ART VALUE.
        TOP. TO STOP THEIR ART VALUE.

GET. BARDS TO CONTINUE TO PUT
SUCH COMMENTS IN BUT,
BRACKET THEM OFF. FOR
USE IN DIFFERENT CONTEXT.

EPILOGUE
FILM. SAGA OF
    TREATED IN THE STYLE OF AMERICAN
GLOSSY MAG". GOSSIP, PHOTOS OF PARTICIPANTS
(MUG, SHOOTS (UNFLATERING) AND LOW DOWN, SCAM
TEXT UNDERNEATH:
    THE SACKINGS ETC.

308

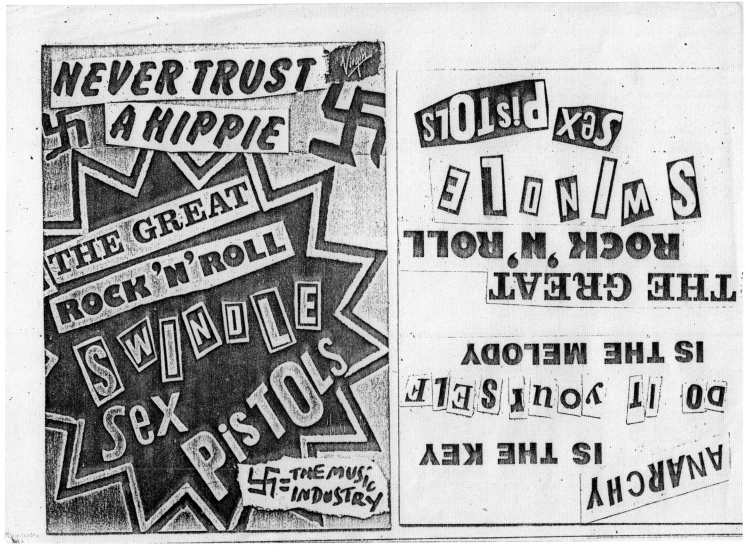

306-308   Late 1978/Early 1979. Jamie Reid's and Malcolm McLaren's notes for the unrealized Sex Pistols book, *When Tutor Takes Over From Practice*.

309   **ABOVE:** 1979. *The Great Rock 'n' Roll Swindle* merchandise display.
BELOW: 1979. Jon Savage/Jamie Reid Sex Pistols graphic.

310 & 311 1959. Source material and execution of a Jamie Reid Sex Pistols graphic.

99

S

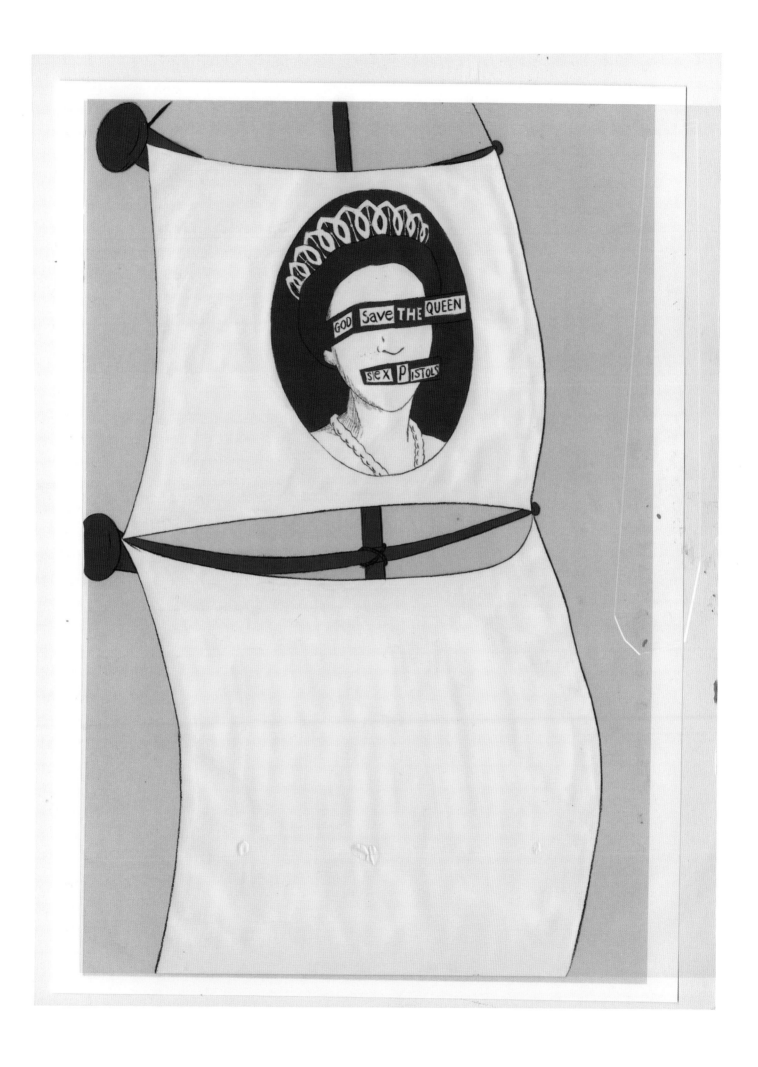

(NY103)NEW YORK, Nov. 21-(AP)-Punk Rocker Sid Vicious, left, enters
court here Tuesday to plead innocent to charges of murdering his
20-year-old girlfriend last month. With Vicious, whose real name is
John Simon Ritchie, is seen accompanied by his lawyer, James Merberg.
Vicious, 21, is former Bass guitarist for the defunct Sex Pistols
Punk Rock group.(APLaserphoto)(ccc31430str-RK)(1978)

SEX PISTOLS (SALES FIGURES)

SWINDL ALBUM I (A) —	VD 2510 —	95,000	TGRAES. I
SOME PRODUCT (A) —	VR 2 —	56,000	SP.
GOD SAVE THE QUEEN (S) —	VS 181 —	208,000	GSTQ
PRETTY VACANT (S) —	184 —	252,000	P.V.
HOLIDAYS (S) —	191 —	178,000	HIS.
(BIGGS — MY WAY) (S) —	220 —	209,000	BIGG, MY WAY.
(SOMETHING ELSE) (S) —	240 —	382,000	S.E.
(C'MON EVERYBODY) (S) —	272 —	251,000	C'MON
(SWINDLE) (S) —	290 —	110,000	GRAES.
(STEPPING STONE) (S) —	339 —	30,000	Stepping stone
(OOLLOCKS) (A) —	V 2086 —	210,000	NMTB
(FLOGGING) (A) —	2142 —	23,000	FADH
(SID SINGS) (A) —	2144 —	43,000	SS.
SWINDLE ALBUM II)	2168 —	42,000	TGRAES II

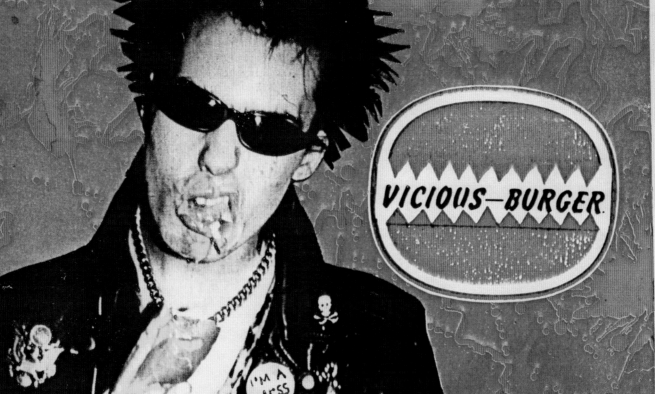

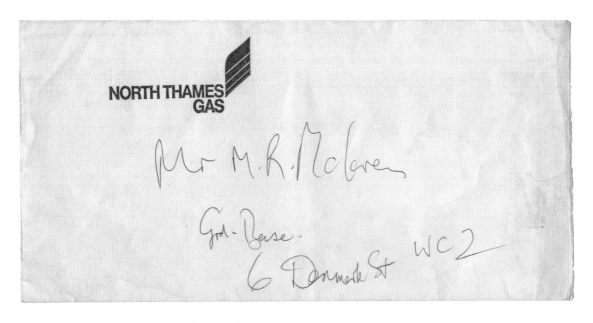

316   1980. Sex Pistols figures in Jamie Reid's hand.

317   1979. Unused Virgin Records graphic for "C'mon Everybody" 7" sleeve by Jamie Reid.

318   18 June, 1979. Gas company shuts off electricity and gas to the Sex Pistols' rehearsal space, London.

319   Late 1979/Early 1980. Steve Jones and Paul Cook in front of *The Great Rock 'n' Roll Swindle* mural at Shepherd's Bush roundabout, London.

DON'T LOOK BACK ON 'GREASE'
LOOK FORWARD TO......
THE GREAT
ROCK 'N' ROLL
SWINDLE
CAFE

WE ARE THE SAVIORS OF ENGLAND!

Punk is Sex Pistols. These four brave and attractive young fellows leapt from the rock scene, and they are very "NOW"— and radical dissenters. Their debut album is called "God Save the Queen," and it inspired much controversy as soon as it came out. It was banned in England, and it is already banned from TV in Japan, but has sold more than 40,000 records already. An old nation, England is very dark, and there is stagnation in everything. In such a nation the Sex Pistols are appealing to the masses with the sound of young energy. Fighting under tons of pressure, we wanted to know what happened after the debut album. We were able to interview them at the Glitterbest offices near Piccadilly Circus in London.

WE ARE STILL AT GUERRILLA WAR!

Q: Did you know you were banned on Japanese TV? **PAUL:** What? In Japan? **STEVE:** Why? [We explained that there was a new article that states it is disrespectful to the royal family and the nation of England.] **STEVE:** Nonsense! [The three others agreed with some excitement.] **Q:** Teddy boys and the National Front see you guys as the enemy. **SID:** In the beginning, yes. We ran into trouble with Teddy boys. Punk bands used to open for Teddy-boy bands, and now that got turned around. They didn't like that. Punk is punk and we have more power, and it's obvious that punks prevail. **JOHNNY:** When the National Front found out about us they tried to use us for their publicity, but it didn't work out. I hear they hate us nowadays. **Q:** I heard you are having hard time performing domestically? **PAUL:** We can't do any concerts in London. **STEVE:** It's horrible. People look at us with contempt. When we appeared on Bill Grundy's TV show, the media started to say we were dirty, dangerous scum and we couldn't do any shows after that. We were supposed to do 25 or 26 shows, but all we could do was 5. All the venues wanted to block us out and it's a mess. **Q:** That's a long guerrilla battle. What is your strategy? **JOHNNY:** The shows outside London went quite well. **Q:** What do you think of England? **JOHNNY:** I hope it gets better, even a little bit. Overcome the situation we are in now. It's in a horrible state. **STEVE:** We can't perform! You understand how we feel? **Q:** What about revolution? **JOHNNY:** What about it? **Q:** Have you ever thought about it? **JOHNNY:** What is this country really doing? The newspapers are not telling the truth. They are just silent when it comes to that. **SID:** Punks will cause a revolution! **Q:** We'd like to know your life story. **STEVE:** I'm 16! No wait, I'm 20. No, I'm actually 21 years old. I was in jail and got the flu before

I joined the band. That was two-and-a-half years ago [bitter facial expression]. **PAUL:** I'm 20 years old and I used to be a truck driver. **Q:** Johnny, you've been playing music since you were a student, right? **JOHNNY:** It wasn't anything big. I used to play moody Irish folk songs. [Everybody cracks up laughing.] **Q:** Why did you start to sing? **PAUL:** When we started the band two-and-a-half years ago, we were looking for a vocalist. We found Johnny hanging out on the street and we made him sing for the band and that's how we started. **JOHNNY:** That's a good explanation. I'm 20 years old, too, by the way. **Q:** What are you most interested in now? **STEVE:** Money and women. **JOHNNY:** I don't like people. Especially boring ones. I like music. **PAUL:** Sleeping, washing my jeans, and being gay! **SID:** Vodka! This is the best! [They started to drink our souvenir cans of beer.]

NY PUNKS ARE TRASH!

Q: You play really hard on stage. Are you being careful with anything? **JOHNNY:** What, our health? **SID:** We're not the Bay City Rollers! **JOHNNY:** First—drink a lot of liquor. Second—eat as little food as possible. **Q:** Do you do any training? **STEVE:** Are you kidding? Is that a question for bums like us? You're killing me... **JOHNNY:** We hardly walk across a street! **STEVE:** Right. We use one of those running machines and train ourselves. I look fat, don't I? **SID:** Yeah, Yamaha ones with an engine. [We discover Steve has a motor bike.] **Q:** Rumor has it that you guys are making a movie? **STEVE:** Not started yet. We might start in mid-November. **Q:** Are you shooting in the USA? **STEVE:** [With puzzled look] We're shooting it here. **Q:** What's it about? **JOHNNY:** It's a documentary about us after the band was formed. It'll get done this year, if everything works out. I heard it's going to Japan too. **Q:** Do you hear anything from Japan about you guys? **PAUL:** No, no. I know people know about us over there. **STEVE:** That's about it. We don't hear anything. **Q:** The album sales are pretty good. [Paul gets excited.] **JOHNNY:** Stop being so loud over small things and shut up. **PAUL:** Why? It's a big thing! **Q:** What do you think about New York punks? **STEVE:** Trash! **JOHNNY:** I smell middle-class on them. All of them. They use the best instruments and live in good neighborhoods. It's just a fashion statement for them.

FAGS? BETTER THAN NORMAL PEOPLE.

Q: Do you have a girlfriend, Johnny? **JOHNNY:** I believe nothing lasts forever. Fuck whenever you feel like it. **Q:** How often do you have sex? **JOHNNY:** Do I have to answer that? I'm a member of the band, what kind of question is that? **SID:** I'll tell you. Johnny is asleep all year around. **Q:** Tell us about fashion. **STEVE:**

We don't like fashion in general. **JOHNNY:** We don't think seriously about what we wear. That's boring. It's the worst when you think you can get the best clothes from the best boutiques. That's wrong. **PAUL:** I'm interested in changes and the current status of fashion, but I'm not going to adjust myself to that. **STEVE:** I always wear same things. Things from the 1950s. **JOHNNY:** No good, like Gene Vincent. He's fat. **STEVE:** [Holding steel bands in both hands] These bands are used to hold your sleeves while playing pool. My style is biker style. It's the style for pushing, not riding. **Q:** I see you [Johnny and Steve] have piercings in your right ears? **ALL:** You're a fag if you wear one in your left! **Q:** What do you think about homosexuals? **STEVE:** They're cool. **JOHNNY:** I don't mind as long as they don't bother me. **PAUL:** They are better than normal people. **SID:** Fags? I don't care. I like girls. **JOHNNY:** I heard there are many gays in New York now. **STEVE:** How's Japan? **SID:** We are talking shit now. **Q:** What kid of men do you like Johnny? **JOHNNY:** Honest ones. Ones with no lies and no deceipt. **STEVE:** That's it. James Bond! **Q:** What is punk? **PAUL:** I don't know. **JOHNNY:** We are the only punk band. We are saviors of England! [said with Hitler-like gesture] **STEVE:** There are like 100 bands that play at being punks, but all of them are fake. We are punk. **Q:** Do you have any plans to perform in Japan? **STEVE:** I don't know... **PAUL:** Someone told me next March. [We are later informed that a few record labels, including Columbia, are teaming up to have them perform in Japan] **Q:** How do you spend your days when you're not performing? **PAUL:** Right now we have one or zero gigs per month, so it's devastating. We meet to talk about new songs and drink. I sleep mostly. **STEVE:** We hide our names on flyers and perform secretly sometimes. **JOHNNY:** We at least get away from the media and boring interviews. This is the first interview in six months.

Many cans of beers are now all over the floor and the band are restless, so we cut off our interview at this point. We had a photo session at a small park in front of the studio and refreshed our minds. They were all in a good mood as soon as we stepped outside. I guess punks don't like to talk that much. Johnny imitating Chaplin, big Steve doing a handstand, Paul messing around with the camera. We could not tell if they were being shy or high. Sid was constantly winking at us and talking to us. From their hard and intimidating stage presence, we were not expecting to see such a lighthearted side to them. They announced the release of their first LP, *Never Mind the Bollocks*, on November 10th, and we hope this will restore faith in the youth of the world. A fresh scar on Sid's left arm